POCKET PRECINCTS

MELBOURNE

A pocket guide to the city's best cultural hangouts, shops, bars and eateries

**DALE CAMPISI &
BRADY MICHAELS**

Hardie Grant
TRAVEL

CONTENTS

Introduction ... v
A perfect Melbourne day ... vii
Melbourne overview map ... viii

Precincts
City East ... x
City West ... 16
Southbank & South Melbourne ... 30
Fitzroy & Collingwood ... 42
Carlton & Brunswick ... 56
Northcote, Thornbury & Preston ... 72
St Kilda & Bayside ... 86
South Yarra, Prahran & Windsor ... 100
Footscray & Yarraville ... 114
Richmond & Abbotsford ... 128

Field Trips
Dandenongs & Yarra Valley ... 142
Mornington Peninsula & Phillip Island ... 148
Great Ocean Road ... 154
Goldfields & Spa Country ... 162

Travel tips ... 168
Maps ... 174
Index ... 202
About the authors & acknowledgements ... 205
Photo credits ... 205

iii

INTRODUCTION

Wominjeka / Welcome

Welcome to Melbourne where we say Wominjeka in the language of the traditional owners of this country, the peoples of the Kulin Nations.

Melbourne is a multicultural and diverse city. There are people from more than 200 different countries here, including the world's oldest continuous culture, the largest Greek population outside Greece, the oldest Chinatown outside China, and the largest Indian and Sri Lankan communities in Australia. Multiculturalism is central to what has made Melbourne one of the world's most liveable cities, and certainly one of the most interesting and exciting.

As a UNESCO City of Literature, it's not short on stories. Melbourne's bookstores, festivals and libraries brim with tales tall and true. Its streets and shopping malls are a shopper's paradise, with fresh local labels embraced as passionately as international designers. The city's art galleries hold covetable collections and exhibitions. The dining scene spoils visitors for choice with some of the world's best cafes and restaurants – renowned for quality coffee, creative interiors and local, sustainable food.

Melburnians love their sport, too, with hundreds of thousands turning out to stadiums for Australian rules football, cricket, the Australian Open tennis grand slam and the Australian Grand Prix.

Like a great yum cha or a progressive degustation, this book is a taster of what Melbourne and its precincts has to offer. Each has its own unique local flavour, reflecting the marvellous multicultural nature and spirit of our city. Then there's field trips beyond the city – to the Mornington Peninsula and Great Ocean Road; the villages of the Dandenong Ranges and wine trails of the Yarra Valley; and the arty towns of the goldfields. Of course, our suggestions are just a starter – there's plenty more to explore and always something new to discover.

Dale Campisi & Brady Michaels

A PERFECT MELBOURNE DAY

The perfect day in Melbourne is like a Choose Your Own Adventure novel, but you can bet there'll be coffee, trams, laneways, lots of looking and maybe even getting lost.

We'd start our day with a coffee and croissant at **Dukes Coffee Roasters** on Flinders Lane (the queue tells you it's worth the wait). Then head for **Hamer Lawn**; find the stairs behind the sculpture *Forward Surge* and wind your way around **Hamer Hall** for an uninterrupted view of the city skyline.

Next stop: the Melbourne Arts Precinct. **The National Gallery of Victoria** (NGV) is the star attraction, and you'll be wowed by contemporary art at **Buxton Contemporary** and the **Australian Centre for Contemporary Art**. Don't forget to make a mix-tape souvenir at the **Australian Music Vault** at **Arts Centre Melbourne**.

Now for the laneways. Enter the labyrinth at **Degraves Street** opposite Flinders Street Station. We love to lunch at casual Italian **Journal Canteen** on Flinders Lane – always at the window to catch the moment that busy **Centre Place** blazes with midday sunshine. Then weave your way past musicians and magicians, through **Centreway** and across Collins Street and admire the cakes in the window of **Hopetoun Tea Rooms** in the ornate **Block Arcade**. Need an umbrella, scarf or gardening tools? Go see **Mr Wares**. Eau de toilette? Head to **Paint 'n Powder** in the **Royal Arcade**.

Spend your afternoon wandering the **State Library of Victoria**'s free exhibitions and magnificent domed reading room, and visit **Curtin House** – for books at **Metropolis**, fashion at **P.A.M.**, or a sunset spritz at **Rooftop Bar**.

For dinner, it's a pita and a bag of beans at **Miznon** on Hardware Lane or **Chinatown** for Tsingtao beer, dumplings and century eggs. Then explore the newest laneway bars or our old favourite **Meyers Place Bar**, relocated to Crossley Street. Cap it off with unexpected gelato flavours: avocado, lime and coriander at **Spring St Grocer**.

As an alternative, take the 86 tram north to Northcote for food trucks at **Welcome to Thornbury**; south to Prahran for a really late night at **Revolver Upstairs**; east to Richmond for beers at **Mountain Goat Brewery** or **The Corner Hotel**; or a train west to Footscray for fragrant flavours at **Pho Hung Vuong** and the laid-back vibe at **Back Alley Sally's**.

MELBOURNE OVERVIEW

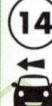

PRECINCTS

1. City East
2. City West
3. Southbank & South Melbourne
4. Fitzroy & Collingwood
5. Carlton & Brunswick
6. Northcote, Thornbury & Preston
7. St Kilda & Bayside
8. South Yarra, Prahran & Windsor
9. Footscray & Yarraville
10. Richmond & Abbotsford

FIELD TRIPS

11. Dandenongs & Yarra Valley
12. Mornington Peninsula & Phillip Island
13. Great Ocean Road
14. Goldfields & Spa Country

CITY EAST

Always the fancy end of town thanks to its gently rising slope, lush civic gardens and grand old buildings, the eastern part of the central business district (CBD) is home to luxury boutiques and theatres on Collins Street, fashionable eateries on Flinders Lane and cool bars, cafes and restaurants in every available nook and crevice, rooftop and basement in between. This is the home of Melbourne's famed laneways (see p. 5) that crisscross the city and enable you to discover hole-in-the-wall cafes, hidden bars, street art and quirky shops. It's also where you'll find Chinatown (see p. 9), a little labyrinth of more than 100 restaurants.

The grand old buildings speak of the city's illustrious history. Parliament House and the Old Treasury Building remind us of the wealth garnered in the 19th century, and the beloved State Library of Victoria is a testament to our belief in public education. The Old Melbourne Gaol, a former prison reborn as a museum, tells the story of Australia's most infamous bushranger, Ned Kelly, among others. Other architecture is modern and memorable, such as Melbourne's contemporary 'heart' at Federation Square (see p. 2), and Melbourne Central (see p. 6), which preserves our industrial history under a giant glass cone.

And then there's the Royal Botanic Gardens (see p. 3), where you can escape the city and gaze on it.

Train: Flinders Street station, Parliament station

→ *Ride the rails from iconic Flinders Street station*

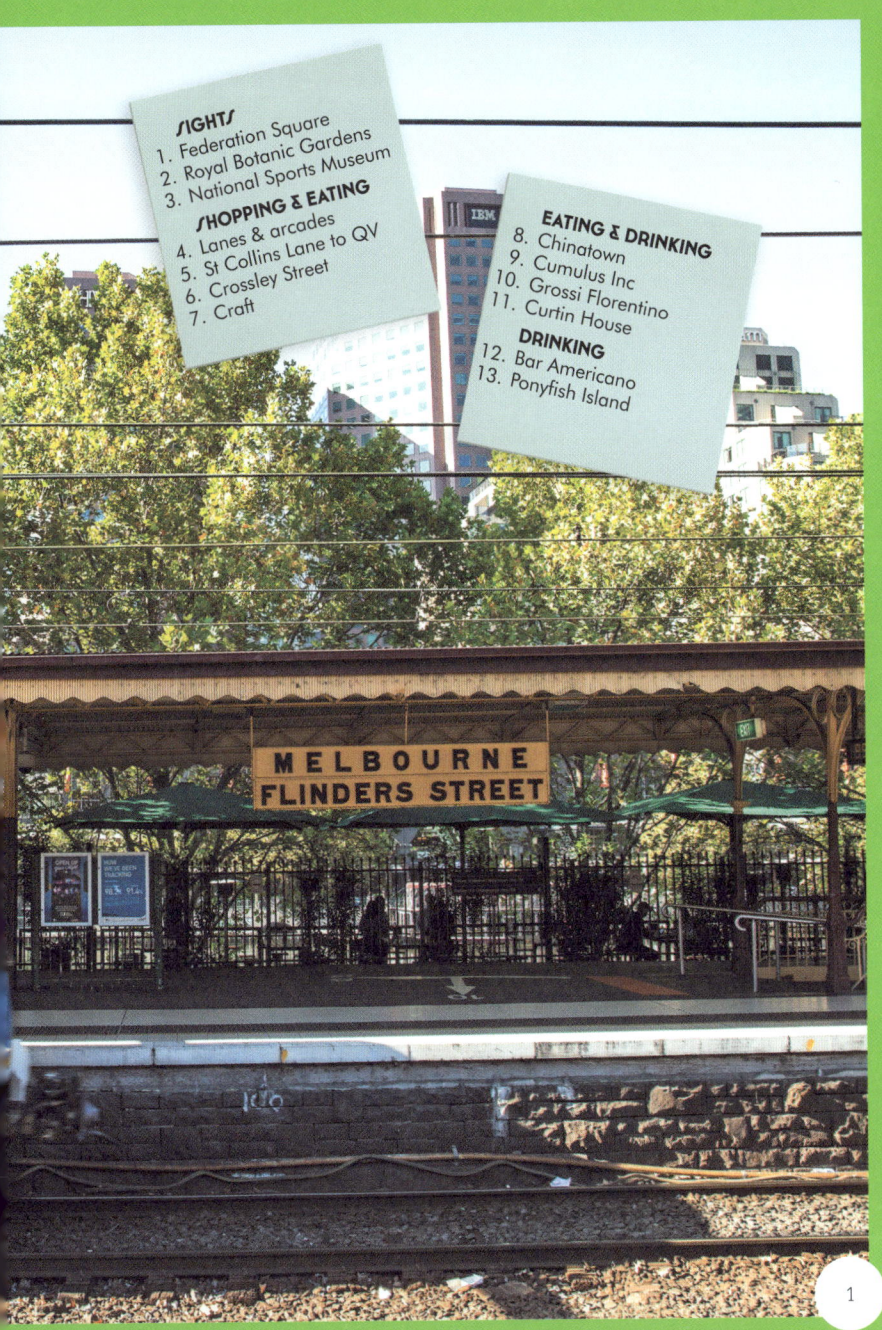

SIGHTS
1. Federation Square
2. Royal Botanic Gardens
3. National Sports Museum

SHOPPING & EATING
4. Lanes & arcades
5. St Collins Lane to QV
6. Crossley Street
7. Craft

EATING & DRINKING
8. Chinatown
9. Cumulus Inc
10. Grossi Florentino
11. Curtin House

DRINKING
12. Bar Americano
13. Ponyfish Island

CITY EAST

1 FEDERATION SQUARE

Cnr Swanston & Flinders sts
www.fedsquare.com
[MAP p. 181 D2]

Not at all square and not even opened in time for the centenary of the federation of Australia, Fed Square is loved by most for its far-out geometric architecture, sloped outdoor public spaces and big screen that runs day and night. Prominently located opposite Flinders Street Station and St Paul's Cathedral, and with more than 10 million visitors every year, it became the beating heart of Melbourne when it opened in 2002. It's home to some of the city's leading cultural institutions, including the **NGV Australia** gallery, where you can see iconic Australian art, historic and contemporary; and the **Australian Centre for the Moving Image (ACMI)** currently undergoing a $40 million transformation, is set to reopen in mid-2020, with new exhibitions and cinemas showing contemporary and classic films. The **Koorie Heritage Trust** shows contemporary art by local First Peoples and reveals Melbourne through Aboriginal eyes on a walking tour of the adjacent **Birrarung Marr** park.

POCKET TIP

There's more than street art down Hosier Lane. Head to Frank Camorra's Spanish restaurants MoVida, MoVida Next Door and Bar Tini, where the vermouth is on tap and tapas is served until 1am.

CITY EAST

2 ROYAL BOTANIC GARDENS

Birdwood Ave, South Yarra
www.rbg.vic.gov.au
[MAP p. 187 E3]

POCKET TIP

The Shrine of Remembrance commemorates Australians' service in wartime. Look out for the face of Aboriginal leader William Barak on a building on Swanston Street in the distance.

Melbourne's lush public oasis is rated among the best botanic gardens in the world. Located on the south bank of the Yarra River and extending to leafy South Yarra, you can get there easily on a tram from the city along St Kilda Road. Established in 1846, it took 60 years to transform a wetland into a wonderland of more than 8500 plant species. Paths and promenades weave through towering stands of majestic trees from all over the world, there are spacious lawns and rotundas for picnicking, and there's punting on the ornamental lake, so don't forget your boater hat! A walk up historic **Guilfoyle's Volcano** (a massive, landscaped water storage tank) has the best city views in the gardens. There are sections of native Australian plants – including many local species – for those who want to learn about what grows Down Under. Guided and self-guided tours are available, including an **Aboriginal Heritage Walk** and a behind-the-scenes look at the **Old Melbourne Observatory**. If you're here in summer, **Moonlight Cinema** is a great way to experience the gardens – and a movie – after dark.

3

CITY EAST

3 NATIONAL SPORTS MUSEUM

Gate 3, MCG
9657 8879
www.nsm.org.au
Open Mon–Sun 10am–5pm
except event days
[MAP p. 194 A3]

The National Sports Museum celebrates the guts and the glory of Australia's diverse sporting culture at the country's most revered sports ground – the Melbourne Cricket Ground (MCG) – the spiritual home of cricket and the Australian Football League (AFL). Featuring interactive zones, 3D holograms, exhibitions and memorabilia of sports heroes, there's numerous exhibitions. The 'People's Ground' is a history of the MCG itself; 'Champions' presents horse racing and the chance to design your own silks; 'Game On' pits you against your mates and sporting legends in a range of sports from cycling to archery, netball to running, such as against Olympian Cathy Freeman; 'Faster, Higher, Stronger' follows Australia at the Olympic Games; and in 'Backyard to Baggy Green' a holographic celebrity cricketer, Shane Warne, is your personal tour guide. Sports merchandise is also available and tours of the MCG take in player boxes, change rooms and the edge of the hallowed turf.

CITY EAST

POCKET TIP
You'll probably need to queue, but the coffee is worth the wait at Dukes Coffee Roasters (247 Flinders La).

4 LANES & ARCADES

[MAP p. 180 B2]

Melbourne is famous for its lanes and arcades, full of cafes, bars, shops and creative businesses. On **Degraves Street** you'll find locally made goods at **Clementine's**; beautiful leather journals and stationery at **Il Papiro**; and cleverly designed bags at legendary Melbourne-born brand **Crumpler**. **Centre Place** is full of street art, cafe-goers, local independent fashion label **Kinki Gerlinki** and **Monster Threads**, which sells cute, quirky and artsy homewares. For lunch on the go at just $5, **B3** serves the city's cheapest take-away baguettes. Across Collins Street, the ornate **Block Arcade** is a Victorian-era shopping palace, home of **Haigh's** chocolates and the **Hopetoun Tea Rooms** – join the queue for cake as Melburnians have done since 1892. **Basement Discs** in adjoining **Block Place** is a music-lovers' institution. The **Royal Arcade** opened in 1870, making it Melbourne's oldest. Local chocolatier **Koko Black** is here; pore over vintage objects at **Hunter Gatherer**; and go on an olfactory journey with the finest French perfumes at the classic **Paint 'n Powder** boutique.

5

CITY EAST

5 ST COLLINS LANE TO QV

Short on space, Melbourne's shopping centres have gone vertical in the central city. **St Collins Lane** is the city's newest, with international fashion labels and a **Leica** photographic store. Melbourne's historic retail heart is the **Bourke Street Mall**, between Swanston and Elizabeth streets. Here you'll find **Myer**, Melbourne's home-grown department store, and Sydney-born upscale rival **David Jones**. Multi-level fashion hub **Emporium** includes more than 200 mid-range and upmarket stores, a food court with views and eats from some of Melbourne's best restaurants and the city's best Banh Mi at **Pho Nom** on the lower ground. **Melbourne Central**, with its underground train station, historic shot tower and giant glass cone, features more than 400 retailers. **Unlocked Tours**, run by yours truly, explore history, architecture and views from the roof. Across the road, **QV** has a subterranean supermarket, big-box discounters, Asian patisseries and take-away tea shops. **No Vacancy Gallery** presents regular art exhibitions on **Jane Bell Lane**.

POCKET TIP

Look up in the Bourke Street Mall for ornate retail architecture and a classic vista up the hill, crowned by Parliament House.

CITY EAST

6 CROSSLEY STREET

[MAP p. 179 A2]

Crossley Street captures the best of Melbourne in one little street. Positioned between Bourke and Little Bourke streets, it was once known as Romeo Lane for its bawdy beginnings. These days the businesses range from the creative to the caffeinated, frequented by cultured hipsters and snap-happy travellers. There's an old-school barber, **Windsor Hair Salon**, clothing stores and iconic Melbourne diner **Pellegrini's Espresso Bar**. A red neon pretzel points you to jewellery and accessories brand **Lucy Folk**, worn by loyal locals and pop stars. **Gallery Funaki** contains the work of Australian contemporary jewellers, with solo and curated group exhibitions. **Romeo Lane** cocktail and tapas bar is tucked away in one of the oldest buildings in the city, and **Meyers Place Bar** is a city institution. Inspired by Asian hawker-style markets and serving up tasty street-style fusion food, **Gingerboy** looks as good as it tastes. **Traveller** by Seven Seeds Roastery serves some of the best coffee in town – look out for the neon shoe.

POCKET TIP
Just around the corner from Crossley Street are two of Melbourne's oldest and best bookstores: Hill of Content (86 Bourke St) and The Paperback (60 Bourke St).

7

CITY EAST

7 CRAFT

Watson Pl, off Flinders La
9650 7775
www.craft.org.au
Open Mon–Wed 11am–6pm,
Thurs–Fri 11am–7pm, Sat
10am–5pm
[MAP p. 181 D1]

Art, craft and design lovers (like us) find plenty to swoon over in this basement shop and gallery that represents many of Melbourne's – and Australia's – leading emerging craft makers and designers. But Craft is much more than a shop – it's also the headquarters of a national not-for-profit organisation, which was founded in 1970 to showcase and support contemporary Australian craft and design, with regular programs, events and markets. Everything here is handmade, from jewellery to ceramics, glassware, bags and art objects that range in price from $15 right up to $1500 (and more!). As well as the sleek retail spaces brimming with beautiful things, there's an adjoining exhibition space that presents a year-round program of free exhibitions by creatives who blur the line between craft and contemporary art, while exploring the role of creativity and sustainability in the 21st century.

POCKET TIP
The Nicholas Building (37 Swanston St) has a beautiful stained-glass ceiling. On the ground floor is Cathedral Arcade with quirky indie retail, galleries and makers throughout.

CITY EAST

8 CHINATOWN

[MAP p. 177 F2, 178 B3]

Melbourne's Chinatown, established in 1851, is the oldest Chinatown outside China. Get the story at the **Chinese Museum** (22 Cohen Pl), and get your fill at more than 100 restaurants representing Imperial, contemporary and regional Chinese cuisines. **Supper Inn** (15 Celestial Ave) is one of Chinatown's oldest restaurants and serves old-school Cantonese until 2.30am. Imperial fine diner **Flower Drum** (17 Market La) has been one of Australia's top restaurants for decades; and three-storey dumpling temple **Hutong Dumpling Bar** across the road has developed a cult following for its shao long bao soup dumplings. Stalwart **Shark Fin Inn** (50 Little Bourke St) does yum cha seven days a week. **Shanghai Village** (112 Little Bourke St) is a favourite with hungry hipsters, thanks to its cheap dumplings and hot pink decor, and **Sichuan House** (22–26 Corrs La) will delight chilli lovers. Chinatown's alleys conceal an array of bars, including one of our faves: **Union Electric** (12 Heffernan La).

9

CITY EAST

9 CUMULUS INC

45 Flinders La
9650 1445
www.cumulusinc.com.au
Open Mon–Fri 7am–11pm,
Sat–Sun 8am–11pm
[MAP p. 181 F1]

Consistently rated among Melbourne's best restaurants since opening in 2008, Melbourne restaurant baron Andrew McConnell's Cumulus Inc is the kind of diner you wish was your local. It's casual yet sophisticated, where the freshest best-quality produce is the hero on the plate. In the morning the place is drenched with light; a delightful spot to start the day with a long black and madeleines with lemon curd or nutella. Think about sharing for lunch and dinner: the whole roast lamb shoulder falls right off the bone and is made for two – perfect with a side of potatoes, confit garlic and sage, and a hearty red. Can't choose? Splash out on the chef's menu from $75 per person. The place hums day and night, so book ahead if you're planning a date. Seats overlooking the bar or kitchen are the best in the house. Upstairs is wine bar **Cumulus Up**.

CITY EAST

10 GROSSI FLORENTINO

80 Bourke St
9662 1811
www.grossiflorentino.com
Open Mon–Sat 7.30am–late
[MAP p. 179 A3]

POCKET TIP

You'll find a subterranean cheese cave at Spring St Grocer (157 Spring St), and house-made gelato too. Butcher's Diner (10 Bourke St) is open 24-hours for cheesy toasties and beefy burgers (cash only).

Guy Grossi is one of Melbourne's most famous chefs, and he's created a little empire of Italian restaurants on Bourke Hill. His flagship **Florentino's** pedigree as Melbourne's leading Italian restaurant can be traced back all the way to the 1920s. Special occasions warrant a visit to Florentino: contemporary Italian cuisine using the finest ingredients and impeccable and attentive service will make for a night you won't forget. **Grill**, **Florentino** and **Cellar Bar** make up Grossi Florentino at 80 Bourke Street; **Ombra Salumi** next door at number 76 is another Grossi venture focused on preserved meats and vegetables; and hard-to-find **Arlechin** (Mornane Pl) makes a mean cocktail and classy midnight munchies under a vaulted cork roof. Ombra and Cellar Bar are more informal – both great for alfresco people-watching in the dappled shade. Ombra does a $25 Sunday roast with all the trimmings, while the bread-moppingly good tagliatelle bolognaise is just $18 (every day) at Cellar Bar.

CITY EAST

11 CURTIN HOUSE

252 Swanston St
www.curtinhouse.com
[MAP p. 177 D3]

The action at Curtin House extends from the ground floor entrance all the way up to its rooftop eyrie. On level 1 you'll find restaurant bar **Cookie**, which has been turning out the city's favourite contemporary Thai food for almost two decades. Prime position is on the two balconies overlooking Swanston Street. Live music venue **The Toff in Town** occupies level 2. There are private booths here, replete with buzzer service. The adjacent stage room features live music and performances most nights of the week, and afterwards DJs transform the Toff into a nightclub long into the mornings. **Mesa Verde** on level 5 boasts one of Australia's largest hoards of tequila and mezcal, and the list of margaritas is long. Good-times Mexican dining is enhanced with a dash of their house-made Hazard hot sauce, and DJs play late on weekends. The **Rooftop Bar** is a beloved Melbourne institution, particularly in summer when you can catch arthouse, classic and recent release films in the open air surrounded by twinkling skyscrapers. For good shopping, pop into hip designer **P.A.M** and indie bookseller **Metropolis**.

POCKET TIP

A hub for Melbourne's arts community, Loop (23 Meyers Pl) is more than a bar: it's a multimedia art space with an ever-changing program of projected visuals, exhibitions and events.

CITY EAST

12 BAR AMERICANO

20 Presgrave Pl
www.baramericano.com
Open Mon–Sat 5pm–1am
[MAP p. 180 C1]

Melbourne's bar scene is sophisticated and complex, perhaps best illustrated by this little hole-in-the-wall by artist and bar impresario Matt Bax. It's certainly Melbourne's smallest bar, with standing-room only for about a dozen people, but squeeze in if you can. This means you'll probably only stay for one or two cocktails. The cocktail list is as small as the bar, distilled into classics only. Try the negroni – the bartender's drink is always a measure of quality, and it won't disappoint. A rotating list of amaro-blended botanicals will intrigue your palette if you can't decide what to drink. Feeling generous? Purchase a caffe sospeso – suspended coffee, amaro or negroni – and make the next visitor feel a little special by paying it forward. Note: no bookings, no cash, no wi-fi, no pictures.

POCKET TIP
Dine on a dime at Om Vegetarian (1/28 Elizabeth St): all you can eat traditional Indian Thali plates are just $7.50.

CITY EAST

13 PONYFISH ISLAND

Evan Walker Bridge
0426 501 857
www.ponyfish.com.au
Open Mon–Sat 11am–1am,
Sun 11am–12am
[MAP p. 180 B3]

The Yarra River, known by the first Melburnians (and us) as Birrarung, has become a hotspot for waterside drinks. The most uniquely located riverside watering hole is undoubtedly Ponyfish Island, accessible only by stairs under the Evan Walker Bridge, in the middle of the river itself. Drinks and snacks are dispensed from a central service core, allowing punters to pull up a stool with a view up and down the river, or to the north and south banks that teem with walkers and cyclists, day and night. The fit-out is logically nautically themed, with ropes, life rings and anchors featuring prominently; passing rowers and cruise boats also provide visual variety. The wine list is short but solid: Seppelt and Veuve Cliquot, T'Gallant and Leo Buring. Then there's the house lager and good-times cocktails: look out for the spiced rum, Malibu and pineapple; or the gin, Midori, apple and pistachio fairy floss. Basic snacks of nachos, toasties and burritos don't cost the earth, but please don't feed the birds.

POCKET TIP
Land lubber? Try Riverland Urban Beer Garden (Federation Wharf, under Princes Bridge) in the former vaults under Federation Square.

POCKET TIP
Looking for a little cabaret with your cocktail? Try the kooky Butterfly Club (5 Carson Pl).

CITY WEST

Originally the working heart of the city in the days of international shipping on the Yarra River, the western part of the central business district (CBD) and its docks was for many years a no-go zone for all but dockside workers, strip club goers and after-hours ravers. But today the western half of the grid, Docklands and North Melbourne are the new frontier in urban renewal.

The area of Little Bourke Street and Hardware Lane has been a popular dining hub for more than twenty years. The atmosphere cranks up a notch at nights and on weekends, when live music fills the lane and hawkers lure crowds of hungry visitors into some of the more tourist-focused eateries. Queen Victoria Market (see p. 18) is one of the last remaining open-air Victorian-era markets in the world, not to be missed for its heritage or its hawkers.

Docklands has been radically transformed since the 1990s, with glass office and apartment towers dominating the water's edge. Take it all in with a spin on the Melbourne Star Observation Wheel (see p. 19). Nearby North Melbourne, full of workers' cottages and converted warehouses, is a heritage outpost that feels more like a country town than an inner-city suburb and a great place to discover local secrets like the exquisite cakes at Beatrix (see p. 25).

Train: Melbourne Central station, Flagstaff station, Southern Cross station

→ *Queen Victoria Market is Melbourne's old-fashioned retail heart*

SIGHTS
1. Queen Victoria Market
2. Melbourne Star Observation Wheel

SHOPPING
3. Outré Gallery
4. Lord Coconut
5. Wilkins and Kent

EATING & DRINKING
6. Miznon
7. Mörk Chocolate
8. Beatrix
9. Hansang
10. The Bottom End
11. Prudence

CITY WEST

1 QUEEN VICTORIA MARKET

Cnr Victoria & Elizabeth sts
9320 5822
www.qvm.com.au
Open Tues & Thurs 6am–2pm,
Fri 6am–5pm, Sat 6am–3pm,
Sun 9am–4pm
[MAP p. 183 F2]

Once the site of the city's main cemetery, including the grave of Melbourne founder John Batman, the Queen Victoria Market was opened in 1878 and is one of the world's last remaining Victorian-era marketplaces. More than 1000 businesses trade in everything from seafood, cut flowers and organic vegetables to souvenirs and local wares. There's treasure – and trash – to be found. The **Deli Hall** is a must-visit for every self-respecting foodie, packed with the finest quality deli goods. Chase down a bargain bratwurst or borek – just look for the milling crowds! The **Ultimate Foodie Tour** will give you the lowdown on the best market eats and treats. **String Bean Alley** is a collection of colourful converted shipping container shops, headed up by local roaster **Padre Coffee**. The market comes alive with seasonal **night markets**, featuring a dizzying variety of multicultural eats and artisan stalls on Wednesday nights in summer and winter.

POCKET TIP

Catch Irish music and poetry, get your Guinness on tap or join in a trivia night at the snug pub The Drunken Poet (65 Peel St, West Melbourne).

CITY WEST

2 MELBOURNE STAR OBSERVATION WHEEL

101 Waterfront Way, Docklands
8688 9688
www.melbournestar.com
Open Mon–Sun 11am–7pm (May to August), Mon–Sun 11am–10pm (Sept to Apr)
[MAP p. 182 A3]

The observation wheel may not be a unique concept to Melbourne (there are currently four big wheels in the world), but it's a fabulous way to see the good, the bad and the beautiful of Melbourne's city and surrounds. Enclosed cabins fit up to 20 people, with plenty of room to move. From the comfort of your cabin you'll see panoramic views of Port Phillip Bay and the Macedon and Dandenong ranges (see p.142) in the distance. Spot the railway network that feeds the city with office workers and day trippers from the west, the industrial shipping metropolis of Coode Island and Port Melbourne, as well as the rejuvenated Docklands and Fishermans Bend. Take your pick from day or night rides; the spectacular view looks prettier after dark and the wheel itself lights up like a giant disco Christmas tree, but you'll see more detail during the day. It's cheaper to book online ahead of time. Just $2 more buys an extra spin!

POCKET TIP

Take Port Phillip Ferries (131 Harbour Esp) to the Bellarine Peninsula town of Portarlington for a dip in azure water or lunch at The Grand Hotel.

CITY WEST

3 OUTRÉ GALLERY

249–251 Elizabeth St
9642 5455
www.outregallery.com
Open Mon–Thurs 10am–5.30pm, Fri 10am–7pm, Sat 10.30am–5pm, Sun 11.30am–4pm
[MAP p. 176 B3]

More than a shop, unusual Outré is a groovy gallery space specialising in what owners Martin and Louise McIntosh describe as: 'contemporary international pop, lowbrow, pop surrealism and underground art'. This pop-tastic art space has been running for over 20 years, representing more than 80 artists from around the world and filled to the brim with framed prints, limited-edition posters and original artworks, with a range of price points. There's a program of exhibitions, including the 'Small Wall Project' that showcases the work of Australian creatives like Melbourne locals Martin Harries, Ghostpatrol and a bunch of street-art stars. If you love mid-century-inspired art and design and pop culture, you'll love Outré. Check out their website and socials for info on upcoming exhibitions and events. Outré also has an outpost in Smith Street, Collingwood.

POCKET TIP
The wet chai is a standout at Sun Moth Canteen & Bar (28 Niagara La).

CITY WEST

4 LORD COCONUT

Level 5, Mitchell House
0450 015 263
www.lordcoconut.com
Open Mon–Fri 11am–6pm,
Sat 12pm–4pm
[MAP p. 176 B3]

Inside this gorgeous Art Deco building, known as Mitchell House, you'll find the city's only dedicated men's jewellery store. A little bit gothic, a little bit industrial and a lot olde-worlde gentleman, Lord Coconut stocks a stunning range of rings, cufflinks, tie bars, brooches and lapel pins for discerning gents and those who love them. Gender aside, we reckon there's something for anyone who appreciates beautiful, creative and unique jewellery by local and Australian artisans. Look out for Ali Alexander's chemical-symbol rings: an offbeat example of art-meets-metal, as well as Fiona Griffith's subway token rings. And while there are some some pretty serious price tags, there's also a selection of more affordable everyday pieces. Regular exhibitions constantly mix things up – and give you another reason to peruse art you can wear. But who is Lord Coconut you ask? You'll have to pop in to find out!

POCKET TIP
Rocksteady Records (Level 1, Mitchell House) has a broad selection of new and pre-loved vinyl, with just about every musical style represented. Keep an ear out for instore gigs, too.

CITY WEST

5 WILKINS AND KENT

372 Little Bourke St
9670 5624
www.wilkinsandkent.com
Open Mon–Thurs 10.30am–6pm, Fri 10am–6pm, Sat 10.30am–5pm, Sun 11am-4pm
[MAP p. 176 B4]

Wilkins and Kent has been a player in Melbourne's furniture and homewares scene since the 1990s. Their furniture – clean, simple and functional, barely embellished – is beloved in homes across the city. Their Little Bourke Street store is a treasure trove of gifts and a delight for tourists exploring Melbourne's laneways. Inside this former map and globe shop (look out for the original signage on the front window), you'll find a selection of locally made, Australian and imported quality goods, including tea towels, Opinel kitchenware, Sunnylife picnic ware, Myrtle and Moss skincare, Harper and Charlie paper goods and city souvenir toys by Make Me Iconic. Coloured glassware is beautifully displayed in windows overlooking the cobblestoned Niagara Lane, and if you're feeling overwhelmed by the choices, the friendly staff will help you navigate the rich pickings on offer.

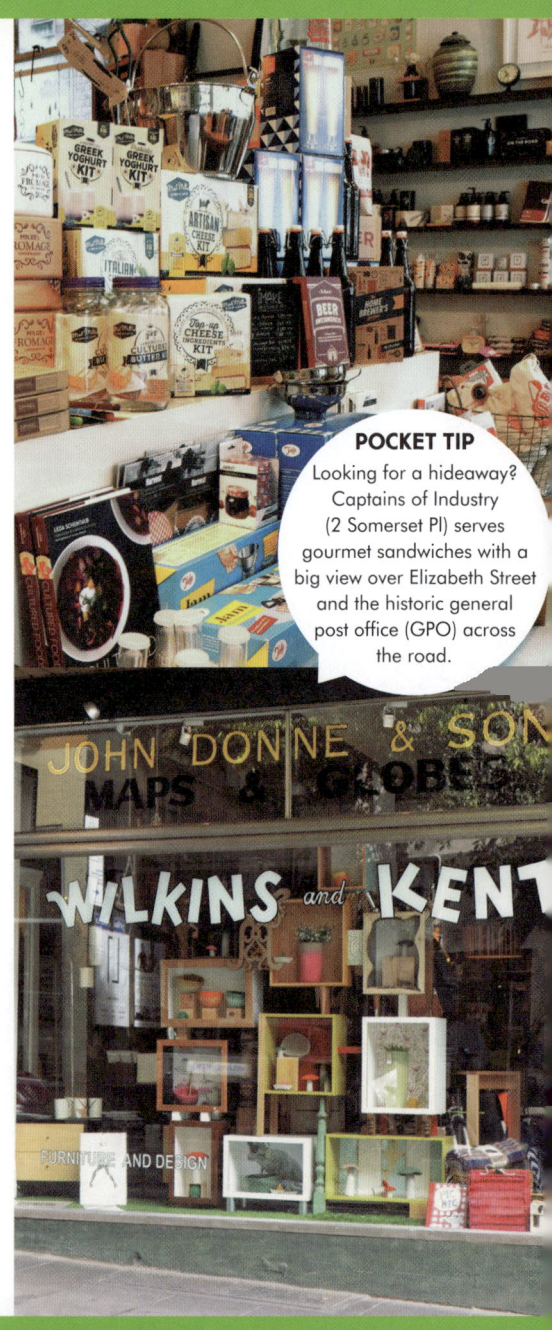

POCKET TIP

Looking for a hideaway? Captains of Industry (2 Somerset Pl) serves gourmet sandwiches with a big view over Elizabeth Street and the historic general post office (GPO) across the road.

CITY WEST

6 MIZNON

59 Hardware La
9670 2861
www.miznonaustralia.com
Open Mon–Fri 12pm–11pm,
Sat 10.30am–11pm.
[MAP p. 176 A4, 183 F4]

Hardware Lane is a hotspot for alfresco dining, so consider yourself warned: it can get hectic! Fortunately, there's respite in Israeli street food outpost Miznon. It's part of an international suite of Israeli street food restaurants by chef Eyal Shani that are full of heart and hearty fare. Fluffy pitas come stuffed 14 different ways, from classic falafel to lamb on the bone. The more-ish Tunisian pita is deliciously simple tuna, potato, pickles, aioli and onion. Whether you eat in or out, everything comes in paper, including whole grilled cauliflower (leaves on) and the no-frills named Bag of Green Beans (literally, a bag of green beans). Don't go past the share-worthy eggplant Sabich and the spicy fish Chraime. The best seats have a view of the friendly open kitchen; we always go casual on the bleachers, adorned as they are with fresh tomatoes.

POCKET TIP

Take in the atmosphere of Hardware Lane over aperitivo and artisanal bites at Kirk's Wine Bar (cnr Hardware La and Little Bourke St).

CITY WEST

7 MÖRK CHOCOLATE

150 Errol St, North Melbourne
9328 1386
www.morkchocolate.com.au
Open Tues–Sun 9am–5pm
[MAP p. 183 D1]

The cacao artisans at Mörk Chocolate make Melbourne's finest quality drinking chocolates. At their brew house in North Melbourne, you can overindulge in their complete range, served myriad ways: with oat milk and cinnamon for breakfast, as a soda or single-origin shake, or layered with vanilla and orange crema catalana for dessert. All their ingredients are ethically sourced: cacao liquor from Sur del Lago in south-western Venezuela; organic, unrefined coconut blossom sugar from a sustainable farm in West Java; and organic cocoa powder from a single farm in Peru. Their signature brew is the Campfire Chocolate: pour the beaker of chocolate into the smoke-filled glass, sprinkle with smoked salt and dip in the house-made toasted marshmallow. Their Sweet Objects treats are made to complement the chocolate: lamingtons, canelles, pralines and even blue-cheese profiteroles. Note: there's no coffee here, but decadent chocolate cereal is available as take-away.

POCKET TIP

Need coffee or lunch? Auction Rooms (103 Errol St) serves renowned St Ali coffee and flavourful Middle Eastern cuisine in a converted warehouse.

CITY WEST

8 BEATRIX

688 Queensberry St,
North Melbourne
9090 7301
www.beatrixbakes.com
Open Mon & Wed–Fri
8am–4pm, Sat 9am–4pm
[MAP p. 182 C1]

OMG the cakes! This is the work of pastry chef Nat Paull, who's worked with some of the best in the business, including Australia's first ladies of food, Maggie Beer and Stephanie Alexander. It's all local, all ethical at this neighbourhood cake house. Come for breakfast and lunch (baguettes and ciabatta rolls, and coffee by Allpress), but dessert is the main event. Vintage beaters hang all over the walls to remind you that heaven is an angel food cake, paradise is a coconut shagg layer cake, and the cocoa meringue roulade with strawberries and crème fraîche is simply to die for. In fact, the seven deadly sins are in most of the rest of the menu. Follow @beatrixbakes on Instagram for mouthwatering pics of the Beatrix cake squad's daily tricks with the beater.

CITY WEST

9 HANSANG

347–349 King St
9995 0867
www.hansang.com.au
Open Mon–Sat 11am–11pm
[MAP p. 183 E4]

Korean eateries have popped up all over Melbourne in recent years, and Hansang is one of the newest in town. Across the road from Flagstaff Gardens, it's located in one of the city's oldest buildings, dating back to the 1850s Gold Rush. This small and stylish restaurant combines pale timber furnishings and quietly creative decor with beautiful exposed bluestone walls, but the food is the real star. Expect Korean home-style classics made with care and bursting with flavour. We ordered the set menu and received our choice of small and main dishes, with several small plates, known as banchan, served on the side. 'Hansang' means 'a table full of food' in Korean, and if you order this way, that's exactly what you'll get! But if you're not feeling like a full-on feast, a main shared between two people should be more than enough for most. Bonus: the beer is cheap and the staff are courteous and attentive. Vegetarians and vegans take note: Koreans love their meat, so this might not be the place for you.

POCKET TIP

Flagstaff Gardens has been a city retreat since 1862. Climb to the top of the hill to catch a glimpse of the bay. There's a bowling lawn, tennis and netball courts and a barbecue.

27

CITY WEST

10 THE BOTTOM END

579 Little Collins St
9629 3001
www.thebottomend.com.au
Open Mon–Fri 11.30am–11pm,
Sat 4pm–6am
[MAP p. 175 D3]

A pub, disco and diner all in one, The Bottom End is just as fun and cheeky as the name suggests. It also refers to the bottom end of town, where this three-level playhouse lives. There's food, fun and games to be had from lunchtime until late, starting with the American-style dive bar/pub on the ground floor, where you can knock back a beer and watch the sports screens from the comfort of your booth. Unflashy as it may be, the Bottom End is both highly ironic and inclusive, with its tongue firmly in cheek. It hosts the popular monthly gay night Swagger, as well as open-minded parties every Friday and Saturday night, with three distinct dance zones on the lofty top floor. Get your fuel for a long night's partying with an all-American burger or hotdog, courtesy of the burger-masters from Easey's in Collingwood. Be warned: you'll need to dance to shake the fat off these bad boys.

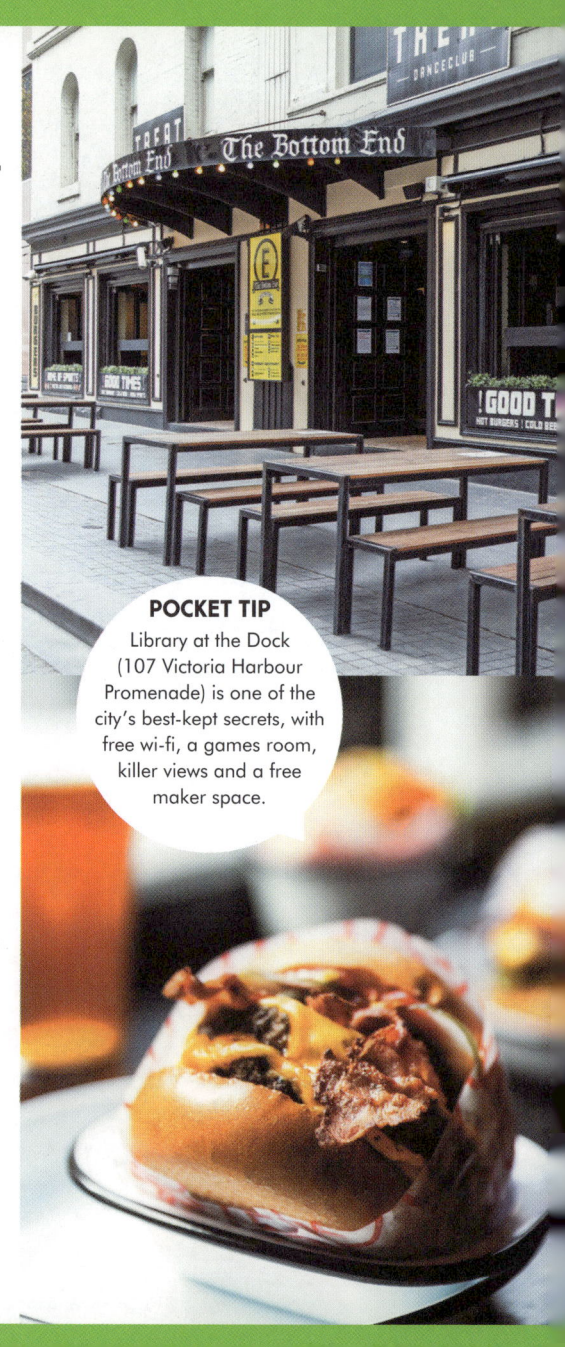

POCKET TIP
Library at the Dock (107 Victoria Harbour Promenade) is one of the city's best-kept secrets, with free wi-fi, a games room, killer views and a free maker space.

CITY WEST

11 PRUDENCE

368 Victoria St, North Melbourne
9329 9267
www.prudencebar.com
Open Mon–Sat 3.30pm–1am,
Sun 3.30pm–11:30pm
[MAP p. 183 E2]

Locals in the know at this shopfront drinking den can tell you that before 2000, Prudence was a record store. That shows in the stacks of vinyl behind the bar and the love for vinyl that the bar staff ooze as they spin their favourite records while serving you your favourite drinks. The dimly lit front bar extends to a sunny courtyard out back. A labyrinth of booths can be found upstairs, lit up with gilded mirrors and ornate chandeliers, and bedecked with deer heads throughout. As for drinks, Prudence regulars favour beer over all other libations. You can choose from a range of rotating craft beers on tap, but not before you've sampled the house-brewed Prudence Lager. There's also a long list of local wines and classic cocktails, including negronis, old-fashioneds, sidecars and Manhattans. Go early for $10 Aperol Spritz, $5 cans of Moritz and Peroni Red, and keep your eyes peeled for regular jug specials. Hungry? Ask to order in from local take-aways.

POCKET TIP

Town Hall Hotel (33 Errol St, North Melbourne) is as unpretentious for a drink as it is nostalgic – sticky carpet and all.

SOUTHBANK & SOUTH MELBOURNE

The industrial heart of Melbourne in the 19th and early 20th centuries, the south bank of the Yarra River, opposite Flinders Street Station, was reborn in the 1990s as a shopping and dining mecca. By the 21st century, the area along St Kilda Road had become known as Melbourne's Arts Precinct. Taking in Sturt Street, there are now more than 20 galleries and theatres showing major exhibitions, concerts, ballet and theatre and an array of public art too. Here you'll find the NGV (see p. 32), Australia's oldest and foremost gallery. For the best view of Melbourne and beyond, head to the Eureka Skydeck (see p. 33) in Melbourne's tallest building, Eureka Tower.

Just across busy Kings Way is the bustling precinct of South Melbourne, which feels like a village away from the city. Clarendon Street is its main road, with some grand old pubs to keep you occupied. Just a short walk from Clarendon Street, boutiques cluster around South Melbourne Market (see p. 35), alongside cafes and eateries where you'll feel like a local. Albert Park Lake (see p. 34) is the area's green space, complete with barbecues, walking tracks, boating and all manner of sports facilities.

Train and tram: Flinders Street station, Route 96

→ *The NGV is a modern architectural masterpiece*

SIGHTS
1. NGV
2. Eureka Sykdeck
3. Albert Park Lake

SHOPPING & EATING
4. South Melbourne Market
5. Onstone

EATING & DRINKING
6. Chez Dré
7. St Ali
8. Railway Hotel
9. The Palace Hotel

SOUTHBANK &
SOUTH MELBOURNE

1 NGV

180 St Kilda Rd
8620 2222
www.ngv.vic.gov.au
Open Mon–Sun 10am–5pm
[MAP p. 186 B1]

At the Melbourne Arts Precinct more than 20 arts venues are clustered into one square kilometre. The National Gallery of Victoria – better known as the NGV – is the main attraction, where you can catch free and paid exhibitions by major artists, old and new. With 75,000 artworks in the permanent collection, you can bet there's gold in here, from Rembrandt to Rothko, treasures from the ancient world and the latest art experiments. The annual Melbourne Winter Masterpieces presents the greats, like Monet, Van Gogh and Picasso, while the NGV Triennial celebrates the world's best contemporary art and design. The serene water wall out front is a Melbourne institution, and Leonard French's stained-glass ceiling in the Great Hall is the largest in the world. The sculpture garden out back with its annual architecture commission is a great spot for a breather, while NGV Friday Nights offers DJs, bars and late-night access to exhibitions. The NGV's **Design Store** has a huge selection of art books and gifts.

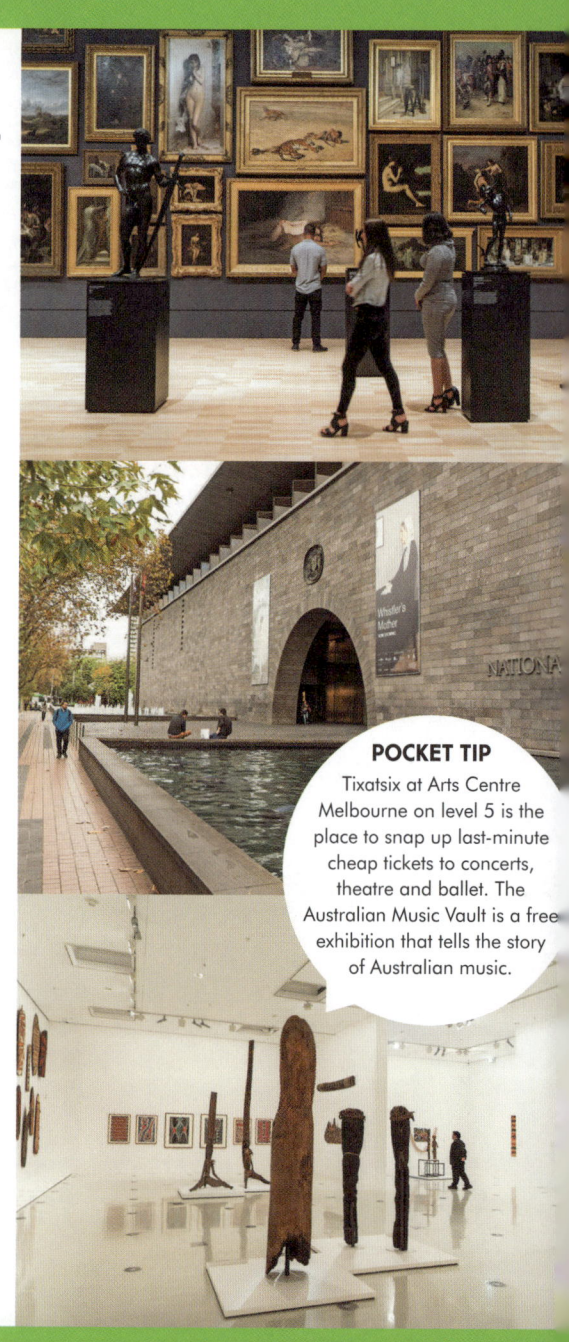

POCKET TIP

Tixatsix at Arts Centre Melbourne on level 5 is the place to snap up last-minute cheap tickets to concerts, theatre and ballet. The Australian Music Vault is a free exhibition that tells the story of Australian music.

SOUTHBANK &
SOUTH MELBOURNE

2 EUREKA SKYDECK

Riverside Quay, Southbank
9693 8888
www.eurekaskydeck.com.au
Open Mon–Sun 10am–10pm
(last entry 9.30pm)
[MAP p. 180 B4]

Melbourne's tallest building is an adventure to find. Follow the giant gold bees that guide you from the riverside Southbank Promenade to the entrance of Eureka Tower, where you can get your ticket to ride to the top of Melbourne like a modern-day Jack and the Beanstalk. (Brace yourself: this lift is fast and with no stops!). On the 88th floor, Eureka Skydeck offers panoramic views of the city, bay and distant mountain ranges from behind glass and also in the open air. By night, the city glitters with light. For a few extra dollars, **The Edge** experience projects thrill-seekers beyond the building in a glass cube for a unique perspective on the city. Don't forget your camera and beware if you suffer vertigo.

POCKET TIP

Entry is free to contemporary art galleries Buxton Contemporary (Southbank Blvd) and ACCA (111 Sturt St). Look out for opening soirees to rub shoulders with the city's arts scene.

SOUTHBANK &
SOUTH MELBOURNE

3 ALBERT PARK LAKE

[MAP p. 175 E4]

Once part of the Yarra River delta, Albert Park Lake and surrounds has been a gathering place for the people of the Kulin Nations for thousands of years. In the south-eastern corner of the park you'll find the giant **Bunurong Corroboree Tree**, believed to be more than 300 years old. Declared a public park in 1864 but not really loved like one until the early 20th century (for a time it was also a tip, a commons farm and a shooting range), the area supports several native bird species, including black swans, magpies, kookaburras and cockatoos. You'll find shaded picnic areas with barbecues dotted around the park, and you can grab breakfast, lunch and coffee at the **Boatshed Cafe** – as well as paddle boats, kayaks and sailing dinghies. The **Melbourne Sports and Aquatic Centre** (MSAC, 30 Aughtie Dr) has indoor and outdoor 50-metre pools, diving facilities and all manner of playing courts. The Australian Grand Prix is also held on a circuit around the lake every March. Look back towards the city for spectacular views of the towering skyline.

POCKET TIP

Kickstart your day with a coffee and a kale and cauliflower salad with miso, almond hummus and poached egg at The Kettle Black (50 Albert Rd, South Melbourne).

SOUTHBANK & SOUTH MELBOURNE

4 SOUTH MELBOURNE MARKET

322–326 Coventry St,
South Melbourne
9209 6295
www.southmelbournemarket.com.au
Open Wed & Sat–Sun
8am–4pm, Fri 8am–5pm
[MAP p. 189 D2]

For picnic supplies and people watching, this bustling undercover market is renowned for its quality produce and specialty foods. Get the flavour of Australia at **Mabu Mabu**, purveyors of native dips, pastes and sauces. Sweet tooths will love **Agathe Patisserie**'s pandan-flavoured flans and croissants, as well as **Atypic Chocolate**'s hot chocolate and whipped-cream sandwiches. But really great retail is what sets this market apart from the city's others. There's brightly coloured handcrafts at **Market Imports**, the latest homewares at **The Super Cool**, ethically focused clothes, toys, bags and books at **Merchants of Change**, hipster haberdasher **Frankie's Story** and a rotating mix of emerging designers at the **SO:ME Space** in the centre of the market. A visit wouldn't be complete without a famous South Melbourne Market dim sim, and lunch among the hubbub of **Claypots** seafood restaurant.

35

SOUTHBANK &
SOUTH MELBOURNE

5 ONSTONE

283 Coventry St,
South Melbourne
8060 9842
www.onstone.com.au
Open Mon–Fri 10am–5pm,
Sat 9am–4pm, Sun 10am–3pm
[MAP p. 189 E2]

Instagram is great and all, but if you really want to make a lasting memory, you've got to lay it down on stone. Using specialist inks printed directly onto stone, Emma and Nick at OnStone turn happy snaps, wedding photos and commemorative portraits into lasting keepsakes. But there's much more at play here beyond the clarity of stone prints. Each is framed in recycled timber and backed with upcycled polystyrene – so far reusing more than ten kilometres of fence palings and 2000 square metres of polystyrene that was otherwise destined for landfill. A visit in store will help you understand how to transform a single image into a multi-piece installation or enrich it as part of a collage. If you're visiting from elsewhere, they'll even ship it home for you.

POCKET TIP
Need to read? Check out Mary Martin Bookshop (ground floor, Southgate), Coventry Bookstore (265 Coventry St, South Melbourne) and Avenue Bookstore (127 Dundas Pl, Albert Park).

SOUTHBANK &
SOUTH MELBOURNE

6 CHEZ DRÉ

285–287 Coventry St, South Melbourne
9690 2688
www.chezdre.com.au
Open Mon–Sun 7.30am–4.30pm
[MAP p. 189 E2]

Tucked down a cobbled alley, with just a little awning to indicate its presence, Chez Dré is hiding something big. Renowned for its coffee, it also has a significant kitchen and a large area for indoor dining: picture marble-topped tables, reclaimed timber and buttoned banquettes. Umbrellas and a big old peppercorn tree provide shade in the courtyard. Breakfast is served all day and is Frenchy in orientation: croque monsieurs and -madames, and French-toast brioche. There are baguettes, salads and sandwiches for lunch and, for afters, petits gateaux: cross-town-worthy macarons, tartes and eclairs.

POCKET TIP
If a patisserie is what you're after, stop into Bibelot out front for some truly decadent delights.

SOUTHBANK &
SOUTH MELBOURNE

7 ST ALI

12–18 Yarra Pl,
South Melbourne
9132 8960
www.stali.com.au
Open Mon–Sun 7am–6pm
[MAP p. 189 F2]

Salvatore Malatesta is the Melbourne coffee baron who revolutionised the cafe scene in Melbourne in the 2000s, and this converted garage is where his famous St Ali empire began almost 20 years ago. Even after all that time, there's still a queue to get in – a testament to the quality maintained in the kitchen. A Barista Breakfast takes in three different St Ali coffees for $10, or you can take the plunge on a coffee adventure with six for $25. The all-day menu ranges from hangover big breakfasts, pancake stacks and cheesy cheeseburgers to poke bowls of roasted broccoli and grains or tofu and wombok. The lunch menu changes daily: you get what's going in this former garage – and you'll love it.

POCKET TIP

Screaming for ice-cream? Don't miss Jock's (83 Victoria Ave, Albert Park) award-winning ice-cream and sorbet.

SOUTHBANK & SOUTH MELBOURNE

8 RAILWAY HOTEL

280 Ferrars St,
South Melbourne
9690 5092
www.railwaypub.com.au
Open Mon 4pm–12am,
Tues–Thurs 12pm–12am,
Fri–Sat 12pm–1am, Sun
12–11pm
[MAP p. 189 D3]

Dating back to the days when pubs were assiduously named for their proximity to infrastructure, South Melbourne's Railway Hotel remains a gem of old Emerald Hill station. In winter, warm your toes by an open fire and in summer relax in the backyard beer garden. There's an enormous L-shaped bar with plenty of space to chat over pots or pints of the dozen ales on tap, including White Rabbit, Little Creatures, Sapporo and Heineken. A broad gastro-pub menu surveys the Aussie classics, including fish and chips, burgers and parmigianas, with several good options for the vegan and vegetarian among us, too. Look out for the daily specials under $20, and Monday night is trivia night.

SOUTHBANK &
SOUTH MELBOURNE

9 THE PALACE HOTEL

505 City Rd, South Melbourne
9682 3177
www.thepalacehotel.com.au
Open Sun–Thurs 12pm–11pm,
Fri–Sat 12pm–1am
[MAP p. 188 A3]

This unassuming pub is one of the friendliest in town – what it lacks in colour it makes up for in community. You can see it in the diverse crowd who call the Palace their local: young and old, kids and canines, suits and students, everyone is welcome. Twelve beers are on tap rotation, from local and international craft beers like Bodriggy, Mountain Goat and 3 Ravens to mainstream favourites Carlton Draught and Tiger. The menu is classic Aussie 'pub grub', so try ordering like a local: say parmy for parmigiana, wings for fried chicken wings, and bangers and mash for sausages and mashed potato. There are specials six days a week for those watching their wallets. There's a beer garden out back and a multitude of sports on the big screen. Visit the website to keep up to date with what's showing.

POCKET TIP

Looking beyond the pubs? Try Hats and Tatts (78 Cecil St, South Melbourne) for more than 100 different types of whisky and cocktails, too.

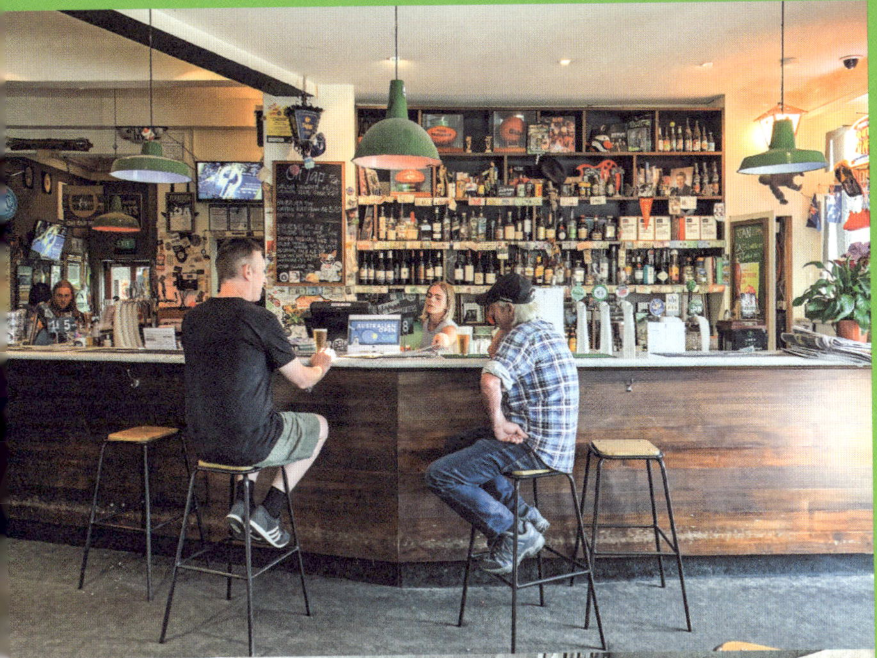

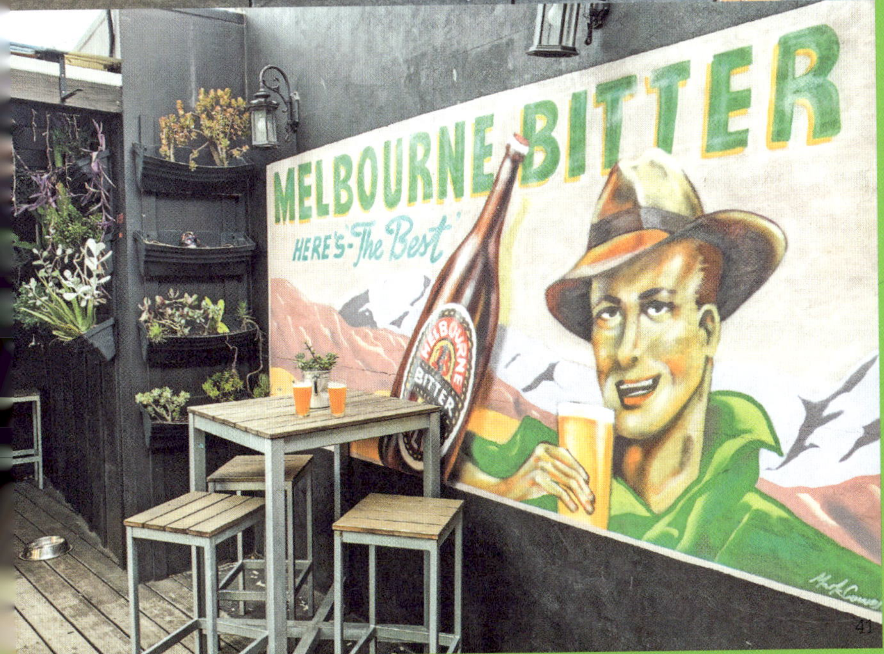
MELBOURNE BITTER
HERE'S "The Best"

FITZROY & COLLINGWOOD

Fitzroy and Collingwood are among Melbourne's oldest and most eclectic suburbs: a magnet for students and artsy types for decades, many of whom can no longer afford to live here. Yes, the gentrification is real but the creative crowd still hang out here and street art (*see* p. 45) can be found on every other wall. Fashion has always been a big part of the Fitzroy scene – people come here to be seen, and the local preference for funky vintage or locally designed threads can be found in the many clothing stores. It's also arguably Melbourne's vegan and vegetarian heartland and now that the vegan trend has gone mainstream, there are even more plant-based eateries than ever.

Brunswick Street and Smith Street are the anchors of these suburbs, each brimming with designer boutiques, vintage stores, cafes, restaurants bars and clubs. Gertrude Street is a hotspot for fashion and Johnston Street is emerging as the new hip strip. Creativity has been brewing in the streets of Collingwood for decades, with more and more artists, art dealers and creative co-working spaces opening their doors. The network of backstreets across both Fitzroy and Collingwood will also reward you with numerous local bars, cafes and classic pubs.

Train and tram: Collingwood station, Victoria Park station, Route 11, Route 86

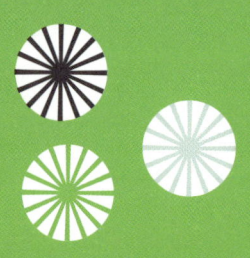

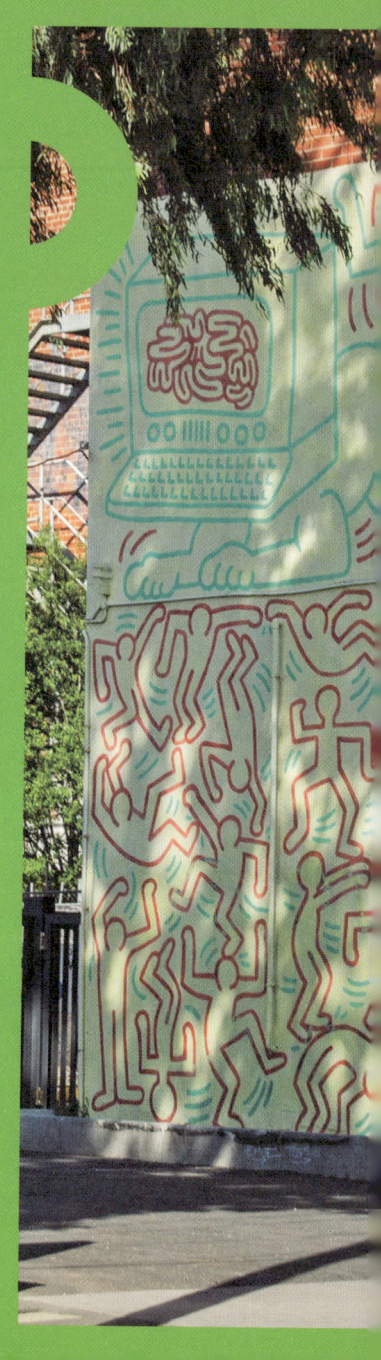

→ *The iconic mural by legendary New York street artist Keith Haring*

SIGHTS
1. Brunswick Street Gallery
2. Johnston Street Art Walk

SHOPPING
3. Third Drawer Down
4. Happy Valley
5. Cottage Industry

SHOPPING & EATING
6. CIBI

EATING & DRINKING
7. Marios
8. Smith & Daughters
9. Paradise Alley
10. Fitzroy Pub Crawl
11. Naked For Satan

FITZROY & COLLINGWOOD

1 BRUNSWICK STREET GALLERY

322 Brunswick St, Fitzroy
8596 0173
www.brunswickstreetgallery.
squarespace.com.
Open Tues–Sun 10am–6pm
[MAP p. 185 D1]

For a taste of Fitzroy's arts scene, Brunswick Street Gallery is your go-to. The unassuming stairs from street level transport you to a world of creativity above. Presenting work from local, Australian and international emerging artists in solo and group shows, the exhibitions across a veritable rabbit warren of installation rooms is diverse: from delicate botanical illustrations to bold and challenging self-expression in paint and mixed-media, sculpture and more. The number of exhibition spaces means there are regular evening openings – a great way to rub shoulders with the local creatives, discover new art and make a new friend or two. Twice-weekly life drawing classes are affordable at just $20 for two hours, materials supplied.

POCKET TIP
The Centre for Contemporary Photography (204 George St, Fitzroy) exhibits the work of emerging and leading contemporary photographers.

FITZROY & COLLINGWOOD

2 JOHNSTON STREET ART WALK

[MAP p. 185 D2]

Creativity has been brewing in Fitzroy and Collingwood for decades, and here you'll find art all over the streets. Using Johnston Street as a spine for a look-see at local street art, you'll be rewarded by venturing down side streets to make your own discoveries. Everfresh's **Welcome to Sunny Fitzroy** (143 Johnston St) is a postcard tribute and an essential souvenir selfie. Further east, Chapel Street – colloquially known as **Juddy Roller Street** after the street art network and gallery (226 Johnston Street) features pieces by multiple artists. Head inside for a look at street art exhibition-style. Down the hill past Johnston Street is Melbourne's most significant street art, the heritage-listed **Keith Haring mural** (60 Johnston St), one of the last remaining outdoor murals that the New York artist painted on his 1980s world tour. Head south (right) on Wellington Street for a look at **Matt Adnate's 20-storey mural** on the side of the public housing tower at 240 Wellington Street. Celebrating Collingwood's multicultural community, it's the largest mural in the Southern Hemisphere.

POCKET TIP
Faraday's Cage (329 Gore St, Fitzroy) is an excellent cafe with seats on Chapel Street so you can take in street art over coffee or lunch.

45

FITZROY & COLLINGWOOD

3 THIRD DRAWER DOWN

93 George St, Fitzroy
9534 4088
www.thirddrawerdown.com
Open Mon–Sat 11am–5pm
[MAP p. 185 E4]

Having made its name in ironic designer tea towels and gaining reproduction rights to the work of international cult artist David Shrigley, among many others, Third Drawer Down has gone onto colonise the world of artistic gifts. Here you'll find banana-shaped table lamps, tube-socked paper weights, inflatable swans and more. This thoroughly eccentric, curated collection of pop cultural iconography is both nostalgic and fresh, and a whole lot of fun. Duck through to the pint-sized Open Closed Mart out back for a surreal mini-market novelty trip. Our current favourites are the Australiana-themed colourful designs from Arts Project Australia, an organisation which supports artists with an intellectual disability. And there are more beautifully printed linen artsy tea towels than you can throw a wet dish at, or even hang on your wall.

POCKET TIP

Hit the weekend Rose Street Market (60 Rose St, Fitzroy) for artisan wares, handmade gifts, jewellery and affordable art. It's also great to grab food from Young Bloods Diner.

FITZROY & COLLINGWOOD

4 HAPPY VALLEY

294 Smith St, Collingwood
9077 8509
happyvalleyshop.com
Open Mon–Wed & Sat
10.00am–6pm, Thurs 10am–7pm, Fri 10am–9pm, Sun 11am–5pm
[MAP p. 185 F2]

Happy Valley owner Chris Crouch has a good feel for what the people of the inner north want in a design store: a mix of cutting-edge and classic designs, locally made goods and first-ever imports of the best that overseas has to offer. The range of books is broad and deep in quality – from classic fiction to art and design coffee table books, and music, travel and cookbooks, too. Better still, this ain't no poky bookstore. The ceilings are double height, and there's loads of natural light. Giftware ranges from handmade badges and brass necklaces to all manner of quirky stationery, mini Melbourne building models by Gin & Apathy, Triumph and Disaster grooming products, reusable designer coffee cups (the *essential* Melbourne accessory), Koko Black chocolate and more. You won't have trouble finding something for your most difficult friends and family, or even your most difficult self.

POCKET TIP

Get your gay on at Hares and Hyenas (63 Johnston St, Fitzroy), a bookstore, cafe and events space for the queer community.

FITZROY & COLLINGWOOD

5 COTTAGE INDUSTRY

67 Gertrude St, Fitzroy
9419 2430
www.cottageindustrystore.com.au
Open Mon–Fri 10.30am–5.30pm, Sat 11am–5pm
[MAP p. 185 D4]

Pene Durston's Cottage Industry is chock full of beautifully presented, ethically made and handcrafted goods – many of which are her own creations. Heavy on nostalgia, Durston's ethos is about repurposing – souvenir tea towels and old-school Welsh blankets become one-of-a-kind cushions, vintage linen is transformed into 'anti-fashion' work smocks and if you're lucky, you might even score a store bag made from old newspapers. Her signature fingerless gloves, made from angora and lambswool, are durable and in a range of colours and lengths. You can also find classic heritage brands such as Stanley (handy thermoses, flasks and lunch boxes) and Falcon enamelware, South African wax print umbrellas, and Durston's own must-have suburban pride-felt pennants – the perfect Melbourne keepsake. You'll probably be met by store cats Jethro and Tully – they're poseurs in the pretty front window.

POCKET TIP
Hunter Gatherer (247 Brunswick St, Fitzroy) offers a hand-picked range of pre-loved clothing that supports charity.

FITZROY & COLLINGWOOD

6 CIBI

31–39 Keele St, Collingwood
9077 3941
www.cibi.com.au
Open Mon–Fri 8am–4pm,
Sat–Sun 9am–4pm
[MAP p. 185 F1]

A slice of Tokyo in the back streets of Collingwood, CIBI is all about space: in your head, in your heart and all around you. The exposed high ceilings and even lighting help convey a distinctly Zen vibe. The name CIBI means 'Little One' and encourages all who enter this peaceful concept store to touch base with their younger, innocent selves. The cafe menu is seasonal and simple, and the Japanese breakfast of grilled salmon, free-range omelette, vegetables, potato salad, brown rice and miso soup makes us feel healthier just thinking about it! The retail component is beautiful; it's full of stylish Japanese gifts and homewares, including quality Hakusan porcelain; precision Allex scissors; colourful Noda Horo enamel cookware and Siwa polypaper bags, wallets and cases. Epitomising Japanese efficiency and thoughtfulness, there's even a grocery store.

POCKET TIP

Friends of the Earth (312 Smith St, Collingwood) serves feel-good fresh, organic, vegan and gluten-free meals. You can even volunteer in exchange for lunch.

FITZROY & COLLINGWOOD

7 MARIOS

303 Brunswick St, Fitzroy
9417 3343
www.marioscafe.com.au
Open Mon–Sat 7am–10.30pm,
Sun 8am–10.30pm
[MAP p. 185 D2]

Marios is a Fitzroy institution. Along with The Black Cat (*see* pocket tip), it's one of the venues that transformed a tired old Brunswick Street into Melbourne's bohemian, creative and alternative place-to-be. Simplicity and attention to detail are the markers of quality at Marios – tables are dressed with white, starched tablecloths, and the waiters (who often double as artists when not at work here) are always neatly attired in vest and tie. They're confident, knowledgeable and decidedly unstuffy, too. Regulars return time and again for an espresso coffee with dairy milk (never soy, never skim), the all-day breakfast and fine fettuccine. Despite the quality of the experience, it doesn't cost the earth to eat here, which keeps the long-time regulars – and celebrities – coming back for more. And there's nowhere quite like the window seat to while away an afternoon under the red neon glow of the iconic 'Marios' neon sign.

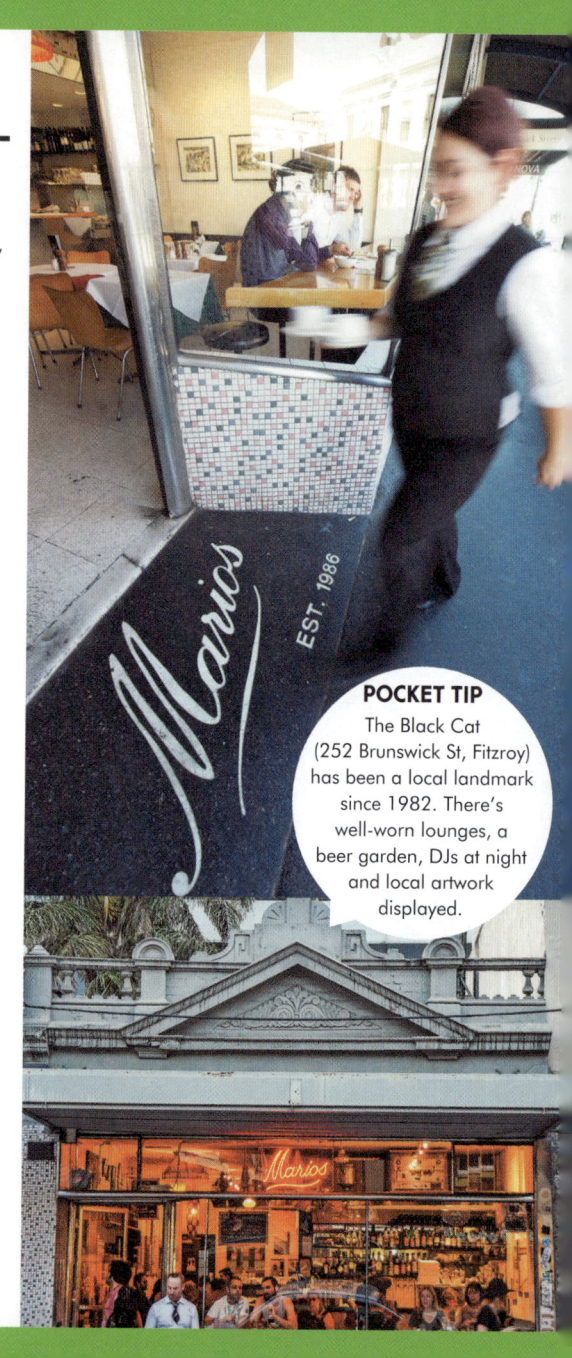

POCKET TIP

The Black Cat (252 Brunswick St, Fitzroy) has been a local landmark since 1982. There's well-worn lounges, a beer garden, DJs at night and local artwork displayed.

FITZROY & COLLINGWOOD

8 SMITH & DAUGHTERS

175 Brunswick St, Fitzroy
9939 3293
www.smithanddaughters.com
Open Mon–Fri 6pm–late, Sat 10am–late, Sun 10am–3pm
[MAP p. 185 D3]

Trailblazers of 21st-century veganism, Mo Wyse and Shannon Martinez' Smith & Daughters is a must-visit restaurant that is challenging the concept of vegan dining. There are some ripper mock-meat dishes here; the 'beef' ragu is made from pressed mushroom and will fool even the most committed carnivore. Flavour and creativity feature across the menu, which is regularly updated: fermented chilli provides the oomph in the melanzane puttanesca, the humble minestrone soup is presented as a salad and the granita is served savoury with an olive crisp. The exposed bluestone walls and salon hang provides an informal dining experience. Grab a seat at the communal benches to get a good look at what everyone else is eating. The drinks and dessert are as artful as the mains. Combine the two with a midnight Manhattan special – a boozy black coffee amaro with walnut bitters, maple syrup and ice-cream.

POCKET TIP

The legendary Vegie Bar (380 Brunswick St, Fitzroy) has been open since 1988. Find meat-free Mexican street food at Trippy Taco (234 Gertrude St, Fitzroy).

FITZROY & COLLINGWOOD

9 PARADISE ALLEY

25 Easey St, Collingwood
9029 8484
www.paradisealley.com.au
Open Wed–Fri 4pm–late, Sat 12pm–late, Sun 2pm–late
Casati's Deli open Mon–Fri 7am–3pm
Backwoods Gallery open Tues–Sun 12pm–6pm
[MAP p.185 F2]

A multi-purpose venue for the cool kids and just about everybody else, Paradise Alley is quintessentially new-Collingwood: a creatively converted warehouse down a side street, accessible only via a dirty, narrow side alley (the name is *meant* to be ironic). It's home to a co-working space, a deli and coffee joint, an art gallery *and* a microbrewery! It's a community of friendly colleagues doing their thing, and doing it well. You can enjoy a quiet soy cappuccino, pastries or a toastie at **Casati's Deli** and explore the art at **Backwoods Gallery** during the day. When the bar opens, you can sample South American street food, courtesy of the **Little Latin Lucy** kitchen, order from the wine and cocktail list or sink beers and eight balls in the dingy pool room – deep into the night.

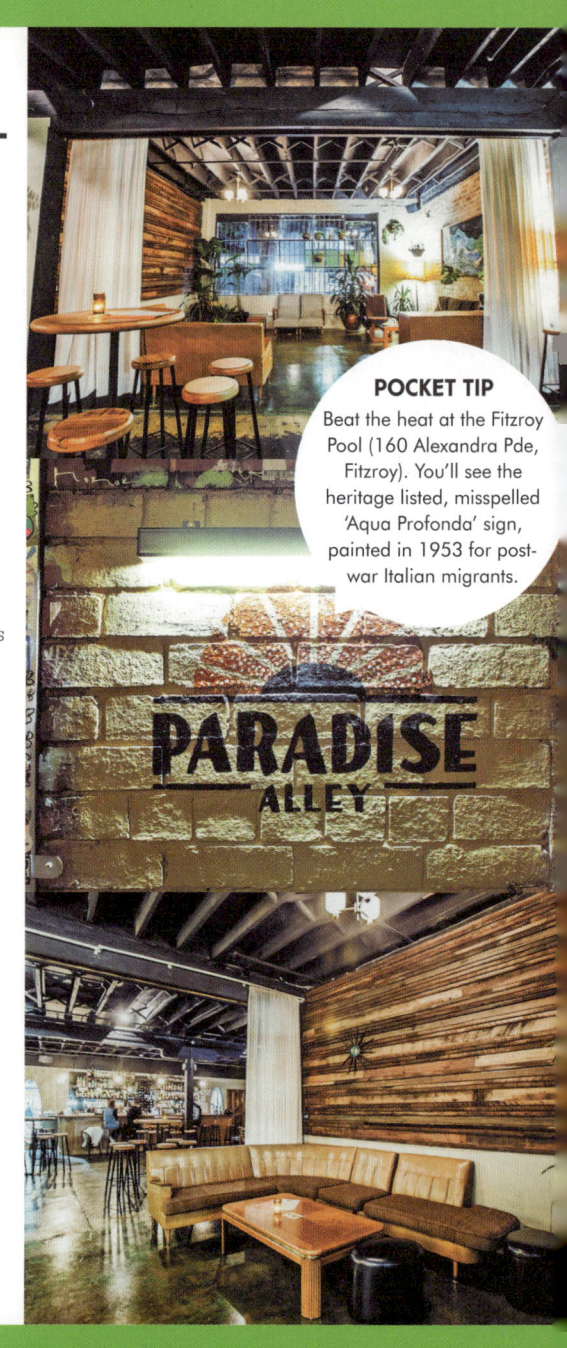

POCKET TIP

Beat the heat at the Fitzroy Pool (160 Alexandra Pde, Fitzroy). You'll see the heritage listed, misspelled 'Aqua Profonda' sign, painted in 1953 for post-war Italian migrants.

FITZROY & COLLINGWOOD

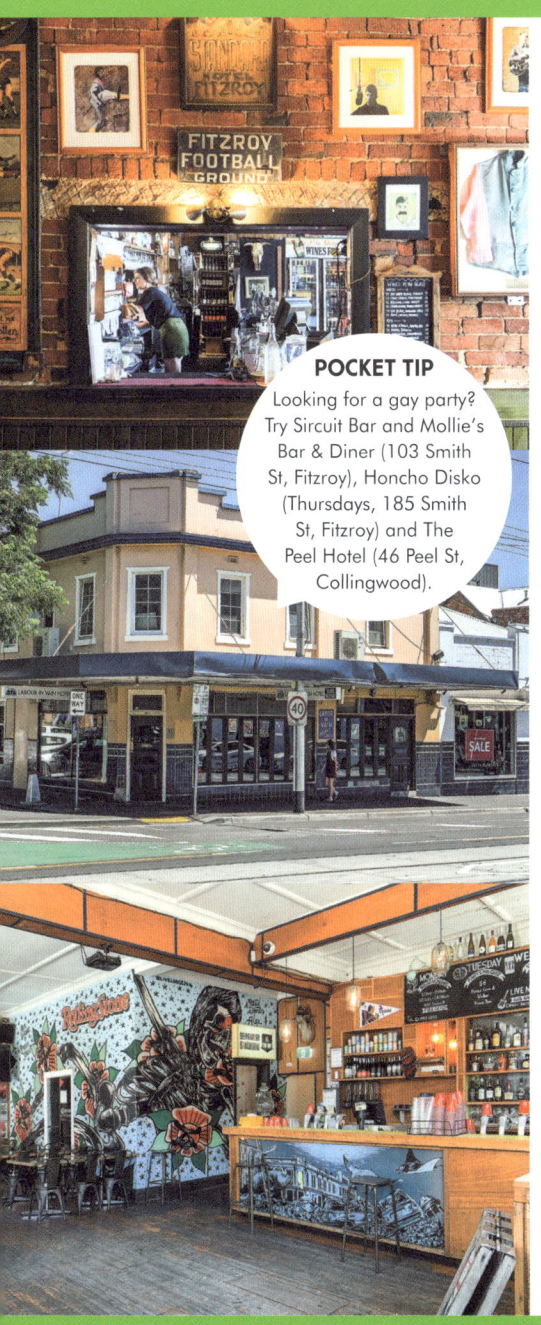

10 FITZROY PUB CRAWL

[MAP p. 185 D4]

Nothing quite reveals Fitzroy's roots like its many old pubs. Conveniently, they're all within easy walking distance of each other, which makes for a good old-fashioned pub crawl. **The Workers Club** (51 Brunswick St) serves pub classics with a twist and hosts regular live gigs. **Labour in Vain** (197A Brunswick St) has a rock'n'roll vibe and a rooftop beer deck. **The Standard** (293 Fitzroy St) is in the quiet backstreets with craft beers and a mouth-watering menu. Live music is a regular feature at **The Rainbow** (27 David St), including excellent blues/soul house band Checkerboard Lounge. The unpolished **Napier Hotel** (210 Napier St) is occasionally raucous, always fun and has an upstairs exhibition space. Our old local, the **Union Club Hotel** serves tasty burgers and parmigiana (with vegetarian options), with regular lunch specials. In Collingwood, you'll find live gigs and nightly dinner specials at **The Grace Darling** (114 Smith St), as well as Melbourne's original punk rock pub **The Tote** (67–71 Johnston St).

POCKET TIP

Looking for a gay party? Try Sircuit Bar and Mollie's Bar & Diner (103 Smith St, Fitzroy), Honcho Disko (Thursdays, 185 Smith St, Fitzroy) and The Peel Hotel (46 Peel St, Collingwood).

FITZROY & COLLINGWOOD

11 NAKED FOR SATAN

285 Brunswick St, Fitzroy
9416 2238
www.nakedforsatan.com.au
Open Fri–Sat 12pm–1am,
Sun–Thurs 12pm–late
[MAP p. 185 D2]

With a name like that, you'd be forgiven for having second thoughts about entering, but once inside you'll remember it's best to keep your clothes on. The new tapas menu now features $6 sliders of fried chicken, beef brisket or haloumi; $9.90 tinned anchovies and sardines; and $14 mussels and chips. Classic and seasonal cocktails are priced from $18 and focus on vodka.

Beyond the dimly lit bar downstairs, you can ride the elevator to **Naked In The Sky** for amazing city views from the rooftop bar, lounge and restaurant, which offers budget-friendly lunch specials Monday to Friday and dinner specials on Sunday (all dishes $11). Get cheesy with the fried cheese and walnut croquettes, crumbed eggplant with honey and blue cheese or go all out on a baked camembert. As for drinks, there's even more vodka excursions up here. Can't decide? Try the ice box of six shooters for $29.

POCKET TIP

Discover emerging performers or rediscover old faves at Bar Open (317 Brunswick St, Fitzroy), six nights a week.

55

CARLTON & BRUNSWICK

Carlton is a vibrant food and cultural precinct just a short tram ride or walk from Melbourne city. It was a slum in the 19th century and a refuge for European immigrants in the 20th century, which has helped shape the suburb's famous Italian food and wine scene on popular Lygon Street. Long the domain of students and academics for its proximity to the University of Melbourne, Carlton is also renowned for its bookshops, notably Readings (see p. 61). Leafy Rathdowne Street and Nicholson Street in North Carlton are local strips of restaurants and cafes, mostly Italian too. Nearby, you'll also find the Melbourne Museum (see p. 60) in the Carlton Gardens. Further north is Royal Park, home to the Melbourne Zoo.

Sydney Road in Brunswick has been a cultural melting pot since the 19th century, more recently anchored by bridal and bonbonnieres stores, and Turkish and Lebanese take-aways. Still hot for foreign foods of the Middle Eastern variety, Sydney Road's influences are now truly international. An influx of younger people to Brunswick in the last decade has brought new bars, cafes, restaurants and boutiques, each vying for attention among the discount variety stores. Once the lesser-known cousin to Sydney Road, the East Brunswick end of Lygon Street has asserted itself as a hip strip of great cafes, bars and boutiques.

Train and tram: Brunswick station, Parliament station, Route 1, Route 19

→ Italian after dark on Lygon Street, Carlton

SIGHTS
1. CERES
2. Melbourne Museum

SHOPPING
3. Readings
4. Brunswick Bound
5. Mr Kitly

EATING & DRINKING
6. D. O. C. Pizza & Mozzarella Bar
7. Los Hermanos
8. The Brunswick Mess Hall
9. Green Man's Arms
10. Carlton Yacht Club
11. Retreat Hotel
12. Howler

CARLTON & BRUNSWICK

1 CERES

Cnr Stuart and Roberts sts,
East Brunswick
9389 0100
www.ceres.org.au
Open Mon–Fri 8.30am–3pm,
Sat–Sun 8.30am–1pm
[MAP p. 175 E1]

An oasis in the suburbs, this community-run sustainability centre and urban farm is an inspiring way to connect with the natural environment. Established in 1982, the Centre for Education and Research in Environmental Strategies (CERES) transformed industrial land into a place of nature and beauty, where you can learn about growing your own food, making your own soap and bread, fixing your bike or taking a deep dive into ancestral lineage healing. Check the website for all the courses CERES has to offer. There's also a retail nursery onsite and regular markets for organic fruit and vegetables, artisan goods and second-hand wares. The **Merri Table** organic cafe serves produce grown on site. The Buddha Bowl brims with healthy freshness, and you'll feel good knowing that all the profits made here go back into CERES, so that they can continue their mission to support the planet.

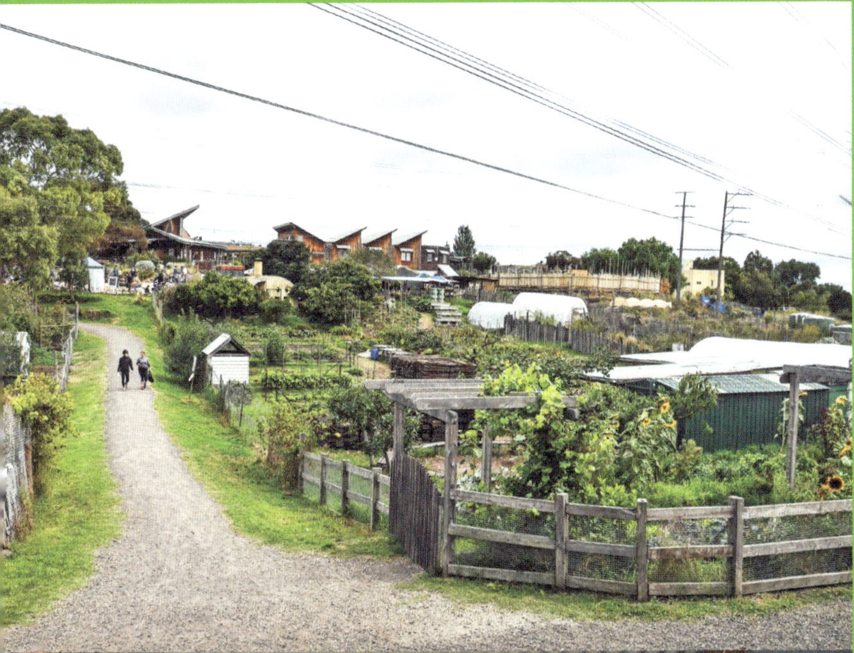

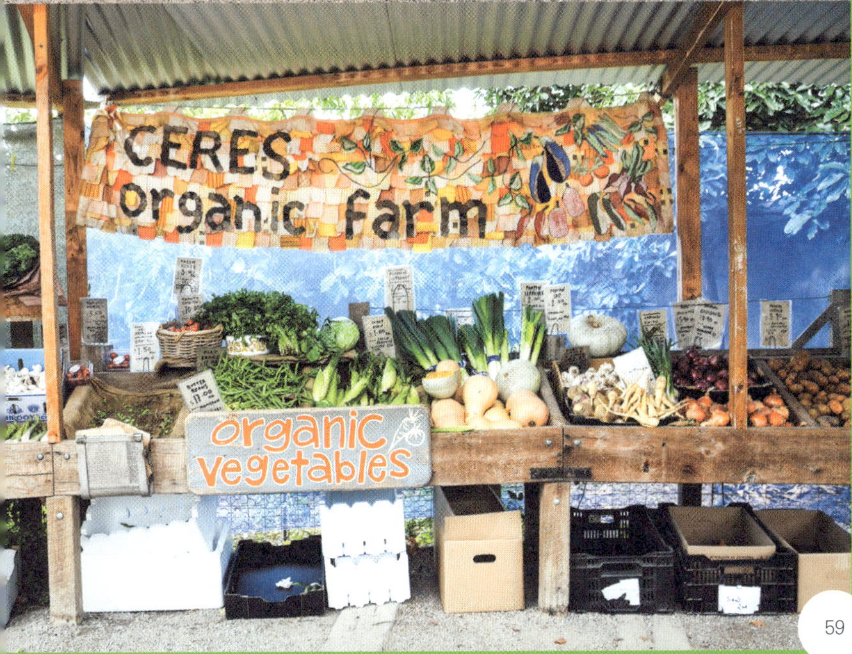
CERES
organic farm
organic
vegetables

CARLTON & BRUNSWICK

2 MELBOURNE MUSEUM

11 Nicholson St, Carlton
13 11 02
www.museumsvictoria.com.au/melbournemuseum
Open Mon–Sun 10am–5pm
[MAP p. 184 B3]

Melbourne Museum in the historic Carlton Gardens tells a very rich history. Its largest collection item is the UNESCO World Heritage listed **Royal Exhibition Building** out front, built in 1880 in multiple architectural styles to demonstrate the city's wealth. Its counterpoint is the year 2000 museum itself: discreetly transparent and contained mostly underground. Inside, an entire whale skeleton is suspended from the ceiling and a forest garden grows within the roofline. The **Bunjilaka Aboriginal Cultural Centre** introduces you to the world's oldest living culture through artefacts, stories and traditions, and the **Melbourne Gallery** tells the story of this city built on gold – and the utopian dreams of its many immigrants. There's regular temporary exhibitions and tours, including a before-hours one with morning tea and the museum to yourself! Museums Victoria also run the **Immigration Museum** in the city and **Scienceworks** in Spotswood.

POCKET TIP

The Counihan Gallery (233 Sydney Rd, Brunswick) exhibits the work of emerging and established Australian contemporary artists, with a regular program of talks and events.

CARLTON & BRUNSWICK

3 READINGS

309 Lygon St, Carlton
9347 6633
www.readings.com.au
Open Mon–Sat 9am–11pm,
Sun 10am–9pm
[MAP p. 184 A1]

One of the great Melbourne independent bookstores, Readings has been a Melbourne institution since it opened in 1969. It's at the heart of Melbourne's literary scene and provides good old-fashioned customer service and careful curation across a vast selection of books and music. This store was renovated in 2018 – with so much more space and light for browsers and booklovers. There's a jam-packed calendar of free and paid literary events, from little-known self-published authors to the big names of the book world. Music focuses on classics and classical, with CDs and vinyl. The famous Readings bargain table is always worth a rummage for cut-price hardbacks; find it at all seven Readings stores across Melbourne. **Readings Kids** bookstore next door is a brightly lit space with Australian and international picture books, non-fiction, young fiction, Young Adult (YA), and has knowledgeable staff.

POCKET TIP

Cinema Nova (380 Lygon St, Carlton) screens arthouse and mainstream movies and serves classic cocktails that you can drink during the movie.

CARLTON & BRUNSWICK

4 BRUNSWICK BOUND

361 Sydney Rd, Brunswick
9381 4019
www.brunswickbound.com.au
Open Mon–Sat 10am–6pm,
Sun 11am–5pm
[MAP p. 198 B2]

Independent retailer Brunswick Bound might look like a bookstore from the street, but there's plenty more to see once you step inside this popular local hangout. There's a selection of hundreds of fiction and non-fiction titles, including beautiful art and design, and illustrated children's books. If you just want a good recommendation, the knowledgeable staff will sort you out. There's also a good range of CDs and vinyl, stationery, jewellery and gifts made by local artists and designers, as well as beautiful 20th-century furniture and objects on the almost-secret second level overlooking Sydney Road. There are comfortable club lounge chairs in nooks for the weary-legged, and an amazing counter made of old books, too.

POCKET TIP

Pop into the cute reader-friendly cafe Foxtrot Charlie next door and enjoy a latte with your latest literary find.

CARLTON & BRUNSWICK

5 MR KITLY

381 Sydney Rd, Brunswick
9078 7357
www.mrkitly.com.au
Open Wed–Sat 11am–6pm,
Sun 11am–4pm
[MAP p. 198 C2]

Climb the floral-carpeted stairs off hectic Sydney Road and you'll find Mr Kitly – a combination retail space and art gallery with a reverence for natural materials and Japanese aesthetics. Here you'll find beautiful handmade and quality manufactured objects that thoughtfully combine form and function. There's design-oriented homewares, jewellery and gifts such as eco-lunchboxes, vases and tidies in ceramic, metal, paper, textile, wood, glass and enamel. Don't miss the simple stoneware and porcelain pieces by Melbourne ceramicist Tara Shackell; fine quality linen clothing by Fog Linen Work; and locally made natural skincare products by Soap Club. There's also an interesting selection of books and magazines on craft, design and architecture, plus a range of indoor plants for small spaces and well-designed tools for urban gardening. Regular exhibitions reflect this thoughtfully considered local store that inspires simplicity and beauty in everyday life.

POCKET TIP
The Boroughs (345 Lygon St) is a beautifully presented store with the best design and craft from Melbourne. East Elevation (351 Lygon St) is a warehouse cafe and chocolate factory.

CARLTON & BRUNSWICK

6 D. O. C. PIZZA & MOZZARELLA BAR

295 Drummond St, Carlton
9347 2998
www.docgroup.net
Open Mon–Wed 6pm–late,
Thurs–Sun 12pm–late
[MAP p. 184 B2]

Pizza and pasta is the main game of the Italian restaurants on Lygon Street, but if it's *your* main game, you'll want to go *off piste* to nearby Drummond Street in search of D. O. C., a flash little pizzeria with the biggest name in pizza. Its approach is simple: best quality ingredients and minimum intervention. Minimalism is also the name of the game in decor; D. O. C. is still a pizza joint, after all. Mozzarella tasting plates compare Australian fior de latte with Italian buffalo mozzarella and smoky Australian scamorza. The pizza bases are yeasty, hand-thrown and authentically uneven. Don't go past the simple margherita or the porcini of wild mushrooms and truffle oil; just don't ask for a half and half. Add some green with an insalata misti, and try the goat's cheese tiramisu for dessert.

POCKET TIP

So successful is D. O. C. that the owners have opened a cafe and delicatessen (326–33 Lygon St), as well as a pizzeria and produce store in Mornington.

CARLTON & BRUNSWICK

7 LOS HERMANOS

339 Victoria St, Brunswick
9939 3661
www.los-hermanos.com.au
Open Mon–Wed 6–11pm,
Thurs–Sat 6pm–1am
[MAP p. 198 A1]

Los Hermanos is a late-night Mexican go-to for local punters, an easy stroll from the bars and venues on Sydney Road. This friendly neighbourhood taqueria feels like the real deal, free of the on-trend hipster Mexican vibe. The best seats in the house are at the bar – where you can watch the bartenders slinging drinks and easily read the menu on the blackboard behind them. The food focus is a variety of cheap tacos filled with mouth-watering ingredients, like slow-cooked lamb, crispy fried fish and field mushrooms with grilled manchego cheese. Our pick is the De Ejotes taco, stuffed with organic green beans, potato and free range oven-baked eggs with jalapeños. While you're at it, why not try the cactus salad, spike-free and marinated in lime juice. Los Hermanos is open at a respectable dinner hour but rolls well into the night, so don't be surprised if your post-party taco stop turns into a fiesta of its own.

POCKET TIP
Coffee and brunch? Nearby Wide Open Road (274 Barkly St, Brunswick) is a former supermarket turned super-cafe and coffee roastery.

CARLTON & BRUNSWICK

8 THE BRUNSWICK MESS HALL

400 Sydney Rd, Brunswick
9388 0297
www.thebrunswickmesshall.com.au
Open Tues–Thurs 5.30pm–11pm, Fri & Sat 5pm–1am
[MAP p. 198 C2]

Pass through the fairly unassuming entrance off Sydney Road and you'll soon be transported into a big and beautiful old masonic hall, complete with high-pitched ceilings and hefty timber beams. Grab a seat and take it all in while you wait for Asian treats from the **Lucky Panda Kitchen**, under the charge of ex-Longrain chef Kampat Suthipong. If you're out with friends, you'll probably be encouraged to bypass the decision making and go straight for the banquet, which also has a vegetarian version. There are fun snacks aplenty – some sweet and some seriously spicy curries. Speaking of hot and spicy, The Brunswick Mess Hall really wants you to drink that heat away with a massive selection of bottled beers and some seriously tempting cocktails. Next door is **Little Mess**, The Mess Hall's smaller, younger sibling who likes to party all the way from the front bar to the beer garden out back.

POCKET TIP
Nearby Royal Park (Flemington Rd, Parkville) is home to the Melbourne Zoo, native gardens, walking tracks, picnic grounds and playing fields.

CARLTON & BRUNSWICK

9 GREEN MAN'S ARMS

418 Lygon St, Carlton
9347 7419
www.greenmansarms.com.au
Open Mon–Thurs 4pm–late,
Fri–Sun 12pm–late
[MAP p. 184 B1]

Once an old-man's pub with a delightful bistro sign, the old Percy's has been reborn as the Green Man's Arms, with a respect for its history. It's a locally unique concept: a vegetarian and vegan pub that fills a meat-free gap in the Melbourne public bar dining scene. But meat eaters are welcome here, too – that is, if you're willing to swap a chicken parmigiana for an eggplant schnitzel or a chickpea flour pancake. The food choices are intentionally limited, making you want to try one of everything; fortunately the bigger dishes are perfect for sharing. It's a bit pricier than a standard counter meal, but it's no standard pub and kitchen. The drinking room is part classic Aussie pub and part eclectic, artsy Carlton drinking hole, with interesting artworks and a retro flavour. We love that they serve only local beers on tap. Cheers to that!

POCKET TIP

Pidapipó (299 Lygon St, Carlton) gelato has become a local obsession. All gelato is made on site using fresh, natural ingredients – the result: join the queue.

CARLTON & BRUNSWICK

10 CARLTON YACHT CLUB

298 Lygon St, Carlton
0412 401 640
www.carlton-yachtclub.com
Open Mon–Wed 5pm–1am,
Thu 5pm–3am, Fri 4pm–3am,
Sat 5pm–3am, Sun 2pm–1am
[MAP p. 184 A2]

It hasn't been around as long as many of the busy tourist-magnet Italian eateries around it, but the Carlton Yacht Club has found its place as one of the bars, if not the only bar, on Lygon Street. This nautically themed joint is frequented by local university students and Carlton cocktail-seekers, and has plenty of life buoys and retro paraphernalia. There's a world of beers to choose from and just enough wines for the vino lovers. It ain't fancy but it's good fun and gets better when the sun goes down and the cocktail making amps up – particularly on Mondays when the meticulously made martinis are only $12. Choose from the list of classic and latest creations, or as the Carlton Yachties say, 'if you're craving something we don't have, let's get some teamwork going and make something up together.' That's the spirit!

CARLTON & BRUNSWICK

11 RETREAT HOTEL

280 Sydney Rd, Brunswick
9380 4090
www.retreathotelbrunswick.com.au
Open Mon–Thurs 12pm–1am, Fri–Sat 12pm–3am, Sun 12pm–1am
[MAP p. 198 B3]

The Retreat Hotel is located on the site of Brunswick's first hotel, which was operated from 1842 by a certain Miss Amelia Shaw. With an old-school front bar and back band room serving live music seven days a week, this local pub keeps it real. Choose from multiple tap beers and honest pub meals and snacks, like parmigianas, burgers and tacos, with bargain daily specials. Settle in for a taste of the local music scene or test your trivia knowledge at the popular Wednesday night pub quiz.

An upstairs cocktail bar named after the Retreat's first licensee, **Amelia Shaw**, is a totally different scene to the pub vibes below. Meticulously renovated and fitted out with Art Deco details, furniture and geometric murals, it's classy with three fireplaces, a round pool table and cane lounges. Try the signature Miss Shaw's Mai Tai with two kinds of rum and you'll soon find yourself in very good spirits.

POCKET TIP

Bouvier Bar (159 Lygon St, Brunswick East) is a sleek Manhattan-esque bar for grown-ups, open until 3am for late-night shindigs and top-notch food.

CARLTON & BRUNSWICK

12 HOWLER

7–11 Dawson St, Brunswick
9077 5572
www.h-w-l-r.com
Open Mon 4pm–11pm, Tues 4pm–12am, Wed–Thurs 4pm–1am, Fri–Sat 12pm–1am, Sun 12pm–11pm
[MAP p. 198 A4]

Quintessentially hipster Brunswick, Howler is half bar, half live entertainment venue that very quickly took its place in the music industry's national touring schedule. On any given night, you can expect anything from indie cabaret or local comedy to an international rock legend in the custom-designed theatre. The indoor-outdoor **Garden Bar** is where punters gather for the best local and international craft beers, burgers and beats from the DJ booth. Here you can mingle with the locals among greenery and admire the clever re-design of this old warehouse space, which includes a glass ceiling and an outdoor bar that is revealed by the opening of a folding timber wall. If you're hungry and on a budget, the burger special (Mon–Thurs) is a bargain deal that includes fries and a beer, and there's drinks specials (Fri–Sun). Howler has a friendly, community feel and is totally bike friendly, too, with creatively designed racks for your wheels.

POCKET TIP
From Howler, walk 15 minutes to local favourite, The Alderman (134 Lygon St). We've been going here for over a decade, and enjoy a cosy cocktail in the front bar or brew in the beer garden.

71

NORTHCOTE, THORNBURY & PRESTON

Perched atop Rucker's Hill, Northcote has long been known as the local music capital of Melbourne, with more resident musicians per capita than just about anywhere else in Australia. Long-standing venues like the Northcote Social Club (*see* p. 83) provide punters with live music most nights of the week. An ethical maker's culture thrives here, with a bunch of designer and craft boutiques.

The once sleepy northern suburb of Thornbury has become a veritable hipster haven with more eateries and bars on High Street than you'll have the time to explore in a single day or night. The old European migrants might have moved out but traces remain in local grocers and small goods stores, and back yards with fig and persimmon trees. You can step back in time at the Thornbury Picture House (*see* p. 75) or hang out with the locals at the permanent food van park, Welcome to Thornbury (*see* p. 82). Spend any longer here and you'll probably want to move in and call yourself a local. The wave of gentrification has pushed north through Preston, bringing with it Gertrude Contemporary art gallery (*see* p. 74).

Train and tram: Northcote station, Thornbury station, Route 86

→ *Enjoy street eats at Welcome to Thornbury*

SIGHTS
1. Gertrude Contemporary
2. Thornbury Picture House

SHOPPING
3. Pinky's
4. Green Horse
5. Vege Threads

EATING
6. Tahina
7. Welcome to Thornbury

DRINKING
8. Northcote Social Club
9. Joanie's Baretto
10. Open Studio

NORTHCOTE, THORNBURY & PRESTON

1 GERTRUDE CONTEMPORARY

21–31 High St, Preston
9419 3406
www.gertrude.org.au
Open Tues–Fri 11am–5.30pm,
Sat 11am–4.30pm
[MAP p. 197 B1]

The place to see young, fresh and edgy contemporary art in Melbourne's northern suburbs, Gertrude Contemporary gallery moved from artsy Fitzroy to suburban Preston in 2018; a shift that reflects the changing demographics of the precinct. The new digs are flexible, light and bright, thanks to skylights and floor-to-ceiling windows along the streetfront. Gertrude has a reputation for being a launching pad for some of Australia's best and most successful contemporary artists, including Reko Rennie and Kate Rohde. A studio program acts as an incubator for up-and-coming art makers, and numerous Gertrude alumni have gone onto represent Australia at the Venice Biennale. But what about the art? You can expect just about anything here – from found object installations to live and video performance-based artworks. Don't miss regular exhibitors' Atlanta Eke's choreographed dance installations and Ali McCann's photographic and sculptural works.

POCKET TIP
Visit vibrant Preston Market (2/30A The Centreway, Preston) for fresh fruit and vegetables, bargain homewares and gifts. Join the two-hour Food Tour for its progressive breakfast.

NORTHCOTE, THORNBURY & PRESTON

2 THORNBURY PICTURE HOUSE

802 High St, Thornbury
9995 0040
www.thornburypicturehouse.com.au
Open Wed–Thurs 5pm–11pm, Fri 10am–11pm, Sat–Sun 2pm–11pm
[MAP p. 197 B1]

POCKET TIP

Head down the hill to Westgarth Village's gorgeously grand Westgarth Cinema (89 High St, Northcote). Stop by the classic Kelvin Bar (84 High St, Northcote).

The Thornbury Picture House is a friendly local cinema with just 57 seats and a screening selection of new releases, documentaries, cult and classic movies and more. Set in an old corner petrol station that dates back to 1912, the building is rich in local history that is celebrated inside and out. Look out for original garage signs and the old petrol pump decorated with a Thelma-and-Louise-themed artwork. The Picture House also features a bar that stands alone as a destination, even if you don't catch a flick. Hang out in the old drive-through or sit inside for a cosy drink or two, including the signature Motor Spirit cocktail and a range of local craft beers. Even the choc-top ice-creams here are locally made. Going to the 'pictures' might seem old fashioned in this era of instant digital entertainment, but why stay in when you can go out and be entertained in such a nostalgic setting?

NORTHCOTE, THORNBURY & PRESTON

3 PINKY'S

28 Gilbert Rd, Preston
www.pinkysstore.com
Open Wed–Sat 10am–4.30pm,
Sun 10am–3pm

Discover the work of local and Australian makers and designers at this cute and colourful shop, founded by one of Melbourne's most beloved designers, Emily Green. Along with stylist Beckie Littler, Green has created a friendly retail store that celebrates the cool, the quirky and the creative, with gorgeous homewares, wearable pieces, books and artworks. We've been following Green's rise as a designer for years, and it's great to see her create a space that reflects her bright and bold aesthetic. Pinky's is also the site of Green's studio, where her popular jewellery and accessories are made behind the scenes. Her latest work can be found on the shop floor, along with that of a handful of her favourite design and craft contemporaries, including jeweller Ada Hodgson and Sacha Jacobsen of Juno and Ace (we heart her kinetic brass wall hangings). Colour really is everything here, reflected in the oh-so-bright hues of the large botanical-inspired wall mural. There's a sweet selection of gifts for little ones, too.

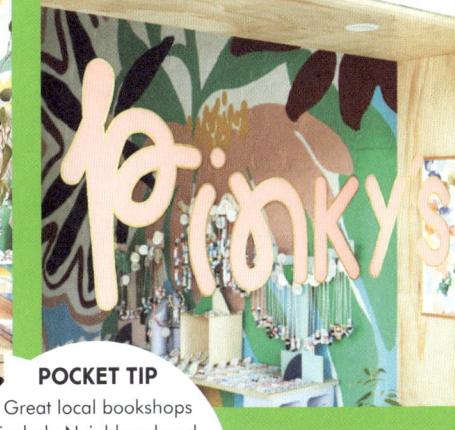

POCKET TIP

Great local bookshops include Neighbourhood Books (55 High St, Northcote), Brown & Bunting (237 High St, Northcote) and Perimeter Books (748 High St, Thornbury).

NORTHCOTE, THORNBURY & PRESTON

4 GREEN HORSE

255 High St, Northcote
9489 5204
www.greenhorse.com.au
Open Mon–Fri 11am–5pm, Sat 10am–5pm, Sun 11am–4pm
[MAP p. 196 B1]

Green Horse is a carefully curated clothing, gifts and homewares store owned and operated by Melbourne entrepreneur and fashionista Jacinta Power. Inside the light and bright shopfront space, you'll find products with a focus on sustainability that don't compromise on style. Choose from timeless women's and men's clothing in organic cotton, merino wool and hemp; chemical-free bath, beauty and cleaning products (including Melbourne-made Ena natural body wash and treatments); and all kinds of lovely things for the home, such as ceramics, fragrances and linen bedding. Green Horse stands behind the products it sells and is more than willing to share the stories behind the brands and the ethical and sustainable processes behind their manufacture. Pop in for a shopping experience that will leave you feeling like you've contributed something small but significant to the planet.

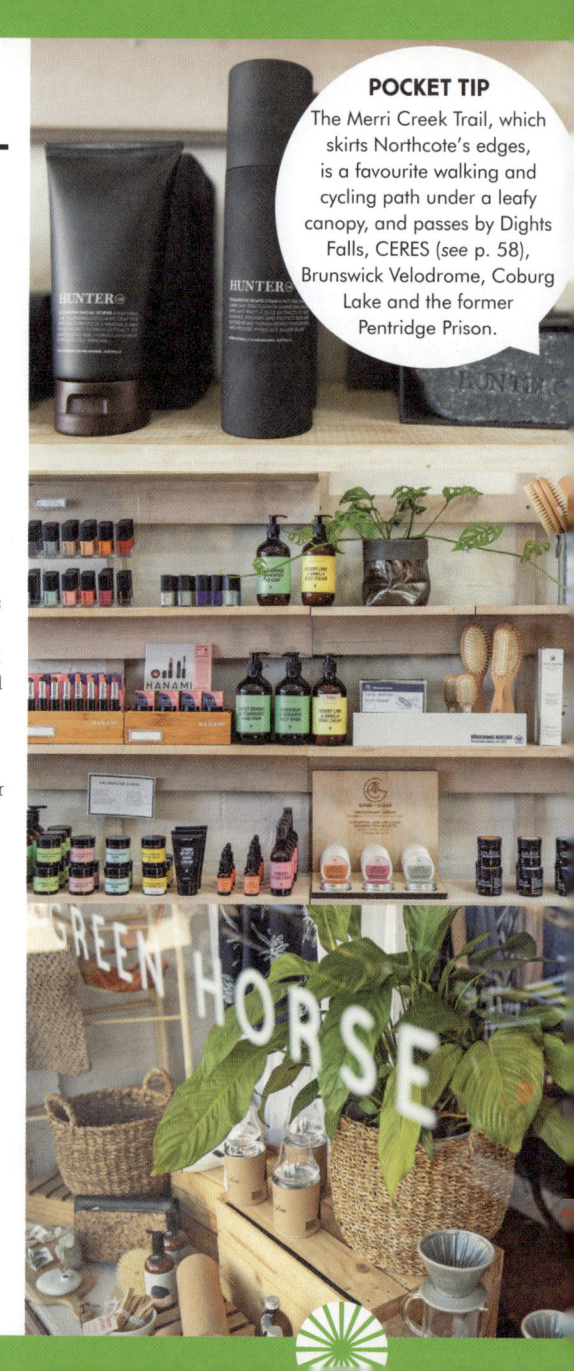

POCKET TIP

The Merri Creek Trail, which skirts Northcote's edges, is a favourite walking and cycling path under a leafy canopy, and passes by Dights Falls, CERES (*see* p. 58), Brunswick Velodrome, Coburg Lake and the former Pentridge Prison.

NORTHCOTE, THORNBURY & PRESTON

5 VEGE THREADS

246 High St, Northcote
www.vegethreads.com
Open Tues–Thurs 11am–5pm,
Fri 11am–6pm, Sat 11am–5pm,
Sun 12pm–4pm
[MAP p. 196 B2]

The ethical, sustainable theme runs deep in Northcote's retail landscape, and few take it more seriously than clothing brand Vege Threads. With a strong online following, founder Amy Roberts decided to open this bricks-and-mortar store in 2018, to cater to locals who want to wear their ethical hearts on their 100 per cent organic cotton and hemp linen sleeves. Bright and simply furnished with a lovely timber feature wall and shop counter, this space features a selection of socks, swimwear, underwear and tees for men and women. All pieces are made with quality, longevity and the environment in mind and are made in Australia using natural dyes and ethical processes. They also support other small manufacturers and businesses, with a percentage of the profits going towards worthwhile environmental projects across the globe. And your whole body is well-covered here, right down to the knitted Australian merino wool socks.

POCKET TIP

All Are Welcome (190 High St, Northcote) was a Christian Science reading room in the 1950s, now a cafe and bakery complete with vintage church pews, delicious breads and pastries.

NORTHCOTE, THORNBURY & PRESTON

6 TAHINA

223 High St, Northcote
9972 1479
www.tahinabar.com
Open Mon–Sun 11am–9pm
[MAP p. 196 B2]

Tahina's fresh take on Israeli street food is made with love and without meat. Inside the former fish and chip shop (you'll see the old shark-shaped sign above the awning), Tahina serves fresh fast-food dishes and superfood smoothies that are as healthy as they are delicious. Try the pita pockets filled with falafel, roasted vegetables and fresh herbs or the traditional shakshuka breakfast platters of eggs, hummus, tahini and pita bread that can be enjoyed at any time of day or night. Time your visit early for lunch or dinner and snare yourself a seat at the bar to watch the bustling open kitchen in action. It's a common story for newly arrived chefs and cooks from across the globe to set up food businesses so they can enjoy – and share – the food of their homeland, and the Tahina story is no exception: owner Israel Roy arrived here in 2012 from Tel Aviv, met and fell in love with partner Nat, and the rest is history. Their food is full of passion for the food Roy grew up with.

POCKET TIP

Tucked away in a back street, Cornerstone (Unit 8, 57 Victoria Rd, Northcote) prides itself on paddock-to-plate provenance, with a focus on healthy and surprising flavour combinations.

NORTHCOTE, THORNBURY & PRESTON

7 WELCOME TO THORNBURY

520 High St, Northcote
9020 7940
www.welcometothornbury.com
Open Mon–Fri 12pm–late,
Sat–Sun 11am–late
[MAP p. 197 B4]

Join Melbourne's biggest outdoor dinner party at the city's first permanent food van park and general fun place to be with an ongoing festival vibe. Melbourne's most popular mobile food vendors gather daily to provide good fast food for hungry folk like you and me. It's located in an old car yard; a fitting location for a bunch of vans on four wheels. There's an ever-changing menu of mobile food by day and by night, so whenever you arrive, there's always something different to try. Expect anything from classic American-style burgers and other dude-food favourites to juicy Greek souvlaki, crispy Vietnamese rolls, Japanese sushi and more-ish Mexican by Melbourne's favourite taqueria **Mamasita**, to name just a few of the international flavours on offer. It's family and dog friendly, and with a capacity of 700, you're pretty much guaranteed a good seat at one of the tables. There's a shipping container bar to satisfy your thirst, too.

POCKET TIP

All Nations Park (Separation St, Northcote), once a rubbish dump, is now a beautifully landscaped community parkland. Walk the spiral path for one of the best views of Melbourne city.

NORTHCOTE, THORNBURY & PRESTON

8 NORTHCOTE SOCIAL CLUB

301 High St, Northcote
9489 3917
www.northcotesocialclub.com
Open Mon 4pm–late, Tues–Sun 12pm–late
[MAP p. 196 B1]

POCKET TIP
One of Melbourne's newest and most intimate music venues, The Merri Creek Tavern (111 High St, Northcote) was established by local music legend Mick Thomas, so it must be good.

Featuring live music most nights of the week, the Northcote Social Club is more than a friendly corner pub – it's an institution. We've been coming here since we lived just a few streets away in the mid-2000s, when the old Commercial Hotel was reinvented for a new demographic of music lovers and locals. Its popularity has paid for some cosmetic upgrades since, but 'The Social' has retained its friendly atmosphere and music focus. The dark-toned front bar is rustic-chic, while the wood and brick dominated outdoor deck and dining area is the perfect spot to watch the sunset over a local craft beer and tasty pub meal. But the intimate band room is the true heart of The Social, showcasing bands and performers, ranging from local up-and-comers to international indie darlings like Melbourne-based Courtney Barnett, who once pulled beers behind the bar. Go on a Monday night for free gigs and look out for lunch, dinner and drinks specials.

NORTHCOTE, THORNBURY & PRESTON

9 JOANIE'S BARETTO

832a High St, Thornbury
9480 5774
www.joaniesbaretto.com.au
Open Wed–Sat 4.30pm–late,
Sun 3.30pm–late
[MAP p. 197 B1]

This friendly shopfront bar pays homage to the Italians who transformed the city's dining culture in the 20th century and invites us all to join in the age-old tradition of after-work drinks and aperitivo. The timber-topped front bar features Italian cultural icons and the framed family photos add a personal feel. Behind the bar you'll find the usual suspects: Campari (served straight up or in a negroni), Aperol, sparkling prosecco and Peroni beer on tap, as well as an all-Italian wine list. Cocktails include the tangy blood orange infused Sicilian margherita. Food offerings include the classic tomato, mozzarella and basil-topped bruschetta and cured meat and cheese boards. There's a handful of more substantial pasta dishes and mains borrowed from **Umberto Espresso Bar**'s menu (see pocket tip), but this baretto is best for starting your night right or ending it with drinks that may turn into an Italian-style family shindig. Saluti!

POCKET TIP

A close relative of Joanie's is Umberto Espresso Bar (822 High St, Thornbury), serving authentic Italian homestyle meals – and espresso coffee made just right.

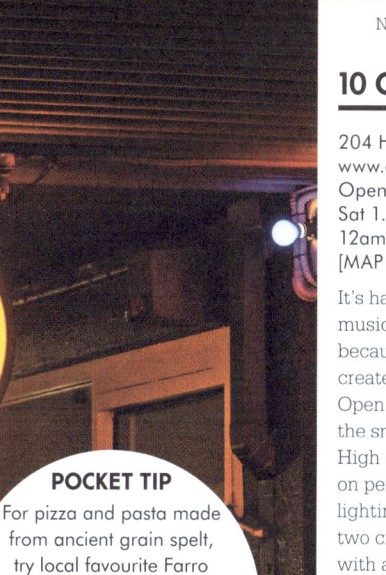

NORTHCOTE, THORNBURY & PRESTON

10 OPEN STUDIO

204 High St, Northcote
www.openstudio.net.au
Open Mon–Fri 6.30pm–1am, Sat 1.30pm–1am, Sun 1.30pm–12am
[MAP p. 196 B2]

It's hard to focus on just one music venue in Northcote, because it takes a village to create a vibrant music scene. Open Studio may be one of the smaller venues on the High Street strip, but it's big on personality. Red walls, dim lighting and candlelit tables for two create a cosy atmosphere with a bohemian vibe that captures the Northcote sensibility before its hipsterfication. You can catch a gig here nearly every day of the week across afternoon, evening, night and late show sessions. Gigs range from jazz and blues to solo storytelling accompanied by guitar and harmonica, and even hip-hop psychedelica. This is a place to catch the niche, the little-known and the esoteric in a venue that is more house party than mass market shakedown. There's craft beer, wine and spirits available at the limited bar, but think big reds, smoky whiskies and vodkas to really get in character.

POCKET TIP

For pizza and pasta made from ancient grain spelt, try local favourite Farro Pizzeria (608 High St, Thornbury). For unexpected Middle Eastern flavours on pizza bases, go to The Moors Head (774 High St, Thornbury).

ST KILDA & BAYSIDE

Just 30 minutes by tram from central Melbourne, seaside St Kilda has always been a place to chill by day and party at night. It's both flashy and trashy – this confluence of style sets St Kilda apart from all other Melbourne suburbs and makes it nationally, if not internationally, famous – if only by virtue of its regular appearances on TV, in film, and in the lyrics of numerous Australian songs. A walk along the beach esplanade (see p. 90) is a must-do for every Melbourne visitor, as is a beer at the legendary Hotel Esplanade (see p. 96) and maybe even a turn on the rides at the historic Luna Park (see p. 90). The local action centres on Fitzroy and Acland streets (see p. 92), but there's plenty to discover across the backstreets and beyond.

Heading south-east along the shoreline you'll encounter laid-back Elwood village, Balaclava and onward to salubrious Brighton, where you can wander the much-photographed Brighton Beach bathing boxes (see p. 88), and sleepy Sandringham, with its historic shipwrecks.

Train and tram: Balaclava station, Brighton Beach station, Route 3, Route 96, Route 16

→ *The open-mouth entrance of historic fun fair Luna Park*

SIGHTS
1. Bayside Trail
2. St Kilda Esplanade

SHOPPING
3. Beyond The Pale

SHOPPING & EATING
4. Acland Street

EATING & DRINKING
5. Cicciolina
6. Matcha Mylkbar
7. Uncle
8. The Hotel Esplanade
9. The Prince Hotel
10. Pontoon

ST KILDA & BAYSIDE

1 BAYSIDE TRAIL

Melburnians are fond of the circle of water known as Port Phillip Bay, and you can easily make a day of it with a walk or ride from the famous St Kilda Beach to picturesque Brighton (8 kilometres, 4.9 miles). Travel further and you'll be rewarded with some of Melbourne's best coastal scenery. Starting from **St Kilda Esplanade**, follow the shoreline via **Elwood** to the quaint and brightly coloured **Brighton Beach bathing boxes**, a tourist drawcard with distant views of Melbourne city. If you're feeling energetic, continue on the **Bayside Coastal Trail**, a scenic 17-kilometre (10.5 miles) journey along beaches and clifftops, with interpretative signs that reveal the area's Indigenous, historic, artistic and environmental heritage. You'll find the wrecks of the World War I-era *J7* submarine at the **Sandringham Yacht Club** and the 19th-century *Cerberus* at beautiful **Half Moon Bay**, overlooked by the dramatic **Red Bluff Cliffs**. Grab a bite at the cute **Cerberus Beach House** on the southern end of the bay before catching the train home from Sandringham.

POCKET TIP

Step back in time at the heritage-listed Jerry's Milkbar (345 Barkly St, Elwood) for a 1950s style milkshake and tasty food fuel for your bayside journey.

POCKET TIP

The Leaf Store village grocer (111 Ormond Rd, Elwood) has all you need for a beachside picnic, including organic produce, fresh breads, deli goods and desserts, too.

ST KILDA & BAYSIDE

2 ST KILDA ESPLANADE

[MAP p. 192 B2]

The St Kilda Esplanade has been pulling crowds for more than a hundred years. First for bathing and promenading, then for the amusements at **Luna Park** theme park, where the big-faced entrance known as Mr Moon has been delighting visitors since 1912, as have the rickety rails of the oldest wooden rollercoaster in the world. Nearby **Catani Gardens** is a popular hangout spot, overlooked by a grand row of Canary Island palm trees, and hosts regular festivals and events. A stroll down the heritage boardwalk of **St Kilda Pier** is a must for panoramic views of the Melbourne city skyline and an ice-cream from the kiosk. Come at sunset for the best chance to see the local penguin colony that lives here, too. The **St Kilda Esplanade Market** happens on Sundays from 10am–4pm (5pm during daylight savings), with handmade goods, street food and live entertainment. **St Kilda Beach** attracts sun seekers from around the world, especially during the warmer months, but if you fancy a swim without the sand, take a dip in the historic **St Kilda Sea Baths**, which also has a gym, bars and eateries.

POCKET TIP
Once a rubbish tip, the St Kilda Botanic Gardens (11 Herbert St) now features an ornamental pond, sub-tropical rainforest conservatory and the iconic Rain Man water fountain.

ST KILDA & BAYSIDE

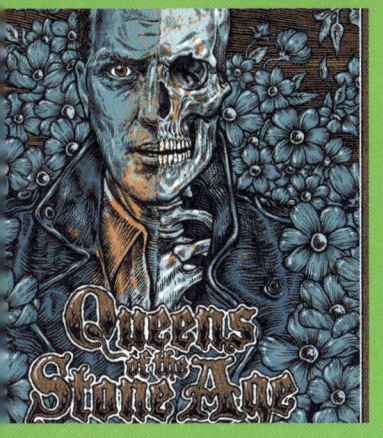

3 BEYOND THE PALE

25 Carlisle St, St Kilda
9593 8900
www.beyondthepale.com.au
Open Tues–Fri 11am–5:30pm,
Sat 11am–4pm
[MAP p. 193 D3]

Rock'n'roll has been the soundtrack to St Kilda for decades and there's no local shop that reflects that more than poster gallery Beyond the Pale. Since the 1990s, this graphic art studio has been producing visuals for local and international bands like The Foo Fighters, Queens of the Stone Age, Arctic Monkeys, Neil Young, Beastie Boys and Florence and the Machine. It's a showcase for the work of the talented Beyond the Pale crew that includes artists Ken Taylor, Vance Kelly, Joe Whyte, Tom Whalen, Hydro74 and Justin Santora. Priced from just $20, this is affordable art, but expect to pay more for your own special commission. There's also a selection of classic band posters and art reproductions featuring Melbourne legends AC/DC and Nick Cave. But it's not all about the music: check out the dark and detailed movie posters by Rhys Cooper and sneaker fetish art by Daymon Greulich.

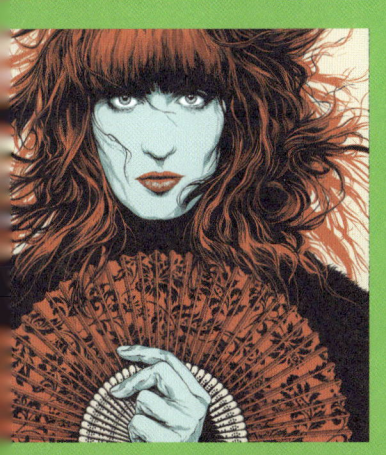

ST KILDA & BAYSIDE

4 ACLAND STREET

St Kilda
[MAP p. 192 C3]

The main section of St Kilda's much-loved and visited shopping, dining and nightlife strip may only run from Carlisle to Barkly Street, but what it lacks in length it sure makes up for in action. Famous for its string of continental cake shops that were opened by European migrants after World War II – with great names like **Monarch**, **Europa** and **Le Bon** – these old-school businesses do a roaring trade, and it's fun to photograph the many cake-filled windows. Here you'll also find the St Kilda branch of Melbourne's favourite local bookstore chain, **Readings** (see p. 61), popular local gift and homewares store **Urban Attitude** and stalwart watering hole **The Vineyard**. The Barkly Street end has become a car-free urban 'park' where the trams end their journey and you're invited to hang with the motley crew of tourists and locals.

POCKET TIP
Woodfrog Bakery (108A Barkly St, St Kilda) serves their celebrated sourdough breads and pastries with good coffee and all-you-can-eat, DIY toast at your table.

ST KILDA & BAYSIDE

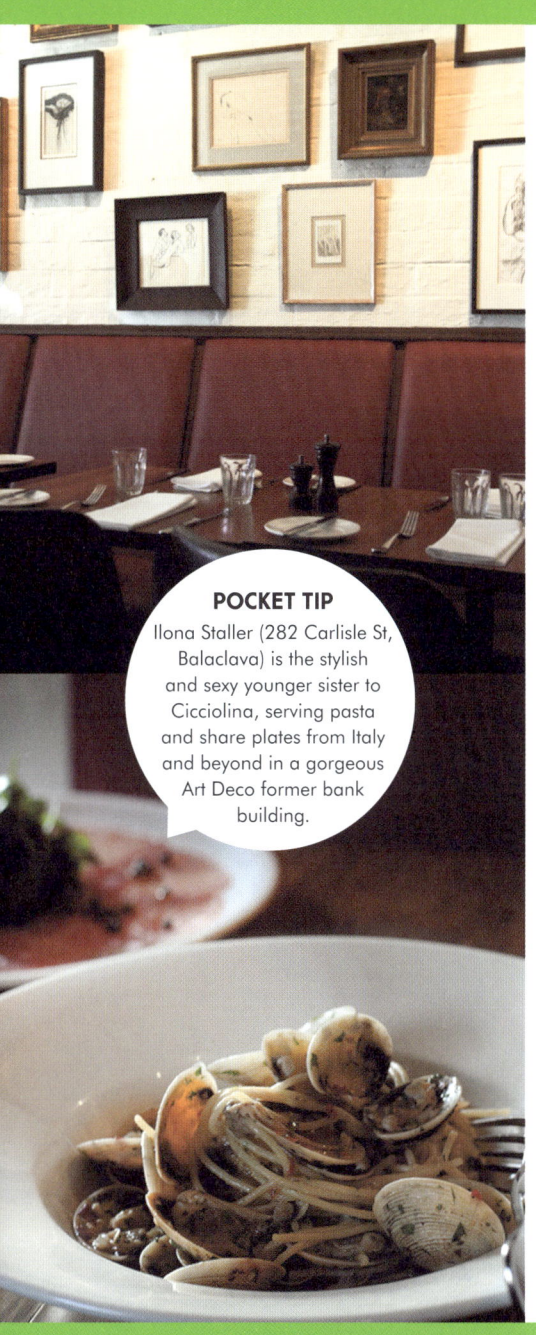

5 CICCIOLINA

130 Acland St, St Kilda
9525 3333
www.cicciolina.com.au
Open Mon–Sat 12pm–11pm,
Sun 12pm–10pm
[MAP p. 192 C4]

POCKET TIP
Ilona Staller (282 Carlisle St, Balaclava) is the stylish and sexy younger sister to Cicciolina, serving pasta and share plates from Italy and beyond in a gorgeous Art Deco former bank building.

With its low-key entrance on busy Acland Street, you could be forgiven for missing this almost-hidden gem, but once you step inside you're in for an authentic Italian-style treat. Cicciolina offers knowledgeable service in the fine-dining tradition, but with an attitude all its own, and sizeable dishes rich in flavour, deftly executed by chefs Michelle Elia and Virginia Redmond. The main menu offers simple Italian fare, including mouth-wateringly silky tuna carpaccio and a whopping 350 gram chargrilled wagyu steak. The cellar boasts over 150 wines from all over the world, 20 of which are available by the glass. With a quarter of a century behind it, Cicciolina is a St Kilda classic that wears its history on its art-covered walls, and has well-worn furniture and a longtime, eclectic clientele. It's almost always full because it really is *that* good, so bookings are recommended. If you're on a budget, try the $25 beer and bolognaise in the **Back Bar**, or go for lunch and save yourself a few dollars.

ST KILDA & BAYSIDE

6 MATCHA MYLKBAR

72a Acland St, St Kilda
9534 1111
www.matchamylkbar.com
Open Mon–Fri 8am–3pm,
Sat–Sun 8am–4pm
[MAP p. 192 C3]

Matcha Mylkbar prides itself on good-looking vegan food that proves that you don't need meat to get your essential nutrients. The light-filled space is dominated by floor-to-ceiling windows overlooking busy Acland Street and its eclectic mix of passers-by, with a decorative brick floor, timber furniture and live greenery inside. The young staff are attentive and happy to explain any of the more curious items on the menu, like the 'vegan egg' made from linseed with a sweet potato 'yolk'. In fact, they're so proud of their fake egg, they've trademarked the recipe. The nourishing bowls are packed with fresh ingredients, and if you're curious about the long list of caffeine-free lattes, try a barista's choice flight of four. There's a novelty factor to some of the dishes and drinks – like the blue algae latte known as 'Smurf' – but it's refreshing to see a health food menu that doesn't take itself too seriously, despite Matcha's mission to save the planet (and your health) one turmeric latte at a time.

POCKET TIP
Galleon Cafe (9 Carlisle St) is a long-time St Kilda favourite, filled with mismatched retro furniture and serving classic comfort food since the 1980s.

ST KILDA & BAYSIDE

7 UNCLE

188 Carlisle St, St Kilda
9041 2668
www.unclerestaurants.com.au
Open Tues–Thurs 5pm–late,
Fri–Sat 12pm–late
[MAP p. 193 E3]

Uncle serves flavour-packed and affordable new-school Vietnamese in this light and fun-filled eatery on the cusp of Balaclava. Pull up a spot at the bar or be seated at a table and take in the cute rickshaw service counter while you enjoy a local craft beer or Vietnamese Bia Hà Nôi. The menu is divided into 'Little Guys' and 'Big Guys' – we like to order a selection of the former, starting with bahn mi – delightfully light and crispy baguettes filled with a choice of tasty ingredients like tofu, crispy pigs ear or our favourite dill and turmeric-infused Hanoi fish. A bowl of steaming pho soup is next, with traditional beef, chicken or vegetarian versions that are fragrant and filling, and there's a mini option, too. Can't decide? The Uncle Knows Best set menu for $55 per person has you sorted. The bar also serves tempting cocktails (try the barrel-aged spiced Pho-Groni, served with basil) that complement the food flavours, and the bamboo-filled rooftop promises good times on high.

POCKET TIP
Big on bagels? Glicks (330 Carlisle St, Balaclava) has been Melbourne's go-to Jewish bagelry since 1968.

ST KILDA & BAYSIDE

8 THE HOTEL ESPLANADE

11 The Esplanade, St Kilda
9534 0211
www.hotelesplanade.com.au
Open Mon–Sun 11am–late
[MAP p. 192 B2]

The 'Espy' is as much a part of St Kilda's identity as the esplanade it's named for. Built as a resort hotel in 1878, this much-loved seaside pub has been a popular live music venue since the 1920s, making it the longest operating live music venue in Australia. After years of renovations, the Espy reopened in 2018, and we think it's better than ever. They've sure let the light in but the paint is still peeling, and with access to rooms previously shuttered, it now feels like a ruin reborn as a contemporary drinking, dining, music and arts complex. There are 12 bars over five levels, including the casual **Espy Kitchen** (think fish and chips, wood-fired pizza, crispy bay bug rolls), and Cantonese-inspired **Mya Tiger** restaurant. Music lovers can catch a gig in the revered and restored **Gershwin Room**, and there's even a program of live and experiential art that you wouldn't expect in a pub.

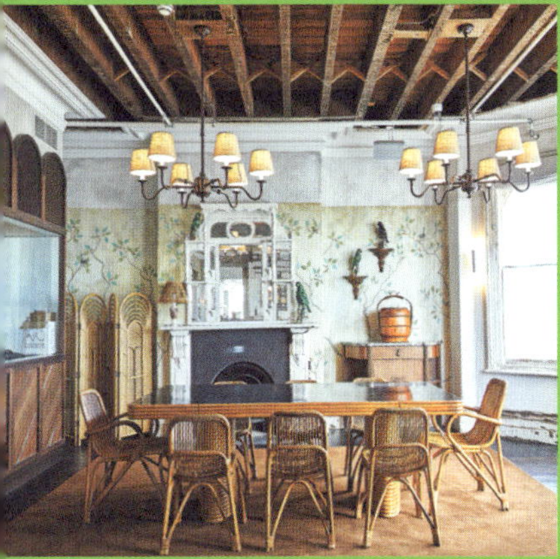
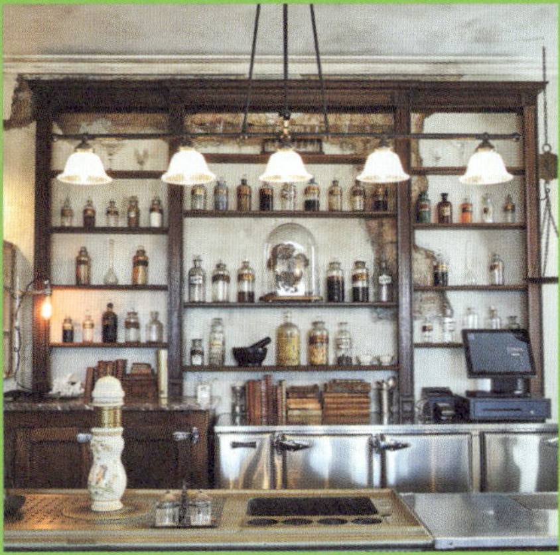
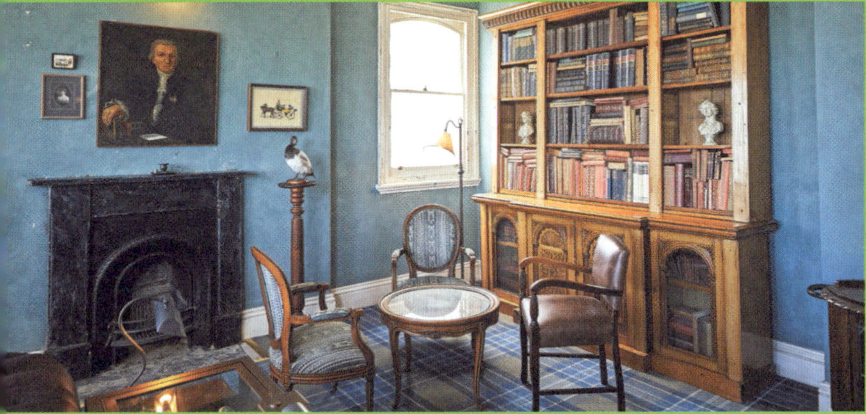
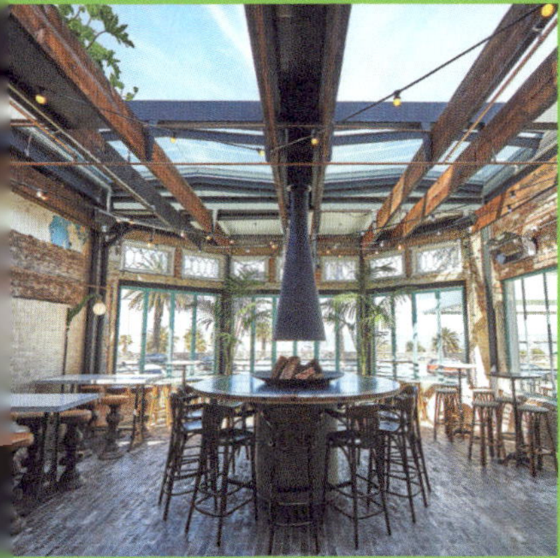
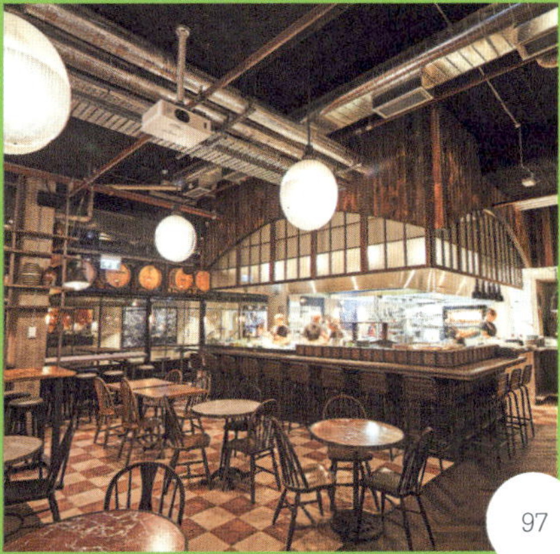

ST KILDA & BAYSIDE

9 THE PRINCE HOTEL

2 Acland St, St Kilda
9536 1111
www.theprince.com.au
Open Mon–Sun 7am–11pm
[MAP p. 192 B2]

The Prince Hotel has been around since St Kilda first became Melbourne's most popular seaside destination in the 1800s. Art Deco additions in the 1930s set the style for the Prince we know and love today. This accommodation, dining and entertainment venue is basically its own principality: you don't need to leave the building. The sleek **Prince Dining Room** serves fire-focused Mediterranean-inspired fare including Flinders Island lamb with fermented chilli; wood-fired zucchini, feta, almond and ras el hanout; and a tagine of lamb, prunes, sesame and tabbouleh for two. The **Prince Bandroom** still hosts a diverse array of bands and DJs; Lenny Kravitz, the Scissor Sisters, Pink and Coldplay have all appeared here. The once grungy **Public Bar** has recently been restored to its former 1930's glory, all sleek lines, deco details and classy atmosphere to match the rest of this royally named destination. Gather here for a craft beer, cocktail or enjoy a streetside Aperol spritz in the sun.

ST KILDA & BAYSIDE

10 PONTOON

30 Jacka Blvd, St Kilda
9525 5445
www.pontoonstkildabeach.com.au
Open Mon–Fri 12pm–late,
Sat–Sun 11am–late
[MAP p. 192 B3]

This casual beachside bar and eatery is about as close to the sandy shores of St Kilda beach as you can get, while enjoying a beer, cocktail and a bite to eat. And it looks good too, with an impressive blonde timber ceiling, tiled floor, tubular steel shelves and muted sand and earth tones throughout, allowing you and the blue sea to stand out. The bar serves about a dozen Australian and international beers on tap and a good selection of wines, spirits and cocktails. And if you haven't heard of a frose or friesling, you might have to try one of these on-trend frozen wine beverages to feel like part of the crowd. The food here includes bar snacks, hand-stretched pizzas from the wood-fired pizza oven and more substantial sea and land-based dishes from the wood grill, with plenty of vegetarian options, too. Pontoon is family friendly and gives good times for anyone who loves a crowd, with a beach club vibe and DJs spinning party tunes on weekends.

SOUTH YARRA, PRAHRAN & WINDSOR

The south side of the Yarra River is where many well-heeled Melburnians live in gracious townhouses and gleaming glass towers. Salubrious South Yarra is revered for chic Chapel Street (see p. 103) and Toorak Road, where high-end designer stores cluster like diamonds. Neighbouring Prahran and Windsor revel in a grittier street cred, but there are still plenty of jewels to discover further south along Chapel Street. Shopping takes in Australian and international brands, as well as vintage and thrift stores, all in a range of architecturally interesting buildings. A destination for fashionistas and party goers the world over, Chapel Street expresses the full gamut from glitz to grunge.

Prahran's streets teem with all types, and they never cease to surprise with a new bar, shop, club or street-style affectation. Look up for traces of Prahran's retail history, including grand old department stores such as the aptly named Big Store. Cruisy Greville Street (see p. 104) is the original hipster street, famed for its independent stores. The Windsor end of Chapel Street is also where you'll find the iconic Astor Cinema (see p. 102), Melbourne's go-to for double-session nostalgic movies, as well as a plethora of thrift stores and boozy bars and restaurants for the party crowd. The precinct is alive long into the night (and morning), so if you like to party you're bound to end up at late night institutions such as Revolver Upstairs (see p. 112) and Poof Doof (see p. 112).

Train: South Yarra station, Prahran station, Windsor station

→ Tusk cafe in Windsor

SIGHTS
1. The Astor Cinema

SHOPPING & EATING
2. Chapel Street
3. Greville Street
4. Vintage shop crawl

EATING
5. Burch & Purchese Sweet Studio
6. Tusk
7. Borsch, Vodka and Tears
8. David's

EATING & DRINKING
9. Lucky Coq
10. Revolver Upstairs

SOUTH YARRA, PRAHRAN & WINDSOR

1 THE ASTOR CINEMA

Cnr Chapel St & Dandenong Rd, St Kilda
9510 1414
www.astortheatre.net.au
Check website for session times
[MAP p. 193 F1]

Opened in 1936 and the last remaining single-screen cinema in Melbourne, the Art Deco-styled Astor is the place for cinephiles to see classic double features, like Hitchcock's *Vertigo* and *Rear Window* or Kubrick's *A Clockwork Orange* and *Full Metal Jacket*. There might only be one screen at the Astor, but at almost 20 metres wide it's a big one! Projections are in 35mm, 70mm, 2K and 4K, so you can expect glorious clarity and detail when the glamourous gold curtains part for your matinee or evening session. Films range from classic to cult with a few quality new releases thrown in. Meet your pals for a drink at the **Overlook bar** beforehand, and don't forget to grab yourself a free program for the back of your bathroom door – something that Melburnians have been doing for decades.

Technically in St Kilda, the Astor is much closer to Windsor – even if it sometimes takes two turns at the lights to cross busy Dandenong Road!

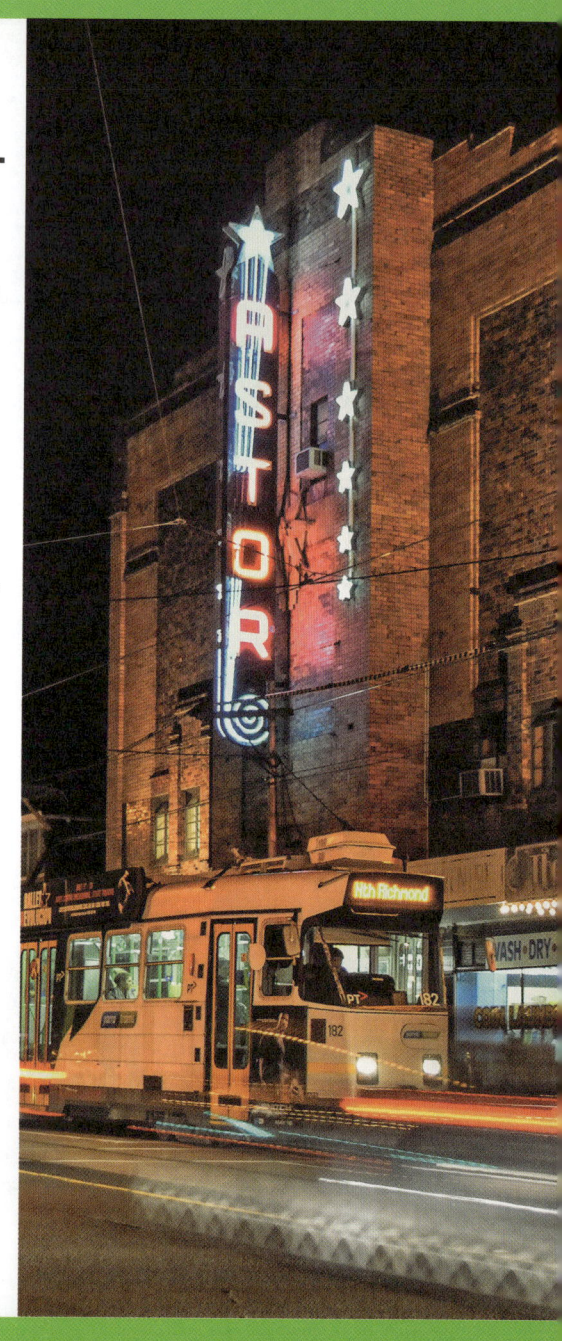

SOUTH YARRA, PRAHRAN & WINDSOR

2 CHAPEL STREET

[MAP p. 190 C1]

Chapel Street is a Melbourne hotspot for fashion and shopping. Start your shopping spree near the corner of Toorak Road, where you'll find **Le Louvre** (2 Daly St) haute couture. **The Como Centre** (cnr of Toorak Rd and Chapel St) is home to the arthouse **Palace Cinema Como**. If you need caffeine and calm, go to **Kanteen** (150 Alexandra Ave), overlooking the Yarra River and Herring Island. The strip between Toorak and Commercial roads focuses on fashion, both local and international. Australian mid-range label **Country Road**'s megastore (women's, men's and kids' clothing, and homewares, too) anchors the corner of Toorak Road, along with bright and bold Finnish design house **Marimekko** (3/576 Chapel St), for an eye-popping range of clothes and homewares. Chapel's roll call of Australian fashion designers includes **Scanlan & Theodore** (no. 566), **Alice McCall** (no. 549), **Arthur Galan** (no. 568), **Gorman** (no. 561), **Saba** (1/576), **Sass & Bide** (no. 531), **Kookai** (no. 527) and **Crumpler** bags (no. 182) at the Prahran end.

> **POCKET TIP**
> Built in 1847, Como House (Lechlade Ave) is a ten-minute walk from The Como Centre and a fine example of Italianate architecture. Book a house tour, wander in the gardens or take high tea in the stables.

103

SOUTH YARRA, PRAHRAN & WINDSOR

3 GREVILLE STREET

Prahran
[MAP p. 191 B1]

Greville Street has been long known for its independent, quirky sensibility – a foil to the big-brand names on Chapel Street. Today it's a vibrant mix of fashion and homewares, cafes and bars, and now boasts one of Melbourne's coolest inner-urban parks, perfect for watching the beautiful people. Local icon **Greville Records** (no. 152) has been supporting independent music for more than 30 years; if it's rare, obscure or important, you'll find it here. There are vivid patterns and chunky knits at **Fool Clothing** (no. 118); Melbourne-made luxe skincare at **Aesop** (no. 143); and affordable limited-edition art and illustration prints by local and international artists at **Signed and Numbered** (no. 153). The artisan pizzeria **Ladro** (no. 162) has expansive digs with outdoor seating; and you can even get your Greville Street selfie made into a wearable souvenir at **Das T-Shirt Automart** (no. 127) as quickly as it takes to enjoy a carefully made, near-perfect flat white at nearby **Pardon** cafe (no. 155).

104

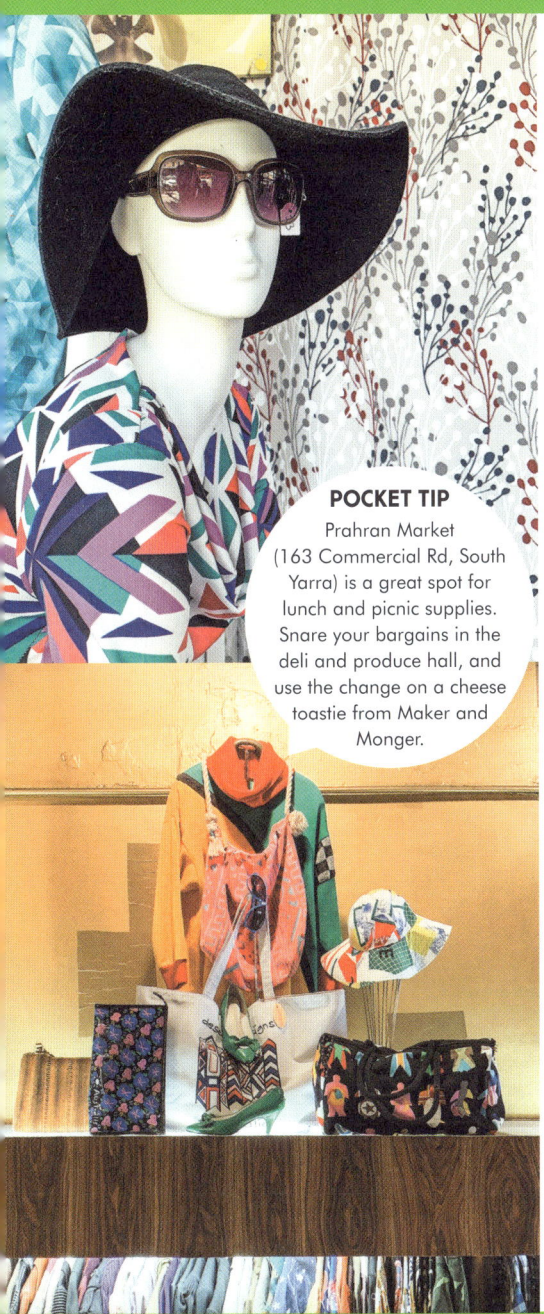

SOUTH YARRA, PRAHRAN & WINDSOR

4 VINTAGE SHOP CRAWL

[MAP p. 191 B2]

The Prahran and Windsor end of Chapel street has more second-hand stores than just about anywhere in Melbourne. These range from classic, overstocked and charmingly musty opportunity shops (aka 'oppies') to treasure troves of vintage clothing, designer rags and objects. Make a day of it by starting at **Chapel Street Bazaar** (271 Chapel St) for vintage vinyl and kitschy homewares. **Prahran Mission** (211 Chapel St) is great for trawling books and **Shag** (130 Chapel St) for kooky kitsch clothing. **Salvos Stores** (115 Chapel St) is easily the best dressed of the bunch: the staff have eyes for good clothing, so expect to pay a little more. **Storehouse Thrift** (77 Chapel St) has quirky costumes in mind, and the **Sacred Heart Mission Shop** (86 Chapel St) is particularly good for furniture. **Save the Children** (59 Chapel St) and **Mecwacare Opportunity Shop** (52 Chapel St) are old-fashioned bargain black holes (careful you don't get lost among the racks of clothing, men's and women's aplenty). Don't be afraid to rummage: they're not called opportunity shops for nothing. Finders keepers!

POCKET TIP

Prahran Market (163 Commercial Rd, South Yarra) is a great spot for lunch and picnic supplies. Snare your bargains in the deli and produce hall, and use the change on a cheese toastie from Maker and Monger.

SOUTH YARRA, PRAHRAN & WINDSOR

5 BURCH & PURCHESE SWEET STUDIO

647 Chapel St, South Yarra
9827 7060
www.burchandpurchese.com
Open Mon–Sun 10am–6.30pm
[MAP p. 190 C1]

There is a unique extravagance about Burch & Purchese, the 'sweet studio' of chefs Darren Purchese and Cath Claringbold. They create and sell a veritable candy paradise of skilfully balanced flavour and texture with jellies, sponges, mousses, crumbles and spreads. It's art you can eat. At first you won't want to, it's so beautiful, but it'll get the better of you in the end, and you won't regret it (even if you do feel a bit guilty!). Love-hearts and pastel pinks dominate the interior, but the name of the game here is take-away. There's a handful of chairs out front, but a better setting is nearby **Rockley Gardens** (Rockley Rd) or down by the river. Wow your pals with individual desserts from $10, floor them with a birthday cake from $55 and return for regular limited-edition creations. No one leaves disappointed.

POCKET TIP
Breads and baked goods? Don't go past Tivoli Road Bakery (3 Tivoli Rd, South Yarra).

SOUTH YARRA, PRAHRAN & WINDSOR

6 TUSK

133 Chapel St, Windsor
9529 1198
Open Sun–Wed 8am–11.30pm,
Thurs–Sat 8am–1am
[MAP p. 191 B3]

Tusk boasts the best corner spot on Chapel street, complete with a plant-filled outdoor dining area that is *the* place to be on a sunny day. This is a classic Windsor establishment, with a charming stained-glass heritage shopfront, as well-worn as any hardworking cafe should be, with classic dark timber fittings and vintage light shades. The modern Australian and Mediterranean menu includes crispy corn cakes, open-faced omelettes and an indulgent pancake stack with blueberries and mascarpone for breakfast; and wood-fired pizza and a ripper mushroom fettuccine for lunch or dinner. Juices are freshly squeezed, coffee is by Merlo. Try the grazing share plate with marinated lamb, saganaki and other Greek delights, or choose from the range of vegetarian plates. There's no stiff, apron-wearing pretentiousness here; the efficient wait staff are fast, friendly and fun to be around.

SOUTH YARRA, PRAHRAN & WINDSOR

7 BORSCH, VODKA AND TEARS

173 Chapel St, Windsor
9530 2694
www.borschvodkaandtears.com
Open Mon–Fri 8am–late, Sat–Sun 9am–late
[MAP p. 191 B2]

This little all-rounder is a Melbourne icon: it's easy-going, friendly and no fuss. The raffish interior – scuffed walls and floor; worn chairs; and a dull green, beige and maroon palette throughout – is comfortable, homely and authentic, recalling the Bohemian hideaways of early 20th-century Europe. The food is home-style Polish, served on solid communist-era patterned tableware – comfort food like bagels and bloody marys for breakfast, kransky, po'boys, Polish dumplings and borsch of course. Vodka comes 100 different ways, which is good to know, because you'll be back for more. And they don't have scotch or tequila, anyway. Na Zdrowie!

POCKET TIP

Fed up with $5 coffee? Revolver Lane (231 Chapel St, Prahran) makes it right – and at $3 it's at the right price too!

109

SOUTH YARRA, PRAHRAN & WINDSOR

8 DAVID'S

4 Cecil Pl, Prahran
9529 5199
www.davidsrestaurant.com.au
Open Mon–Wed 12pm–3pm & 6–10pm, Thurs–Fri 12pm–3pm & 6–10.30pm, Sat–Sun 11.30am–3pm & 6–10.30pm
[MAP p.191 C2]

Many Chinese restaurants attempt to reflect the diversity and complexity of Chinese food, but David's keeps it local, sticking to the regional cuisine of Zhouzhuang, a river town outside Shanghai. This is full-flavoured food: lots of ginger, sometimes whole chillies and cloves of garlic, and liberal amounts of soy and sugar. Signature dishes include DIY pork-belly buns, duck wraps and Grandma's 8 – a combination of scallop, shrimp, chicken, pork, bamboo, shiitake, cashews and chestnuts. From the moment you step inside, you'll be calmed by the serenity of the whitewashed interior – just the counterpoint to the exciting hubbub you'll encounter on weekend all-you-can-eat yum cha sittings at 11.30am and 1.30pm. There's no quaint trolleys, but for a flat fee ($40 Saturdays, $45 Sundays), it's exceptional value for the hungry and/or greedy! Plus they mix a mean cocktail.

SOUTH YARRA, PRAHRAN & WINDSOR

9 LUCKY COQ

179 Chapel St, Windsor
9525 1288
www.luckycoq.com.au
Open Mon–Fri 11:30am–late,
Sat–Sun 12pm–late
[MAP p. 191 B2]

Your first reason to visit Lucky Coq is the $4 pizzas, available every lunch and dinner and all day Sunday, too. You'll come again for the pizzas because they're not just cheap – they're good, too! Available in 27 different combinations, there are as many options for vegetarians as carnivores. The playful interior – geometric shapes, road signs, neon and a truck parked inside – sets the good-times vibe. There's always something new to try among the dozen beers on tap, and even more by the bottle. At $30, jugs of mixed drinks, such as sangria and Pimms, are an affordable way to live it up inside or out on the rooftop late into those long summer nights. Weekly events include bingo, trivia, rock and retro nights, and of course there's plenty of room for dining and lolling about.

POCKET TIP

Need a gift? The Shelley Panton Store (440 Malvern Rd, Prahran) has the best in local design with something for every budget.

111

SOUTH YARRA, PRAHRAN & WINDSOR

10 REVOLVER UPSTAIRS

229 Chapel St, Prahran
9521 5985
www.revolverupstairs.com.au
Open Tues–Wed 5pm–4am,
Thurs 5pm–6am, Fri 5pm–Sat 12pm, Sat 5pm–Mon 9am
[MAP p. 191 B2]

Australia's best-known club – an institution for punters, players and industry alike – has been attracting throngs of gig-goers and late-night clubbers up its steep stairs since 1997. The reasons to come here are myriad: DJs and live bands in multiple rooms and **Colonel Tan's Thai** restaurant (half price for local residents on Thursdays). Revolver's walls feature permanent artworks by renowned artists Banksy, Dabs Myla and more, and there's regular exhibitions, too. Visit the website for the gig guide and ticket sales. The 24-hour liquor license means it's a last destination for clubbers citywide. Careful on your way out – those stairs are even steeper after a long night!

POCKET TIP
Poof Doof (386 Chapel St, Prahran) – the self-proclaimed gay club for homos – features some of the gay scene's best DJs.

113

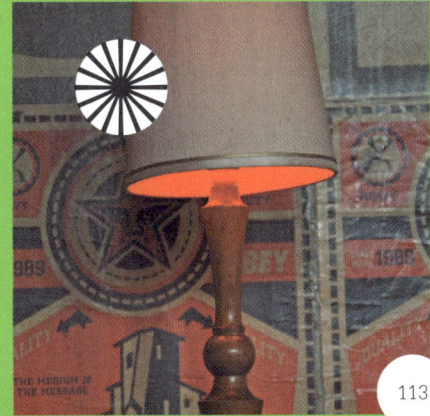

FOOTSCRAY & YARRAVILLE

The inner suburb of Footscray has long been the hub for new arrivals, including Europeans, Vietnamese and more recently the African community. The demographic keeps changing, with students and creatives flocking to the west, where the rents are cheaper. The vibrant street life and diverse culture and cuisine is a drawcard for any curious traveller, from the budget conscious to the reasonably well-heeled.

Further south, Yarraville is Melbourne's secret little village in the west. Built right on the train line, its tight network of streets gives it a decidedly country town feel, with all the coffee and culture of an inner-city suburb. The restored Art Deco Sun Theatre (*see* p. 117) is a glamourous local treasure showing the latest in cinema and is worth a visit in its own right. The excellent Sun Bookshop (*see* p. 117) is a community hub for the locals – and the village vibe of shops and cafes will make you feel like a local, too.

Train: Footscray station, Yarraville station

→ *The ever-changing city view from the Footscray Community Arts Centre*

SIGHTS
1. Footscray Community Arts Centre
2. Sun Theatre

SHOPPING
3. Perfect Splash
4. Village Idiom

EATING & DRINKING
5. Konjo Cafe
6. Pho Hung Vuong Saigon
7. Cornershop
8. Bar Josephine
9. Back Alley Sally's
10. Victoria Hotel

FOOTSCRAY & YARRAVILLE

1 FOOTSCRAY COMMUNITY ARTS CENTRE

45 Moreland St, Footscray
9362 8888
www.footscrayarts.com
Open Mon–Fri 9.30am–5pm,
Sat 10am–4pm
[MAP p. 201 F3]

Community spirit and creativity come together at this neighbourhood arts complex with a view. Set in a charming old bluestone building and custom-designed gallery and meeting space, it has performance and exhibition spaces, as well as music, theatre, dance, exhibitions, and workshops that showcase the talents of local artists and performers. The Indigenous cultural program is outstanding, and linguistically diverse migrant communities, refugees, people with a disability, trans and gender diverse people are all welcomed. While you're here, pop into **Andy's Remedy cafe** for spicy sriracha scrambled eggs for breakfast, or check out the tapas menu featuring patatas bravas, deep-fried caulipops, meatballs and polenta. There's live music from Thursday to Sunday, making the place a popular spot for after-work drinks on the lawn overlooking the Melbourne city skyline.

POCKET TIP
Book a scenic ride up the Maribyrnong River on a Blackbird River Cruise, complete with charming live commentary.

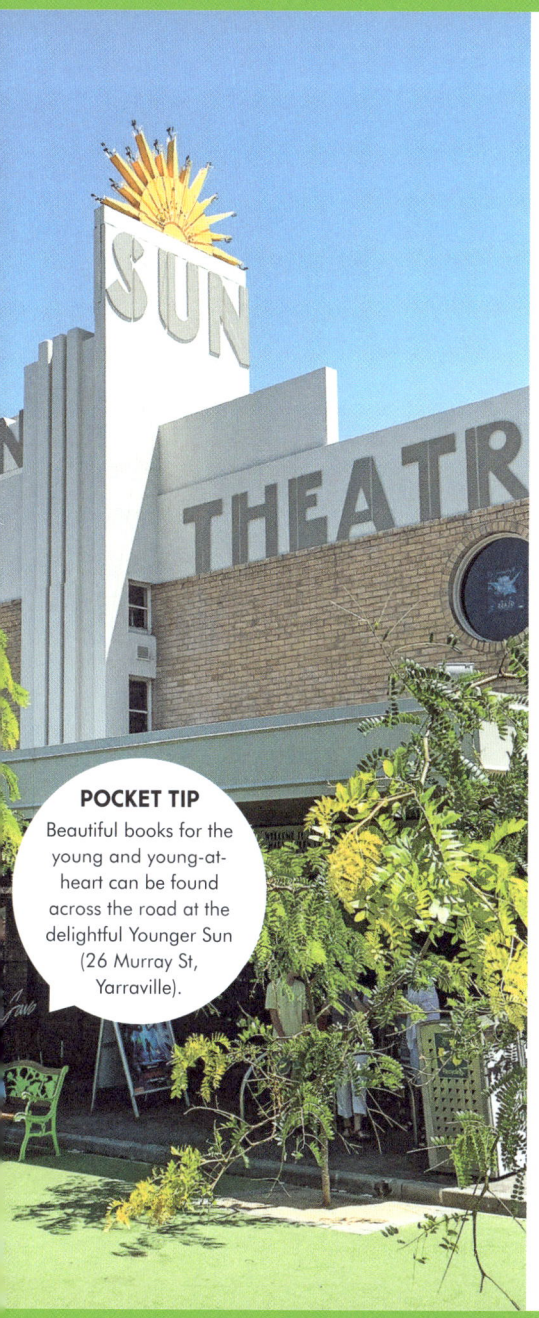

FOOTSCRAY & YARRAVILLE

2 SUN THEATRE

8 Ballarat St, Yarraville
9362 0999
www.suntheatre.com.au
Open Mon–Sun 9:30am–late
[MAP p. 199 B2]

The much-loved gorgeous Art Deco Sun Theatre is the cinematic heart of the Yarraville village, screening a diverse selection of new-release, popular and arthouse films from around the world. The theatre first opened its doors in 1938 but like many other small suburban cinemas struggled with the advent of television and eventually closed down, remaining unloved and derelict for 20 years. Thankfully it was saved in the 1990s and gradually brought back to its former glory as an icon of the inner west. Today it's a beautifully restored gem that contains eight luxurious cinemas of various sizes, each with its own Art Deco-inspired decor and many gorgeous original details. The theatre building is also home to the popular **Sun Bookshop**; a lovely local, independent bookstore with a great selection of fiction, non-fiction and beautiful art, photography and craft titles. As you wait for your film, you can also relax like a local in the urban park right outside the theatre entrance, overlooked by the iconic Sun Theatre neon sign.

POCKET TIP

Beautiful books for the young and young-at-heart can be found across the road at the delightful Younger Sun (26 Murray St, Yarraville).

FOOTSCRAY & YARRAVILLE

3 PERFECT SPLASH

61 Victoria St, Footscray
8590 3112
www.perfectsplash.store
Open Wed–Fri 10am–5pm,
Sun 9am–3pm
[MAP p. 200 B2]

This cute-as-a-button local shop is operated by talented creative siblings Annabelle and Alana and sells Melbourne-made goods that will make your heart sing. Perfect Splash is the colourful front to their studio space out back, where they make functional and decorative ceramic pieces under the name Paradise Structures, and design and produce their own line of limited-edition clothing for men and women. The garments feature hand-dyed, natural and upcycled fabrics and customised prints that you won't find anywhere else. The perfectly petite shop is also a showcase for a community of similarly minded local creatives, including jewellers Rani Rose, Zaric and Dorkus Design (love that name!), ceramicist Hannah Simpkin and designer Cadia Belante, who makes jackets and bags from upcycled sleeping bags. They also stock a small selection of records and tapes of local bands that they love.

POCKET TIP

Head a little south to Seddon, where you'll find a small local shopping area with independent businesses, including cafe Common Galaxia (130 Victoria St) and homewares store Sedonia (41 Gamon St).

119

FOOTSCRAY & YARRAVILLE

4 VILLAGE IDIOM

34 Anderson St, Yarraville
8060 6142
www.villageidiom.com.au
Open Mon–Fri 10am–6pm, Sat 10am–4pm, Sun 11am–4pm
[MAP p. 199 B3]

A haven for lovers of all things vintage and retro, Village Idiom is unashamedly kitsch, colourful and full of fun. The cute pastel pink entrance sets the tone for this jam-packed shop of the similarly pink-haired owner Elise Hopper, a cheery presence among the treasure trove. Here there's vintage-inspired clothing, funky jewellery and all manner of gifts and homewares from Melbourne and beyond. Expect anything from hand-painted Matryoshkya nesting dolls from Russia featuring rock'n'roll icons, locally-made Kester Black nail polish, Status Anxiety leather goods and Mexican folk art to adorable cat-themed ceramics from Japan. But that's just the tip of this candy-coloured iceberg, which you simply need to see for yourself. Clearly Elise is living her quirky shop girl fantasy, and you're all invited to the party, with plenty of brightly patterned retro-inspired frocks to get you in the mood.

FOOTSCRAY & YARRAVILLE

5 KONJO CAFE

89 Irving St, Footscray
9689 8185
www.konjo.com.au
Open Mon–Sat 9am–8.30pm,
Sun 9.30am–6pm
[MAP p. 200 C2]

For an authentic taste of Ethiopian cuisine that's made with love and easy on the wallet, you can't go past Konjo. It's owned and operated by a husband-and-wife team whose passion is to share the culture and flavours of Ethiopia, with rich, earthy and perfectly-spiced dishes. Many of Konjo's vegetable and meat-based stews use a traditional spice blend that includes cinnamon, fenugreek, cardamom, garlic, ginger, basil and chilli. For breakfast, there's silts (Ethiopian scrambled eggs), and ful (a broad-bean-based stew with hard-boiled eggs). Try coffee with organic Ethiopian rainforest beans, freshly roasted and ground on the spot. It takes a while, but the aromatic experience – which includes the ceremonial burning of incense – is worth the wait. We recommend the bargain all-you-can-eat buffets, including a vegan feast on Wednesdays and Thursdays (lunch and dinner), a mixed buffet lunch on Fridays and Saturdays and monthly vegan feasts.

POCKET TIP

Cafe Lalibela next door also serves home-style Ethiopian food served with the famous injera sour bread pancake that will make your mouth water and your belly full.

FOOTSCRAY & YARRAVILLE

6 PHO HUNG VUONG SAIGON

128 Hopkins St, Footscray
9689 6002
Open Mon–Sun 9am–8pm
[MAP p. 201 D1]

Get your fill of some of the city's best pho soup at this bustling Vietnamese eatery. It's regularly full of hungry local families, workers and those who travel to Footscray just to eat here. The glass-fronted space is bright and not too trendy: grab a window seat for the best spot to watch the action on colourful Hopkins Street. The atmosphere is fast and fun, with pop hits playing on the stereo and young, light-footed staff who make the place run like clockwork. The signature steaming bowls of pho come in small, medium and large, all served with the customary bean shoots, Vietnamese mint and fresh chilli, with the traditional beef the broth of choice for most. The grilled chicken is also delicious, rich in flavour and delicately spiced. The crispy deep-fried spring rolls wrapped in fresh iceberg lettuce are served with a sweet, salty and fishy dipping sauce. Note: not so great for vegetarians.

POCKET TIP

Visit To's Bakery (122 Hopkins St, Footscray) for bargain bahn mi (salad baguettes) and delectable Vietnamese take-away sweets.

FOOTSCRAY & YARRAVILLE

7 CORNERSHOP

9 Ballarat St, Yarraville
9689 0052
www.cornershopyarraville.com
Open Mon–Wed 7.30am–4pm,
Thurs–Fri 7.30am–5pm, Sat
8am–5pm, Sun 8am–4pm
[MAP p. 199 B3]

Proudly local, the perfectly placed and appropriately named Cornershop is one of the most popular cafes in the west. Overlooking the sweet little urban park opposite the iconic Sun Theatre (see p. 117), Cornershop serves locally roasted coffee and a breakfast, brunch and lunch menu in a light, bright and pastel green-tiled space with a lovely little courtyard out back. Breakfast and brunch include an intriguingly unconventional coconut dahl dosa with poached eggs, lime and curry leaves, as well as hearty egg-based favourites. The lunch menu is decidedly Middle Eastern and Mediterranean-inspired: think Lebanese salads, pan-fried sardines with skordalia and harissa oil, or slow-roasted lamb shoulder with tabouli, preserved lemon, smoked yoghurt & almonds. Yum! Cornershop really pumps at brunch time on weekends, so you'll have to be patient: it's first come, first served but worth the wait.

POCKET TIP

Dad and Dave's (27–29 Birmingham St, Yarraville) is a small cafe in a former milk bar that serves healthy meals and is conveniently located right next to Yarraville station.

FOOTSCRAY & YARRAVILLE

8 BAR JOSEPHINE

295 Barkly St, Footscray
9077 0583
Open Mon–Sun 1pm–1am
[MAP p. 200 B1]

Josephine is a friendly neighbourhood shopfront bar with a focus on local craft beers and good times for all. Lovingly fitted out with vintage furniture, 1970s Italian tiles, well-worn books and an impressive timber bar top, this place looks older than it is (it's only two!), but has fast become the go-to drinking hole for Footscray locals and their inter-suburban friends. Bar owner Aaron Donato has created an inviting space with a laidback vibe, even when it's full of punters, which might include a (non-drinking) neighbourhood dog or two. Melbourne, Australian and international craft beers are served on regularly rotating taps, including the local Blackmans Brewery and Belgian Chimay. There's a modest list of decent, affordable wines, but why sip on a wine when you can quaff a quality brew thoughtfully selected by those in the know? The staff are more than willing to help you choose.

POCKET TIP

Bad Love Club (shop 5, 68–82 Hopkins St) is Footscray's 'boozy bakery', serving coffee and delectable house-made baked goods by day and cocktails after dark.

FOOTSCRAY & YARRAVILLE

9 BACK ALLEY SALLY'S

4 Yewers St, Footscray
9689 6260
www.backalleysallys.com.au
Open Mon–Wed 5pm–11pm,
Thurs 4pm–12am, Fri & Sat
12pm–12am, Sun 1pm–10pm
[MAP p. 201 F2]

Walk down a grungy laneway towards the Maribyrnong River and you'll be transported to the coolest warehouse bar in the west. You'll find yourself in the uber-cool **Slice Girls West** pizzeria, with its cute and compact dining space, hole-in-the-wall servery and a selection of humourously named pizzas: Viva Forever (aka margherita) or the Say You'll Beet There, with house-made beetroot paste and goats cheese. Head up the old wooden stairs to the main attraction: a massive bar filled with creative details that pay homage to its industrial heritage – from bar tables made from old front doors to clever lighting and original factory fittings. Sally's offers craft beer and even wine on tap, as well as house-designed cocktails, such as its take on the classic Tom Collins – the Sally Collins, with Haymans Old Tom gin, crushed lemonade and fresh mint. There's also an impressive selection of gin, rum, whisky, bourbon and tequila.

POCKET TIP

Set in three cleverly repurposed shipping containers, Rudimentary (16–20 Leeds St, Footscray) is a cafe with a sustainability focus and menu of cafe fare and small batch coffee.

FOOTSCRAY & YARRAVILLE

10 VICTORIA HOTEL

43 Victoria St, Footscray
8320 0315
www.victoriahotelfootscray.com
Open Mon–Thurs 4pm–late,
Fri & Sat 12pm–late, Sun
12pm–late
[MAP p. 200 B2]

This old-school corner pub has been reimagined without losing its character and charm, with a menu of classic counter meals and nouveau pub cuisine. While it still looks much the same from the outside, the Victoria Hotel has had quite a bit of work done since it was known as Harts Victoria Hotel. The sticky carpet is gone, the floors have been polished and there's enough warm timber and subdued lighting to balance the concrete beneath your feet. The tap beer offering has expanded beyond the traditional worker's brew Carlton Draught (still available), to include Young Henry's natural lager, Mountain Goat and the new house-favourite pilsner by Hop Nation. The wine list includes on-tap varieties from the Adelaide Hills and about a dozen bottle options. But it's the food that stuck in our minds since our first visit; specifically the kingfish collar with perfectly crispy skin and succulent, miso-infused flesh.

POCKET TIP

A long-standing local pub that welcomes a diverse crowd, the Dancing Dog (42A Albert St, Footscray) is delightfully shabby, with a daytime cafe, local brews and live entertainment at night.

RICHMOND & ABBOTSFORD

The once-industrial inner city suburbs of Richmond and Abbotsford are now full of warehouse apartments and mid-rise flats towering over 19th-century workers cottages, with residents taking advantage of the precinct's proximity to the city and the green space surrounding the Yarra River. The garment trade had a long history in Richmond, but while the manufacturing has mostly moved on (along with the critical mass of factory outlets that once made Bridge Road a destination du jour), you'll still find vintage and seconds stores, as well as family run shopfront sewing centres.

Victoria Street is the vibrant centre of Melbourne's Vietnamese community, with restaurants and grocery stores aplenty. Contemporary and vintage furniture stores are concentrated on Church Street and the east end of Bridge Road, while Swan Street is a busy bar and restaurant strip. Yarra Bend Park (see p. 132) is perfect for picnicking, promenading and even a spot of boating on the Yarra River; or you can spend a day at Abbotsford Convent (see p. 130). Brewing dominates the area's past and present and Australia's two most popular beers are made here – Carlton Draught and Victoria Bitter – as well as boutique brewers Mountain Goat (see p. 139), Moon Dog and Burnley Brewing.

Train and tram: Richmond station, North Richmond station, Route 12, Route 78

→ *Abbotsford Convent mixes historical grandeur, art, food and open spaces*

SIGHTS
1. Abbotsford Convent
2. Yarra Bend Park

SHOPPING
3. Trophy Wife Nail Art
4. Global Vintage Collective

EATING & DRINKING
5. Au79
6. I Love Pho
7. Feast of Merit
8. Purvis Beer
9. Mountain Goat Brewery
10. The Corner Hotel

RICHMOND & ABBOTSFORD

1 ABBOTSFORD CONVENT

1 St Heliers St, Abbotsford
9415 3600
www.abbotsfordconvent.com.au
Open daily 7.30am–10pm
[MAP p. 195 A4]

This grand 19th-century former convent – which once housed 1000 women and children until the mid-20th century – has been reinvented for the 21st century, with office space for not-for-profit organisations, artists' studios, galleries, cafes, restaurants and community markets. The convent's expansive grounds are great for picnics, and you can buy fresh produce from the monthly **Slow Food Farmers Market**, or take your pick from the eateries open daily: Japanese soul food cafe **Kappaya**, pay-as-you-feel vegetarian **Lentil as Anything**, the **Convent Bakery** and **Cam's Kiosk**. Looking around the buildings is encouraged, as is a look at the contemporary art at **St Helier's Street Gallery** and **c3 Contemporary Art Space**. Check the website for regular events, such as vintage and makers' markets and wellbeing workshops. Proceeds from art, social history and French language tours fund the convent's ongoing restoration.

POCKET TIP

The adjacent Collingwood Children's Farm is a working farm. Milk the cows, feed the chickens, cuddle a guinea pig or take in the sounds of farm life over a coffee at the Farm Cafe.

RICHMOND & ABBOTSFORD

2 YARRA BEND PARK

[MAP p. 195 B3]

Melbourne's largest natural green space is home to significant sites for First Peoples, as well as Victorian-era boathouses, golf courses, ruins, endangered species, city views and walking tracks aplenty. Accessible from Johnston Street, Abbotsford, the **Dights Falls Loop Trail** takes in an historic weir, the indigenous **Koorie Garden** and the last remnants of a 19th-century lunatic asylum. Skiffs, kayaks and canoes are available for hire at both **Studley Park Boathouse** and **Fairfield Boathouse**, where you can also get stuck into a classic Australian barbecue for breakfast or lunch. From the viewing platform at the **Bellbird Picnic Reserve**, you can see a large colony of endangered grey-headed flying foxes and keep your eyes out for the elusive platypus, too. The **Main Yarra Trail** hugs the river all the way to **Heide Museum of Modern Art** (*see* pocket tip) in Bulleen, eight kilometres away.

POCKET TIP

Once home of art luminaries John and Sunday Reed and a coterie of artists, Heide is one of Australia's best art experiences, combining social history, architecture and exhibitions in a garden and sculpture park.

RICHMOND & ABBOTSFORD

3 TROPHY WIFE NAIL ART

2b Bridge Rd, Richmond
0422 052 874
www.trophywife.com.au
Open Tues–Thurs 10am–8pm,
Fri–Sat 10am–5pm
[MAP p. 194 B2]

The human fingernail may be a tiny canvas, but nail artist Chelsea Bagan and her band of nail ninjas have perfected the miniature form since setting up in 2010. Chelsea's creativity with claws is what really sets the place apart from other salons. But Trophy Wife Nail Art isn't just about nails: inside this '80s-inspired 'anti-salon' you'll also find **Gin Castro Hair and Makeup**, **Nails by Kirsten** and **Melinda Grace Beauty**, meaning you can get a complete makeover, including waxing, hairstyling, make-up and more. Whether you're paying homage to Keith Haring, Camille Walala, Daria or just looking to convey a little Christmas cheer, Trophy Wife Nail Art has your nails covered in a dizzying range of colours and designs. Check out the pricing guide online: plain nail polish starts at $45 for 30-minutes' work. You can even choose chrome or holographic gels for a full metal or psychedelic effect.

RICHMOND & ABBOTSFORD

4 GLOBAL VINTAGE COLLECTIVE

245 Church St, Richmond
0419 500 199
Open Mon–Fri 12pm–5pm,
Sat 11am–4pm
[MAP p. 194 C3]

At Global Vintage Collective you'll find the best in print and slogan T-shirts – historic and ironic; jumpsuits, overalls and onesies; sunglasses that are oversized, whacky, cool and classic; and almost anything you need to complete that crazy costume for your next festival. All stock is personally sourced by owner Ashley Tell on seasonal sojourns to the US. Pricing is arranged by the colour of the rainbow; roughly $20 to $100. For those who like to rummage, there's even more to score out back: denim for days, leather in all manner of persuasions and a veritable pantone chart of mechanics' overalls. You'll find more recent vintage from the 1990s, and there is gold to be found from the 1950s and 1960s, too. Need alterations? They're conveniently available right next door.

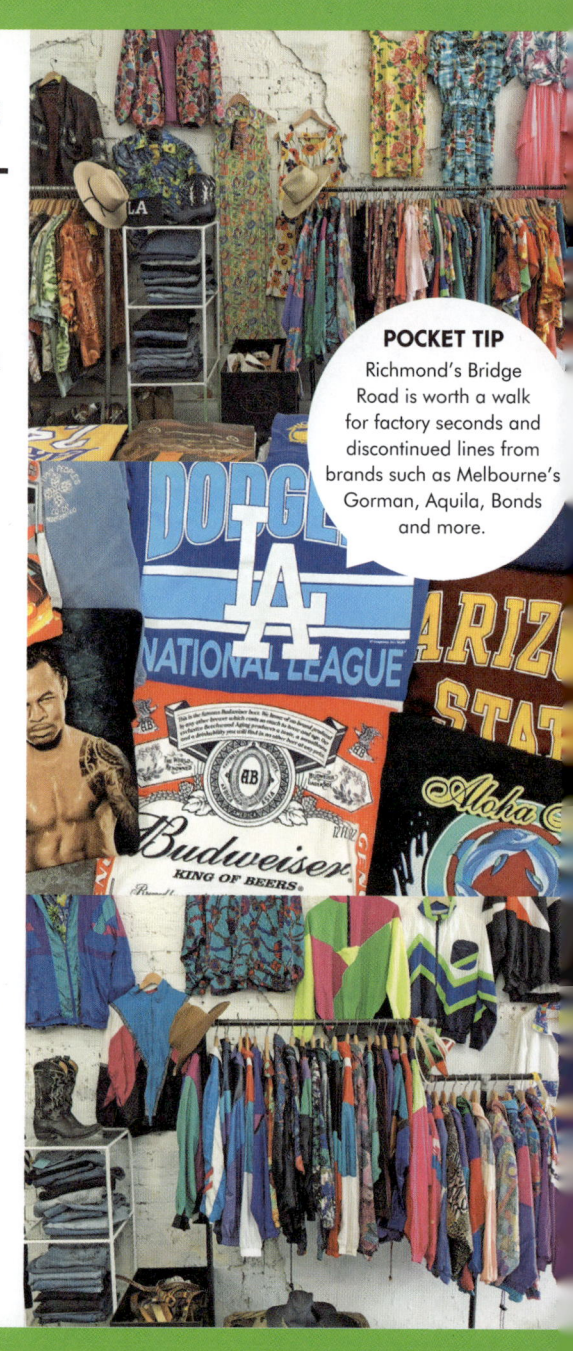

POCKET TIP

Richmond's Bridge Road is worth a walk for factory seconds and discontinued lines from brands such as Melbourne's Gorman, Aquila, Bonds and more.

RICHMOND & ABBOTSFORD

5 AU79

27–29 Nicholson St, Abbotsford
9429 0138
www.au79cafe.com.au
Open Mon–Fri 7am–4pm,
Sat–Sun 8am–4pm
[MAP p. 194 C1]

Making the most of a space is often attributed to tiny hole-in-the-wall cafes, but AU79 has taken that concept to an all-new level in the opposite direction. Transforming an old mechanics' garage, AU79 features an on-site roastery, bakery and patisserie – and there's still room for 200 patrons! But this ain't no big-barn breakfast hall. Lush greenery abounds – as do Insta-happy patrons snapping at the baby pink tabletops and the polished concrete floors. Breakfasts are beautifully presented: porridge is brightened up with blueberries, strawberries and orange; and scrambled eggs are given an Asian flair with chilli and miso. Banana brûlée waffles come with popping candy and the French toast is made from brioche with lashings of peanut butter, whipped cream cheese and peanut brittle. Match your meal with a turmeric, matcha or chai latte. The soba noodle salad and charred greens served with avocado and beetroot hummus are healthy counterpoints on this all-day menu.

POCKET TIP

Making handcrafted tofu since 1982, the casual Tofu Shop International (78A Bridge Rd, Richmond) offers healthy vegetarian meals and fresh salads that are simply tofu-licious.

RICHMOND & ABBOTSFORD

6 I LOVE PHO

264 Victoria St, Richmond
9427 7749
www.pholove.com.au
Open Mon–Sun 9am–10.30pm
[MAP p. 194 C1]

No prizes for guessing what's on the menu here! But if choice on Victoria Street is a burden – or you're on the hunt for the best pho in Melbourne – you won't want to miss this place. Not familiar with pho? It's a fragrant, brothy Vietnamese soup that's loved by many Melburnians. The menu here is grouped by flavour: beef, chicken or vegetable. Simple! The real crowd pleaser is the beef pho. The broth is fragrant, the noodles silken, the meat tender and it comes with plenty of Vietnamese mint, bean sprouts and lemon on the side. Don't forget the chilli! Crunchy spring rolls are in the mix, too. I Love Pho does not feature the latest fashionable fit-out; it's simply furnished for high-turnover lunches and dinners. Photos and a pet tortoise give it a personal touch. But what it lacks in glamour it makes up for in flavour because, after all, it's what's on the inside that counts. If you're looking for a pho with a little extra oomph, giblets, heart, liver, tendon and tripe also available.

POCKET TIP

Looking for more than pho? Try the Insane Fish or the Shaker Shaker Squid at Minh Minh Saigon Soul (94 Victoria St, Richmond).

RICHMOND & ABBOTSFORD

7 FEAST OF MERIT

117 Swan St, Richmond
9428 8480
www.feastofmerit.com.au
Open Wed–Sun 5pm–late
[MAP p. 194 B4]

Enter this rustic-chic cafe and restaurant and feast on the diverse flavours from across the Middle East. The decor boasts an innovative use of reclaimed materials that complement the exposed brick and showcase the real star: the food. Chef Ayhan Erkoc has created a menu of exotic dishes that look as good as they taste, including crispy falafel, slow-cooked lamb shoulder and our breakfast favourite shakshuka, with baked eggs, tomato, banana peppers and flatbread. They serve Melbourne's acclaimed St Ali coffee, too. The dinner menu takes it up a notch, offering small, large and share plates featuring roasted, fried and baked deliciousness, with plenty of vegetarian options. We love the Karnibabar of roasted cauliflower with green harissa, and the naughty but nice grilled haloumi with apricots, beetroot and almonds. Order the banquet and graze the night away on sweet, savoury and spiced flavours. Upstairs, there's a rooftop bar.

POCKET TIP

A Thousand Blessings (251 Highett St, Richmond) serves breakfast and brunch with healthful organic and biodynamic ingredients.

137

RICHMOND & ABBOTSFORD

8 PURVIS BEER

292 Bridge Rd, Richmond
9078 2779
www.purvisbeer.com.au
Open Sun–Thurs 12pm–7pm,
Fri–Sat 11am–8pm
[MAP p. 194 C3]

Australians love a beer, and we spend more than any other country on the amber liquid. Here, at Australia's largest beer retailer, you can find almost any beer from breweries big and small, Australian and international. So whether you need to track down a home favourite or some boutique barrel-aged brew you encountered in Belgium, you're bound to find it. There's literally more than 1000 types available. Of course the staff know their alcohol by volume! Their impressive range of canned beers also means this is the place to acquire your festival supplies. Take advantage of Friday night tasting events to find your favourite.

POCKET TIP
Still can't find the beer you're looking for? Try Beer 360 (468 Bridge Rd, Richmond).

RICHMOND & ABBOTSFORD

9 MOUNTAIN GOAT BREWERY

80 North St, Richmond
9428 1180
www.goatbeer.com.au
Open Wed 5pm–10pm, Fri 5pm–11pm, Sun 12pm–6pm
[MAP p. 175 F3]

Mountain Goat Brewery was among the original craft breweries that paved the way for the boutique beer boom that has taken Australia – and the world – by storm. Drawing on a much longer history of beer brewing in Richmond and Abbotsford, this backstreet brewery bar is as laid-back and approachable as their beers. Over twenty years on, they're still brewing beers unrestrained in flavour, technique and creativity – from their Organic Steam Ale, one of Australia's first organic beers, to their award-winning Rare Breeds and Barrel Breeds. Their brewery and bar still operate in the backstreets of Richmond, and is a favourite drinking spot for Melburnians on Wednesday and Friday nights and Sunday afternoons. There's foosball, the occasional food truck and charity keggers, too; check their Facebook page for the latest. Free tours of the brewery take place 6.30pm Wednesdays and 1.30pm Sundays.

> **POCKET TIP**
> Brogan's Way gin distillery is just across the road (61 North St, Richmond). Similar hours, tastings, tours and food, too!

RICHMOND & ABBOTSFORD

10 THE CORNER HOTEL

57 Swan St, Richmond
9427 7300
www.cornerhotel.com
Open Mon 4pm–12am,
Tues–Thurs 12pm–1am, Fri–Sat
12pm–3am, Sun 12pm–12am
[MAP p. 194 B4]

Adjacent to busy Richmond station, The Corner is a landmark in Melbourne's live music scene. Presenting the hottest new local and international acts since the 1990s, it's known as the place to see bands *before they get famous*. And then there are the old-timers back for a good time, like Joan Jett, Teenage Fanclub and Aussie favourites The Whitlams. The refurbished rooftop bar and kitchen is an affordable adventure through pub grub with a contemporary twist: the fried chicken comes Korean-style with kimchi and kewpie mayo, the fish is pan-fried barramundi and the panna cotta comes piña colada style. Plus you'll also find classic burgers, parmies and Scotch fillet – and the staff will even match your drinks. The Corner's proximity to the sports and entertainment precincts means it's also a popular spot for rendezvousing footy fans and post-show punters, so the crowd is always mixed.

POCKET TIP

Need a pizza? Look no further than Baby Pizza (631 Church St, Richmond).

141

FIELD TRIP

DANDENONGS & YARRA VALLEY

Beyond the suburbs east of Melbourne are the Dandenong Ranges, offering expansive vistas of the city and countryside, winding drives through towering forests, beautiful walking tracks and picturesque hillside villages steeped in history. Take the time to explore the many cool-climate gardens endemic and exotic here, including the Dandenong Ranges Botanic Garden (see p. 144). It's an easy daytrip from the city, but don't rush it when you can make a weekend of it.

Just north of the Dandenongs is the Yarra Valley, its rolling hills ribbed with rows of vines that have made the region famous for its wine. The Yarra Valley feels a world away from the hustle and bustle of Melbourne, even though it's only an hour by car. While many citysiders make a daytrip, you can easily spend two or three days exploring some of Australia's most prestigious wineries, breweries and distilleries, restaurants and art galleries. Start in Coldstream (see p. 147) and don't miss Tarrawarra Museum of Art (see p. 146) or your chance to get up close and personal with Australian wildlife at Healesville Sanctuary (see p. 146).

It's best to have your own car to meander at your own pace, but regular tour buses with bonus designated driver depart daily. See www.visitdandenongranges.com.au and www.visityarravalley.com.au for more inspiration.

→ *The Yarra Valley offers stunning views and sublime food and wine*

143

DANDENONGS & YARRA VALLEY

POCKET TIP

Take the historic Puffing Billy (1 Old Monbulk Rd, Belgrave) steam railway through the lush fern gullies and towering mountain ash trees of the Dandenong Ranges.

DANDENONG RANGES

The Dandenong Ranges is famous for its towering mountain ash (the world's tallest flowering trees), lush fern gullies, waterfalls and quaint mountain villages. The **Dandenong Ranges National Park** provides access to some of the best nature spots, with numerous walks and picnic spots to stop and take in the serenity. If you're feeling fit, try the challenging 1000 Steps **Kokoda Walk** to **One Tree Hill** – it's a workout, but there are plenty of opportunities to stop and catch your breath. For a less challenging walk, take the **Lyrebird Track** to the same location. For a scenic drive, the **Mount Dandenong Tourist Road** is a winding road that passes through the villages of **Sassafras** and **Olinda**. The **Olinda Tea House** is popular for high teas, with three sittings per day. Not far from here is **Dandenong Ranges Botanic Garden**, which becomes a riot of colour in spring when the rhododendrons, azaleas, camellias and daffodils burst into bloom. For panoramic views of Melbourne and beyond, a drive to the top of **Mount Dandenong** is a must. **SkyHigh Mount Dandenong** is a sleek dining space that provides access to those amazing views away from the elements.

DANDENONGS & YARRA VALLEY

THE PIGGERY CAFÉ

1 Sherbrooke Rd, Sherbrooke
9691 3858
www.piggerycafe.com.au
Open Mon–Fri 10am–5pm,
Sat–Sun 9am–5pm

Any trip to the Dandenongs would be incomplete without a visit to the Piggery, a beautifully restored former piggery and stables set among the serene forest surroundings of the Burnham Beeches estate. Rich in history and with a fairytale sense of place, this is the spot to stop and get your fill of the fresh and hearty fare on offer at the Piggery Café. The menu includes classic egg-based breakfasts, beef and vegetable burgers and the ever popular Pig Platter grazing plate. All bread is baked on site, vegetables and fruit are sourced from the kitchen garden, and other ingredients come from a select list of local and Australian producers, ensuring quality and provenance. Established by Melbourne's famous chef/entrepreneur Shannon Bennett, this mountainside gem is blessed with both old-world atmosphere and new-world cuisine. The Piggery also invites all-ages play on the outdoor bocce, croquet and lawn bowls greens.

POCKET TIP

The fabulous Art Moderne-style Burnham Beeches mansion, built in 1929, is being transformed into Australia's first six-star luxury retreat – wander along old pathways through the impressive heritage gardens.

DANDENONGS & YARRA VALLEY

POCKET TIP

Tarrawarra Estate (311 Healesville-Yarra Glen Rd) offers tastings of local wines and beautiful gardens. Innocent Bystander (316–334 Maroondah Hwy) serves pale pink moscato, chilled on tap.

HEALESVILLE

Healesville Sanctuary (Badger Creek Rd) is no ordinary zoo. It's dedicated to the welfare of Australian native animals, set among native bushland and divided into habitat zones accessible on easy walking paths. You can meet animals such as wallabies, kangaroos, wombats, dingoes and emus, over 200 varieties of birds, the elusive platypus and koalas grazing among gums. Don't miss the awe-inspiring **Spirits of the Sky** show – included in the entry fee – it runs twice daily, and you'll be stunned by the size and power of the wedge-tailed eagle. Be sure to visit the **Australian Wildlife Centre** – a hospital that treats thousands of sick and injured native animals every year.

Tarrawarra Museum of Art (313 Healesville-Yarra Glen Rd) is privately funded and impressive for both its striking low-rise architecture and innovative, seasonal exhibition program showcasing modern and current Australian art. It has an enviable collection of mid-20th century and 21st-century art by well-known Australian artists, including Brett Whiteley, John Olsen, Rosalie Gascoigne, Russell Drysdale and Danila Vassilieff. The Tarrawarra Biennial is held August to November in even-numbered years.

DANDENONGS & YARRA VALLEY

COLDSTREAM

POCKET TIP
Yering Station (38 Melba Hwy, Yering) is the valley's oldest vineyard and is a stunning contemporary winery.

The valley town of Coldstream offers a feast of food and wine experiences, with numerous cellar doors, microbreweries and farmgates connected on an easy 13-kilometre driving route. In the township, the **Yarra Valley Gateway Estate** (667 Maroondah Hwy) serves homestyle treats and fresh produce grown on the 110 acre farm – look out for the big strawberry! Nearby, **Coldstream Brewery** (694 Maroondah Hwy) was set up by a bunch of mates with a passion for beer – try a tasting paddle of brews at their friendly bar. One of the smaller players in the Yarra Valley winemaking scene, **Maddens Rise** (cnr Maroondah Hwy and Maddens La) has a humble cellar door with tastings of their homegrown, handpicked and handmade wines. For lunch, the pizza at **400 Gradi Pizzeria at Rochford Wines** (880 Maroondah Hwy) is as revered here as at their flagship restaurant in Brunswick – and it goes well with a Rochford wine (or two).

FIELD TRIP

MORNINGTON PENINSULA & PHILLIP ISLAND

The Mornington Peninsula is Melbourne's summer playground. Families have been camping, caravanning and holidaying on the peninsula for generations. These days, it's part of the greater Melbourne conurbation but still retains its feeling of being a place apart. The Mornington Peninsula Freeway cuts through the seaside suburbs of Mt Eliza, Mornington and Dromana, where you begin to get that holiday feeling. A short detour up Arthurs Seat reveals expansive views of the bay and peninsula – calm bay beaches on one side, wild ocean on the other. Onward, the Point Nepean Road hugs the coastline, revealing glimpses of serene blue-green bay beaches.

The area has been a renowned food and wine destination for years, with award-winning cellar doors, restaurants and farm gates aplenty, particularly in Red Hill and Flinders (see p. 152). The further you travel from Melbourne, the fancier it gets, with the towns of Sorrento and Portsea among the most exclusive postcodes in the country. Sorrento (see p. 150) and Point Nepean (see p. 151) are key sites in Victoria's European immigration story.

Further afield, Phillip Island (see p. 153) is another popular city escape, with families flocking here during school holidays and on weekends, while the popular little penguins live here all year round. The National Surfing Reserve is also here.

The Mornington Peninsula is about 90 minutes by car from Melbourne. Regular bus tours visit wineries and other attractions in the area. You'll need to book ahead if you're planning to stay during peak periods, such as summer and public holidays and on long weekends.

→ *Coastal scenery to take your breath away*

149

MORNINGTON PENINSULA & PHILLIP ISLAND

SORRENTO

The lovely coastal town of Sorrento is an important part of Victoria's story. This is where Europeans first tried (and failed) to establish a settlement – more than 30 years before Melbourne. Since then, the picturesque seaside town has grown to become a desirable holiday destination. For a scenic history lesson, head to **Collins Settlement Historic Site**, where Lieutenant Colonel David Collins landed in 1803 in an attempt to establish a coastal settlement. Lack of fresh water foiled his plans, and today the only remaining evidence is four graves and some detritus on the eastern headland. The area has been re-vegetated and features a pathway for exploring the area on foot. **Ocean Beach Road** is dominated by grand historic limestone buildings, which today house antique and homewares stores, designer clothes boutiques, galleries, eateries and drinking holes, including the classic **Continental Hotel**. Sitting atop a hill overlooking Port Phillip Bay, the popular **Hotel Sorrento** boasts a restaurant, several bars, hotel rooms and the best views in town. The **Sorrento-Portsea Artists Trail** takes in the views captured by renowned local and international artists.

POCKET TIP
You can also catch the Searoad ferry from Sorrento across Port Phillip Bay to the historic town of Queenscliff; a scenic 40-minute journey.

MORNINGTON PENINSULA & PHILLIP ISLAND

POINT NEPEAN NATIONAL PARK

www.parkweb.vic.gov.au
Open daily 10am–5pm

This beautiful nature reserve, with a rich history and panoramic views of Bass Strait and Port Phillip Bay, is located at the tip of the Mornington Peninsula. Point Nepean was originally used by the Boon Wurrung people, who foraged for shellfish and other coastal foods, and was later used by early European settlers as a quarantine station and Melbourne's main military fort. There are numerous heritage-listed buildings to explore, including military forts and tunnels and the historic **Quarantine Station**. Point Nepean was made a national park in 1988, and there's a range of habitats, including coastal dune scrub, woodlands and rare remnant grasslands, all of which support diverse plant and wildlife communities including threatened orchids, Melaleuca trees, the long-nosed bandicoot, black wallaby and a variety of birds. The waters are famous for scuba diving, but be careful – this is where Australian prime minister Harold Holt disappeared. The park is accessible by vehicle and bikes are available for hire from the **Information Centre**.

POCKET TIP
Rare Hare Wine & Food Store (166 Balnarring Rd, Merricks North) offers a dining experience with views of vineyards.

MORNINGTON PENINSULA & PHILLIP ISLAND

FLINDERS

Flinders is the historic but hip town on the Mornington Peninsula that looks away from the bay and out to the wild seas of Bass Strait. Snorkelers and divers love it here for the elusive leafy sea dragons, which are often spotted around the local pier, and the sub-tidal reefs at **Mushroom Reef Marine Sanctuary**. Several walks take in the raw power of the ocean from the safety of land; don't miss the **Flinders Blowhole** west of town. Back in town, foodies are spoilt for choice on Cook Street. Toasties, breads and baked goods from **Flinders Sourdough** (no. 58) are good to go, or stay a while for a gourmet breakfast and cooking class in serene surrounds at **Georgie Bass Café & Cookery** (no. 30). The **Mornington Peninsula Chocolaterie and Ice Creamery** (no. 45) has more than 180 chocolates to choose from, with tasting sessions and workshops for kids and adults. The 125-year-old **Flinders Hotel** (cnr Cook & Wood sts) does fine dining and accommodation, too. You can admire the historic streetscape; visit **Cook Street Collective** (no. 2/41) gallery with its resident jeweller, painter, photographer, woodworker, sculptor and printmaker; and while away time in the clothing and homewares stores.

> **POCKET TIP**
> Award-winning Montalto Winery (33 Shoreham Rd, Red Hill) has a sculpture trail, olive grove, orchard, cafe and restaurant.

MORNINGTON PENINSULA &
PHILLIP ISLAND

PHILLIP ISLAND

In Western Port Bay, Phillip Island is a family friendly holiday destination with good surf breaks and a pristine coastline. **Cape Woolamai**, **Smiths Beach**, **Summerland** and **Cat Bay** are collectively known as the **National Surfing Reserve**, in recognition of the island's rich surfing heritage. **Cape Woolamai** offers stunning views from four coastal walking tracks, including the striking pink granite rock formations known as **The Pinnacles**. The **Nobbies Centre** is an ecotourism venture that hosts **Antarctic Journey** – a family friendly virtual reality experience that brings the icy southern continent to life before your eyes. There's a seal colony at **Seal Rock** just offshore, or you can take a cruise from Cowes for a close-up look at the 25,000 residents. See koalas at **Koala Conservation Centre** and abundant birdlife at **Rhyll Inlet** wetlands. But the undisputed superstars of Phillip Island are the adorable little penguins, who attract hordes of visitors for the nightly **penguin parade**, when they waddle from **Summerland Bay Beach** to their sandy burrows. **The Penguin Parade Visitor Centre** at Phillip Island Nature Park provides a range of penguin-watching experiences for all budgets.

POCKET TIP

Churchill Island is a small island and historic estate that offers hands-on farm experiences and scenic coastal walks.

153

FIELD TRIP

GREAT OCEAN ROAD

One of Australia's great scenic drives, the Great Ocean Road reveals stunning sea cliffs, iconic surf beaches and ancient rainforests abundant with wildlife. Built by returned servicemen after World War I, the Great Ocean Road is a major engineering feat. From the surfing town of Torquay (see p. 156), the road twists and turns for more than 200 kilometres (124 miles) to end at the quaint fishing village of Port Fairy (see p. 160). In-between you can climb lighthouses at Aireys Inlet (see p. 157) and Cape Otway (see p. 159), linger in the seaside retreat of Lorne (see p. p. 157), stop for sightseeing and food in Apollo Bay (see p. p. 158), or venture into the Otway Ranges (see p. 159) to waterfalls and walks. The dramatic limestone coastal formations known as the 12 Apostles (see p. 160) are a must-see, with numerous lookouts along the way offering more spectacular views. This is shipwreck coast, so be on the lookout for these stories, too.

We recommend staying at least two nights to get the most out of your trip down the Great Ocean Road. If you're hiring a car, be warned that the road is winding, the turns are sharp and the drops are vertiginous. Driving can be slow at peak times, as there are few opportunities to overtake. There are many coach companies that offer one-day drives or short stays. Visit www.visitgreatoceanroad.org.au for information on accommodation options, events and other local attractions. If you're staying during Victorian school holidays or public holidays, book well ahead as even the campsites book out.

→ *The spectacular coastline of the Great Ocean Road*

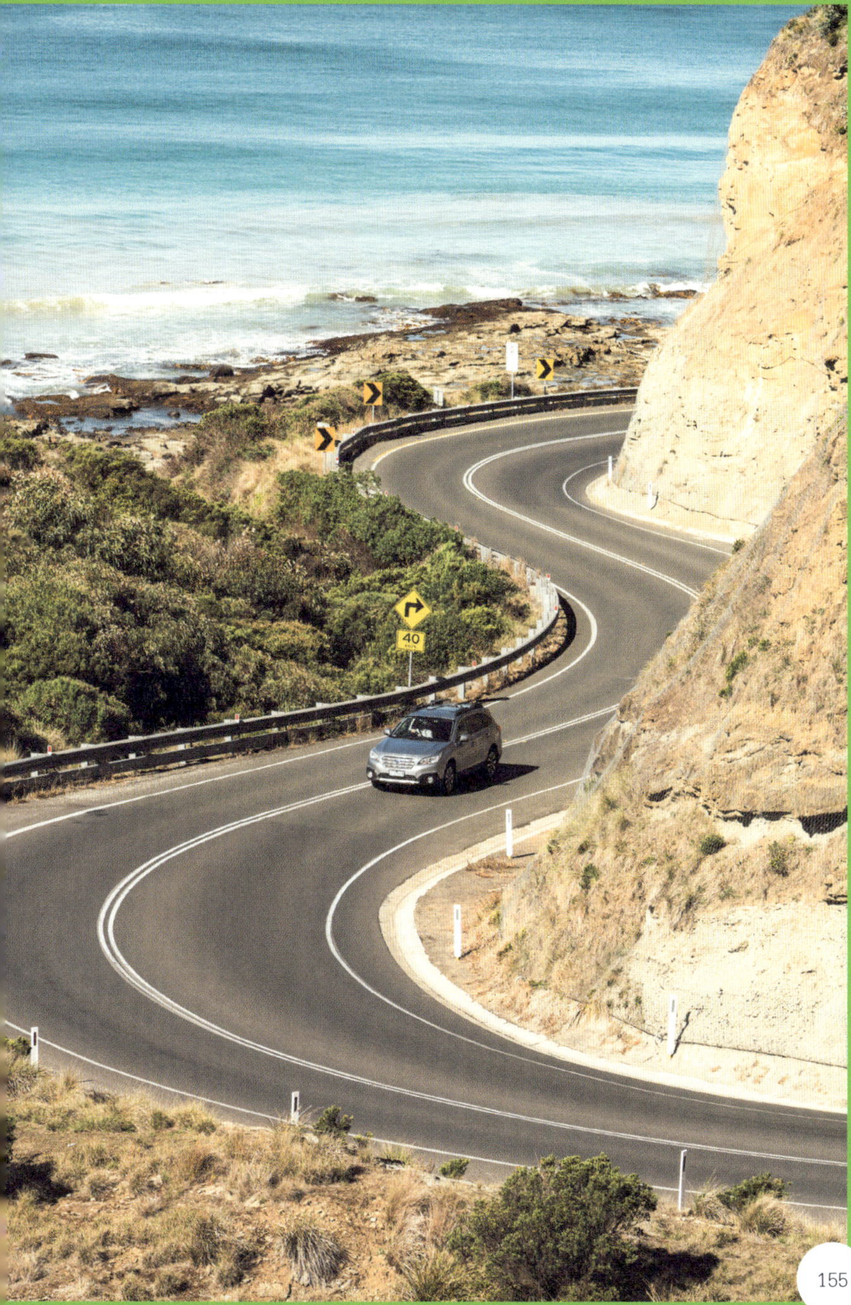
40

GREAT OCEAN ROAD

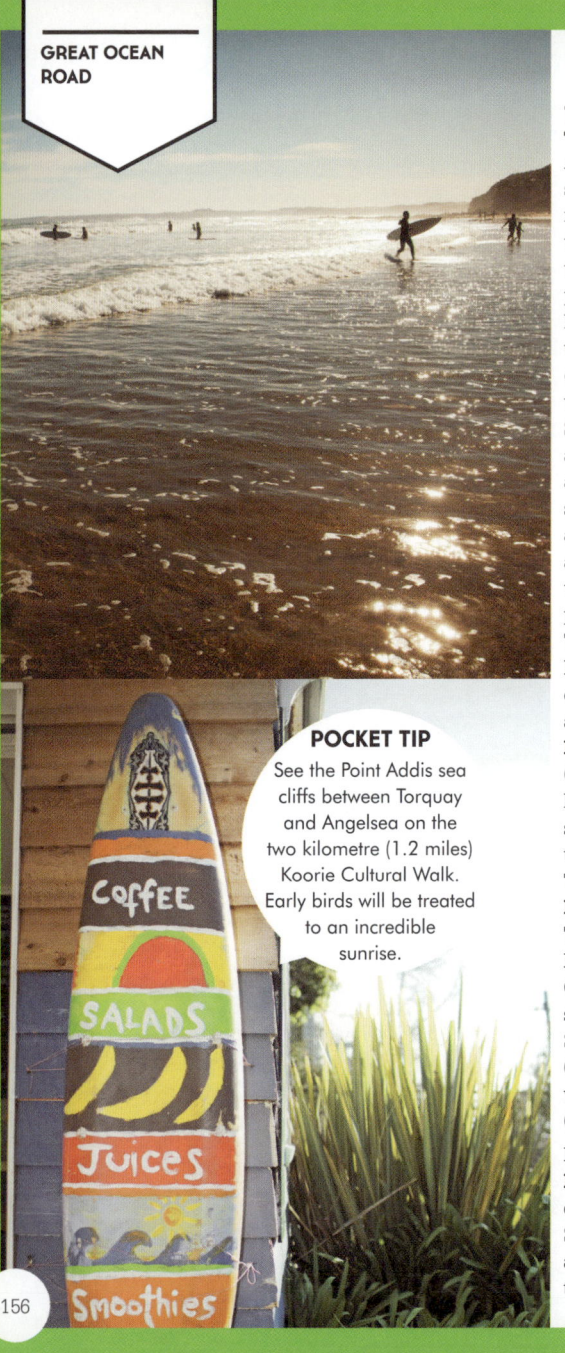

TORQUAY & BELLS BEACH

Australia's surf city of the south, the popular coastal resort town of Torquay is the official starting point of the Great Ocean Road. It pumps in summer, but can be refreshingly quiet at other times of the year. Keen walkers can explore the coastline on the epic 44 kilometre (27 miles) **Surf Coast Walk**, which starts at nearby **Point Impossible** and can be enjoyed in shorter sections along the way. There are several beaches in and around Torquay – be sure to only swim in lifeguard-patrolled areas and note that Torquay back beach is a surf beach. Discover the history of Australia's surfing history and culture at the **Australian National Surfing Museum** (77 Beach Rd). Afterwards, browse through the many surf shops and factory outlets round the corner on Baines Crescent. Try the beer at **Blackman's Brewery** (26 Bell St), head to **The Salty Dog Cafe** (47 The Esplanade) for local Ocean Grinder coffee, get those summer feels with a pair of Saltwater sandals from **Kittos** (30 Bell St) and have lunch with ocean views at **Growlers** (23 The Esplanade).

Near Torquay is famous **Bells Beach**, which features an exposed reef and impressive Southern Ocean swells that attract surfers from around the world, especially during

POCKET TIP
See the Point Addis sea cliffs between Torquay and Angelsea on the two kilometre (1.2 miles) Koorie Cultural Walk. Early birds will be treated to an incredible sunrise.

GREAT OCEAN ROAD

the **Rip Curl Pro** surfing competition during Easter. Non-surfers can appreciate this beach for its dramatic cliffs and natural amphitheatre, which can be enjoyed from the clifftop or the water's edge below.

ANGLESEA & AIREYS INLET

Angelsea feels a little like the proper gateway to the Great Ocean Road. As you drive through the town, you catch glimpses of the dramatic cliffs, coves and expanse of sea to come. It's a popular town for camping and a great spot to pick up supplies. If you need a coffee, stop at **Anglesea General Store** (119 Great Ocean Rd). Just 10 kilometres (six miles) from Anglesea is the striking red-topped **Split Point Lighthouse** at Aireys Inlet. Stop for a browse or buy at **Great Escape Books** (75 Great Ocean Rd, Aireys Inlet), an independent bookshop beautifully displaying its deftly curated selection.

LORNE

The seaside town of Lorne has long been a favourite holiday destination and bursts with holidaymakers over summer. It's a beautiful place to stop and break up the winding drive, and there is a variety of accommodation, boutique shopping, cafes and restaurants, a beautiful beach

POCKET TIP

Look out for the Pole House in Fairhaven. It's literally a house on a pole. It's available to rent, but it doesn't come cheap.

GREAT OCEAN ROAD

POCKET TIP

Don't miss the Wye River General Store (35 Great Ocean Rd). You'll pop in for a coffee and a paper and end up staying for brunch.

and a foreshore playground. The foreshore trampolines and mini-golf will trigger nostalgic holiday feelings. The **Lorne Visitor Information Centre** (15 Mountjoy Pde) houses a small **museum** detailing the building of the Great Ocean Road. If you need lunch, stop at **The Bottle of Milk** (52 Mountjoy Pde) for mouth-watering hamburgers, or for dinner at newly opened **MoVida** (176 Mountjoy Pde), for Melbourne's iconic Spanish fare. And if you haven't packed your reading material, don't miss one of the best independent bookshops in Victoria, **Lorne Beach Books** (108 Mountjoy Pde), with a covetable selection of interior, architecture, travel and children's books. Nearby, the **Lorne Corner Store** (142 Mountjoy Pde) sells a beachy range of menswear (Banks Journal, Salty Crew and essential Hawaiian holiday shirts), womenswear and cool stuff for your house. If you love Byron Bay's Spell & the Gypsy Collective range, don't miss **Midi Boutique** (146 Mountjoy Pde) in a cute little white weatherboard place.

APOLLO BAY

Apollo Bay is the next major town along the Great Ocean Road from Lorne, nestled between **Great Otway National Park** (*see* p. 159) and the sea. There's a wide

GREAT OCEAN ROAD

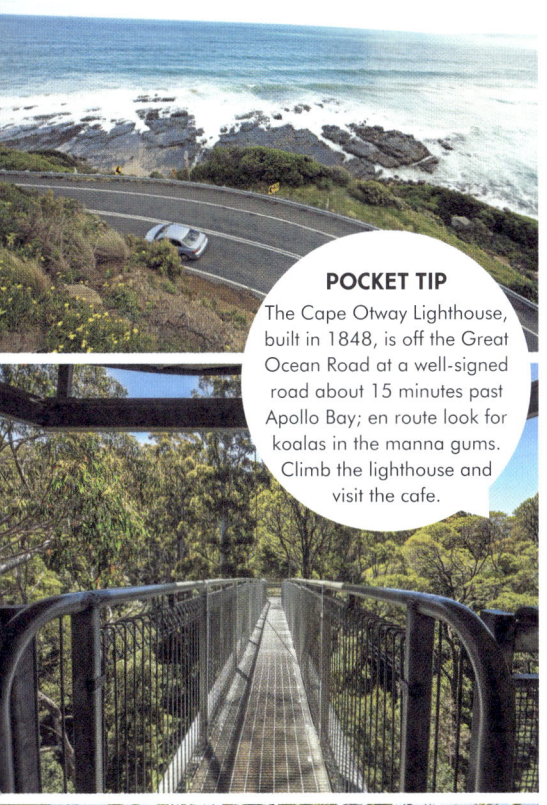

variety of accommodation, cafes and take-away eateries where you can get freshly caught fish (and chips), such as at **The Fishermen's Co-op** (Breakwater Rd). The harbour beach is beautiful for a walk or a brave dip or snorkel in the cold of Bass Strait. **The Great Ocean Road Brewhouse** (29–35 Great Ocean Rd) has craft beer, local wines, a substantial menu, a large deck and a beer garden.

THE OTWAY RANGES

The Great Otway National Park provides some of the best coastal scenery and rainforest experiences in Victoria. Situated within the Otway Ranges, the park contains a wealth of ancient plants and wildlife, including towering trees, abundant birdlife and a local koala population. About an hour from Apollo Bay, the **Otway Fly Tree Top Walk** (360 Phillips Trk, Weeaproinah) provides a bird's eye view of the lush, temperate rainforest below and ends at a spectacular 47-metre high lookout. The national park features numerous waterfalls and scenic walks, picnic spots and campsites, with the 91 kilometre (56 miles) **Great Ocean Walk** covering much of the coastal section.

POCKET TIP
The Cape Otway Lighthouse, built in 1848, is off the Great Ocean Road at a well-signed road about 15 minutes past Apollo Bay; en route look for koalas in the manna gums. Climb the lighthouse and visit the cafe.

GREAT OCEAN ROAD

> **POCKET TIP**
> May through October is whale-watching season. A great vantage point to see southern right whales is Logans Beach Whale Watching Platform (11 Logans Beach Rd, Warrnambool).

12 APOSTLES, ARCHES AND GORGES

The star attraction of any Great Ocean Road adventure is undoubtedly the spectacular 12 Apostles. This collection of towering, offshore limestone stacks are the result of erosion caused by the powerful Southern Ocean, providing an unmissable photo opportunity from one of the many lookout spots. Besides the famous apostles – of which there are only eight left – there are many more awe-inspiring wave-sculpted natural formations on this section of the coastline, including our favourite spot, **Loch Ard Gorge**. The stunning natural gorge is a surprisingly calm refuge from the tempestuous coastline. Named after the famous shipwreck of the *Loch Ard* in 1878 (one of several hundred shipwrecks along the coast) and featuring scenic walks that take in caves, dramatic arches and views of nearby **Muttonbird Island**, this gorge is an essential stopping point on any Great Ocean Road journey. Information and refreshments can be found at the **12 Apostles Visitor Information Centre**.

PORT FAIRY & BUDJ BIM NATIONAL PARK

The historic fishing village of Port Fairy is a fairly sleepy seaside village for most of

GREAT OCEAN ROAD

the year, except when the annual **Port Fairy Folk Festival** rolls into town on the first weekend in March, and it's busy again at Easter. It's also the last stop for many on their Great Ocean Road adventure, and the perfect spot to slow down and take in the historic streetscapes, heritage-listed buildings and impressive Norfolk Island Pines that dot the shoreline. There's boutique shopping here and plenty of cafes. **Rebecca's** (74 Sackville St) is famed for its homemade cakes and tubs of mini biscuits – but you can never eat just one. To walk off the guilts, head to **Griffith Island** to visit the small but spectacular **Port Fairy Lighthouse**, built in 1859.

Less than an hour drive inland from Port Fairy, **Budj Bim National Park** is Victoria's first national park to be co-managed by the traditional owners of the land, the Gunditjmara people. Nature trails around the rim of a volcanic crater provide impressive elevated views of the crater and surrounding forest. Ancient lava flows have created a unique landscape and environment that teems with wildlife; you might spot koalas, possums, eastern grey kangaroos, and there's too many bird species to mention.

FIELD TRIP

GOLDFIELDS & SPA COUNTRY

Melbourne is a city built on gold, and its wealth in the 19th century came from its hinterland about 100 kilometres (62 miles) north of the city. The legacy of the gold rush is still visible in grandiose Victorian architecture, though these days the region is as well known for its art galleries, restaurants, nature reserves, natural springs and charming country communities. Home to the Pyrenees and Heathcote wine regions, Victoria's Goldfields isn't short on award-winning wineries or wine trails. And you'll find plenty of award-winning breweries, cideries and distilleries, too.

Less than two hours from Melbourne, the Goldfields towns of Ballarat (see p. 164), Bendigo (see p. 166), Castlemaine (see p. 167), Clunes and Daylesford (see p. 165) are popular weekend destinations for Melburnians. Ballarat is a small city with grandiose architecture, a thriving cafe scene, a renowned art gallery (see p. 164) and acclaimed Sovereign Hill (see p. 164); Bendigo's streets are also evidently built on gold and its art gallery (see p. 166) hosts regular international exhibitions; Castlemaine is smaller with an artistic community; picturesque Clunes is classic movie-set material and Daylesford is the heart of spa country with a long-standing arts scene. Spend a day or more uncovering stories of the past, discovering secret spots for a swim, zigzagging the wine trails across the region and visiting craft breweries, distilleries, farm gates and antique stores.

→ *Daylesford combines nature, history and hospitality with style*

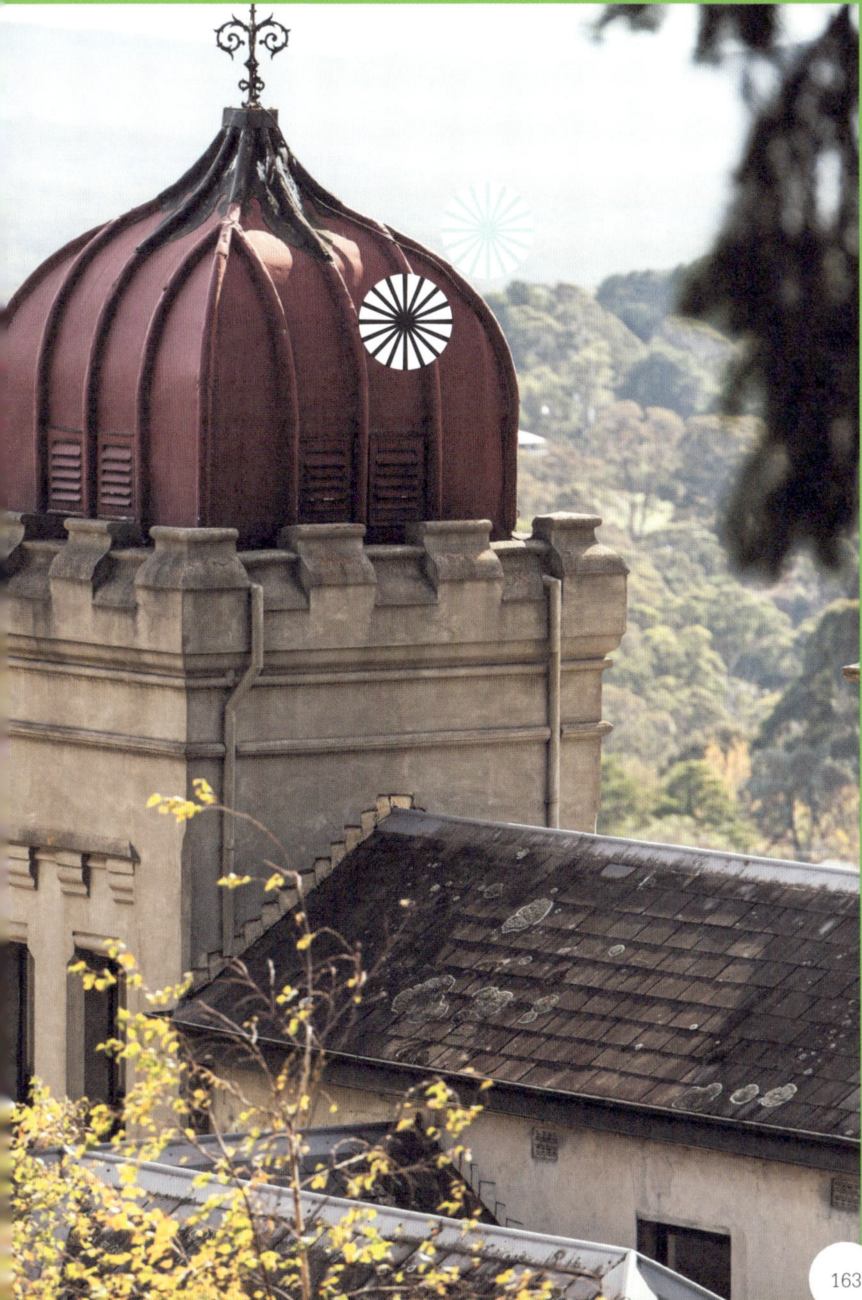

GOLDFIELDS & SPA COUNTRY

POCKET TIP

Ballarat's thriving craft brewing scene includes Cubby Haus Brewing (884 Humffray St South) for seasonal brews, The Mallow (20 Skipton St) for a large range of local brews, and brewer Red Duck alongside Kilderkin Distillery (11a Michaels Dr, Alfredton).

BALLARAT

Ballarat is famed for the gold rush and its grand 19th-century architecture. The **Ballarat Art Gallery and Museum** (40 Lydiard St North) contains an outstanding collection of Australian art. **Lake Wendouree** is a scenic spot for a stop. For caffeine or wine, **L'Espresso** (417 Sturt St) is a long-standing local favourite. Look for hidden gem shops like **The Crafty Squirrel** (cnr Errard and Urquhart sts) for vintage gifts and **The Foundry** (411 Mair St), with Jasper coffee and a beautifully curated selection of gifts.

Regularly named Australia's best tourist attraction, **Sovereign Hill** (Bradshaw St, Golden Point) is a museum and theme park. You can pan for real gold (finders keepers), visit the underground mine, watch a gold pour or craftspeople at work in the forge, candleworks, wheelwright's plant and confectionery works. Costumed characters play out historic scenes in the streets – careful not to get caught up in a public whipping! The **Gold Museum** explores the story of the gold rush, and at night the spectacular **Blood on the Southern Cross** light show reimagines the 1854 Eureka Rebellion, in which miners took on the military.

GOLDFIELDS & SPA COUNTRY

DAYLESFORD & HEPBURN SPRINGS

The twin towns of Daylesford and Hepburn Springs are the heart of Victoria's spa country with wellness centres and a diverse and inclusive community of creatives and tree-changers. There's an experience to suit all budgets: you can fill your water bottle for free at more than 60 mineral springs, each with its own unique mineral profile; take a dip in the historic **Hepburn Pool** or spoil yourself rotten at the **Hepburn Bathhouse** with massages and treatments. There is food and wine aplenty, from cafe fare at **Cliffy's** (30 Raglan St, Daylesford) to casual rustica at **Frank & Connie's Kitchen** (97 Main Rd, Hepburn Springs), quality pub grub at the **Farmers Arms** (1 East St, Daylesford) to the famous fine dining at **Lake House** (King St, Daylesford). Don't miss Daylesford's weekly **Sunday Market** for local goods, produce and a ride on the historic train. There are spectacular views – and three levels of art at the **Convent Gallery** (top of Hill St) overlooking the town. Just outside of Daylesford is picturesque **Lavendula**, a Swiss–Italian farm with European gardens, an 1850s' stone farmhouse and a cafe for antipasto, cakes and wine.

POCKET TIP
Time your visit to coincide with one of the many local community celebrations – most notably in March for Chill Out, the largest rural queer pride festival in Australia.

165

GOLDFIELDS & SPA COUNTRY

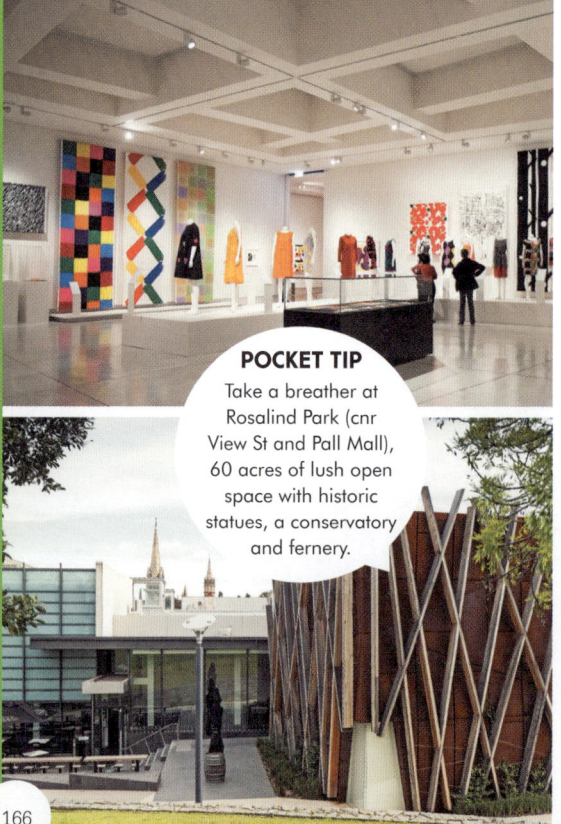

BENDIGO

Built on the back of the world's richest gold rush, Bendigo is a vibrant regional city about two and a half hours by car or train from Melbourne. The ornate Victorian architecture, tree-lined streets and historic tram line provide a beautiful setting for fossicking in the emerging food and wine scene. Located in the middle of the city, the **Central Deborah Gold Mine** (76 Violet St) operated for 100 years until 1954. Reopened as a museum experience in 1971, you can now join tours to explore as far as 220 metres underground. Established in 1863, **Bendigo Pottery** (146 Midland Hwy, Epsom) is Australia's oldest working pottery, now with hands-on experiences, including wheel throwing and clay play. Built in 1887, the **Bendigo Art Gallery** (42 View St) is one of the oldest and largest art galleries in the country. It is also increasingly regarded among the best. The Australian collection dates all the way back to Bendigo's foundation in the 1850s, and includes iconic colonial-era works by Heidelberg painters Frederick McCubbin and Tom Roberts. But it is the contemporary collection and blockbuster retrospectives that are attracting crowds from far and wide.

POCKET TIP

Take a breather at Rosalind Park (cnr View St and Pall Mall), 60 acres of lush open space with historic statues, a conservatory and fernery.

GOLDFIELDS & SPA COUNTRY

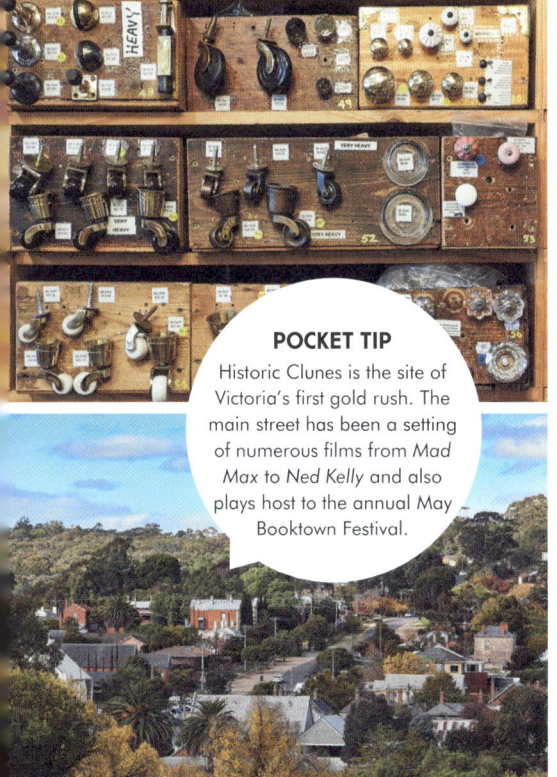

CASTLEMAINE

Jokingly referred to as North Northcote for its influx of creative tree changers from Melbourne's artsy northern suburb, Castlemaine's artistic credentials date all the way back to its gold rush origins. The town is a treasure trove of vintage wares, with several antiques stores on Mostyn and Barker streets, including the wall-to-wall relics at the **Restorers Barn** (129 Mostyn St). Established in 1913, the **Castlemaine Art Museum** (14 Lyttleton St) exhibits historic and contemporary art, as well as local artefacts, all in a gorgeous 1931 Art Deco building. Live entertainment can be found at the **Theatre Royal** (30 Hargraves St), which started out in 1854 and now plays hosts to regular indie performers, film screenings and a bistro. Food, artisan wares and craft can be found at **The Mill** (9 Walker St), a historic woollen mill that has been transformed into a vibrant food, art and makers hub. Here you can enjoy a coffee at **Das Kaffeehaus** and sample sweet pastries and cakes from **Sprout Bakery** and **St Cloud Cakes** before exploring the artist studios and old wares at the **Castlemaine Vintage Bazaar**.

POCKET TIP

Historic Clunes is the site of Victoria's first gold rush. The main street has been a setting of numerous films from *Mad Max* to *Ned Kelly* and also plays host to the annual May Booktown Festival.

167

TRAVEL TIPS

GETTING TO MELBOURNE

Arriving by plane

Melbourne Airport (locally known as Tullamarine Airport) is Melbourne's main airport and Australia's second busiest.

It is connected to Southern Cross Station in the city via a regular **SkyBus** (www.skybus.com.au, every 6–15 minutes, 20-minute journey). SkyBus also operates services from Melbourne Airport to Southbank and Docklands, St Kilda, the Mornington Peninsula, Werribee and Avalon Airport.

Public Transport Victoria **Bus Route 901** (ptv.vic.gov.au) provides a regular bus transfer to Broadmeadows Station (every 15–20 minutes), where you can catch a connecting train to the city and northern suburbs. Route 901 also operates between Melbourne Airport and Frankston. All route 901 buses depart from the bus terminal outside Terminal 4 (T4).

Taxis are available at ranks at T1, T2 and the T4 transport hubs. An airport access fee of $3.65 applies to all pick-ups from an airport taxi rank. The access fee is paid by the passenger to the taxi driver and is included in the taxi fare. There is no airport charge for drop off.

Or, you can order an **Uber** (or other car-sharing service). For terminal T1, T2 or T3 arrivals, the UberX pick-up zone is lane 1 of the main terminal forecourt. The T4 pick-up zone is located at the level 2 transport hub. Look for the signs. There are also several car hire companies and smaller bus transfer operators.

Avalon Airport is greater Melbourne's second busiest airport, located 50 kilometres (31 miles) west from Melbourne and 21 kilometres (13 miles) from the regional city of Geelong. Avalon operates regular direct international flights between Avalon Airport and Kuala Lumpur – if you're flying to Melbourne with AirAsia, this is where you'll arrive. **SkyBus** (www.skybus.com.au) operates express transfers to Melbourne city (every 30–60 minutes, 50-minute journey) and Geelong.

Arriving by road

Melbourne is connected to most Australian capital cities and major regional centres via the National Highway, with several passenger bus services.

Arriving by ferry

The **Spirit of Tasmania** ferry service (www.spiritoftasmania.com.au) operates between Port Melbourne and Devonport, Tasmania.

Arriving by train

Melbourne is accessible by train from most capital cities and many regional centres. **VLine** (www.vline.com.au) provides train and bus services to/from regional Victoria, including the major regional centres of Geelong, Ballarat and Bendigo.

GETTING AROUND MELBOURNE

Walking

Melbourne is a great city to explore on foot, with a well-ordered network of big and little streets, laneways and historic arcades. For a guided exploration of Melbourne's much-loved inner city laneways, take a Lanes and Arcades tour with **Hidden Secrets Tours** (www.hiddensecretstours.com) for a fun and friendly introduction to these iconic thoroughfares.

The inner suburbs are relatively flat and well serviced with an extensive network of easy walking/cycling paths, all easily accessible from the main city grid. Many of the inner suburbs can be reached via lovely historic gardens, including Carlton Gardens, Fitzroy Gardens, Flagstaff Gardens, Alexandra Gardens and the Royal Botanic Gardens.

A walk along the Yarra River via Birrarung Marr rewards you with scenic city views that eventually give way to native bushland.

The 29-kilometre (18 miles) **Capital City Trail** circles the city centre and some inner eastern and northern suburbs. A good starting point is Princes Bridge next to Federation Square, heading east towards Dights Falls.

Public Transport

Melbourne has a good public transport system that includes trains, buses and our much-beloved trams. Visit **Public Transport Victoria** (PTV, www.ptv.vic.gov.au) for public transport maps and information or download the PTV mobile app. Avoid travelling during the peak times, as trains and trams can get jam-packed.

Tickets

MYKI cards are travel cards that cover all metropolitan (and some regional) transport and can be purchased online (www.mymyki.com.au), at train station service counters and from hundreds of businesses including all 7-Eleven stores. You have two options for travel: Myki Money is the pay-as-you-go option for occasional users, Myki Pass is for users who travel often on consecutive days and predetermined routes. You can buy a Myki Pass for 7 days or anywhere between 28 and 365 days. There are three fare groups, based on metropolitan zones: Free Tram Zone, Zone 1+2 and Zone 2 only.

Train

Melbourne's Metro rail network is undergoing expansion. Each line fans out from the central City Loop, which includes Flinders Street station, Melbourne Central station, Parliament station, Flagstaff station and Southern Cross station. You'll need to tap on your Myki when entering a station, and tap off when exiting.

Tram

Melbourne boasts the largest tram network in the world, and boy does it boast! Getting around on trams is one of the best ways to explore the city, as the lines wind their way into the outer suburbs via roads, tramways and even through parks and gardens. It's free to ride trams in the city centre, so you can keep your MYKI card in your pocket and save some coin, but be sure to tap on when exiting the free zone.

When boarding trams, always allow passengers to alight first. Space is often at a premium onboard trams. If you carry a backpack, take it off and hold it in front of you. Never leave bags unattended or on seats. If you're standing, hold onto a handrail. When alighting, always check for cars and cyclists before stepping onto the road.

The free **City Circle Tram** is an informative way to explore the city in old-fashioned comfort in a historic W Class tram. The 60-minute loop runs along the city's edge and passes through the sleek-and-modern Docklands waterside precinct while providing pre-recorded audio commentary.

Taxi

If all else fails, you can always hail a cab! Taxi ranks can be found at Flinders Street station at the corner of Swanston Street, on Queen Street (between Little Collins and Bourke Streets), on Bourke Street (near Russell Street) and on King Street (near Flinders Street). If the rooftop lamp is lit, the ride is yours. You can ride in the front or back seat, and pay by cash or card.

Boat

Numerous boat tours depart from Southbank and Princes Walk, Birrurung Marr and Docklands. Choose from charming historical cruisers or modern comfort machines – you can even ride on a floating tram! River tours take in Docklands, Southbank, NewQuay, Waterfront City, Port Melbourne, Williamstown and beyond. Fancy a day trip? Catch the commuter ferry from Docklands to the lovely beachside township of Portarlington on the Bellarine Peninsula.

Cycling

Melbourne is, for the most part, a bike-friendly city and loads of Melburnians use bikes for travel and leisure. There's a handful of major on-road thoroughfares that are well used by cyclists, including Royal Parade, Canning Street and Rathdowne Street through Carlton, Swanston Street, La Trobe Street and Exhibition Street in the CBD, Albert Street in East Melbourne and St Kilda Road in Southbank. There are various off-road shared cycling and walking paths, including the Yarra River Trail, Moonee Ponds Creek Trail, and Maribyrnong River Trail, as well as the combined Capital City Trail (*see* p. 168). Helmets are mandatory.

Melbourne Bike Share has loads of hire stations throughout the city and inner suburbs, from Fitzroy to St Kilda. For $8 a week, you can take as many 45-minute rides as you like. Just look out for the blue bikes and visit www.melbournebikeshare.com.au for more information.

TRAVEL TIPS

Driving

All visitors planning to drive in Australia must carry a valid international driving permit, as well as the driver's licence issued in their country. Australians drive on the left-hand side of the road. Road distances are measured in kilometres, not miles.

Speed limits are strictly enforced in Australia, with speed cameras operating in metropolitan and regional areas. In Victoria, the default speed limit is 50km/h in built-up areas and 100km/h for highways and freeways, unless marked otherwise. School zones are strictly 40km/h during specified, signed times. Speed limits also apply to 'road related' areas like car parks and public spaces. Always look out for pedestrians and cyclists.

Melbourne has its own rules for navigating roads and trams, including the 'hook turn', which is unique to Melbourne and can be confusing to both locals and visiting drivers. Also, never drive a vehicle past a tram at a designated stop, unless the tram is stopped at a cordoned-off stop with barriers. **VicRoads** (www.vicroads.vic.gov.au) provides useful information on the rules and nuances around driving in Melbourne and Victoria.

It's best to avoid driving during the peak traffic periods, to aid congestion and save yourself an unpleasant journey. Melbourne traffic peaks from 6.30am to 9am and 3pm to 6.30pm.

Parking in Melbourne and its inner suburbs can be like playing a game of pot luck, so be patient and keep your eyes peeled. Hourly parking rates differ across the city, depending on demand for parking in each area. In the central business district (CBD), most car spaces have a limit of 1P (one hour) during the day, with most restrictions ending at 8.30pm. No coins? You can pay with credit card at most parking bays. There are plenty of privately operated car parks, too.

Melbourne has two toll roads: EastLink and CityLink, which both charge a fee for use. Toll pass information can be found on the **VicRoads** website (www.vicroads.vic.gov.au) and toll passes can be purchased beforehand or up to three days after travel from the **Linkt** (www.linkt.com.au) or **Eastlink** (www.eastlink.com.au) websites and from any 7-Eleven store.

MEDIA & TOURIST INFO

Visit Melbourne (www.visitmelbourne.com) is a great resource for Melbourne's many attractions and events, as are **Time Out** (www.timeout.com/melbourne) and **Broadsheet** (www.broadsheet.com.au/melbourne). If planning to visit a number of major ticketed attractions, you can purchase an **iVenture** visitor card (www.iventurecard.com/au/melbourne) and save yourself enough money for at least another $5 latte.

TIME ZONE

From April to October, Melbourne is on Australian Eastern Standard Time (AEST).

From the first Sunday in October to the first Sunday in April, clocks go forward one hour to daylight saving time.

CLIMATE

Melbourne is famous for giving you four seasons in one day, so it's best to be prepared for anything. The climate is temperate, with average temperatures ranging between 14–25°C (57.2–77°F) in summer and 6.5–14.2°C (43.7–57.6°F) in winter. Melbourne receives only half as much rain as Sydney. Summer can get very hot, with consecutive days over 30°C (86°F) not uncommon. But for the most part, the weather is pleasant and winters are tame by Northern Hemisphere standards. The **Bureau of Meteorology** (www.bom.gov.au) provides up-to-date weather information and has a handy mobile app.

WI-FI

Wi-fi can be found just about anywhere: public libraries, cafes and other businesses, including shopping centres. There are free wi-fi hotspots at all Melbourne city train stations, the Bourke Street Mall and Queen Victoria Market – select 'VicFreeWiFi' to access. The State Library, City Library and Federation Square also offer free wi-fi.

PEAK SEASONS

There is at least one major festival or event happening in Melbourne at any one time, so anytime is good to visit. The peak tourist seasons are December to February, when locals take their annual holidays, hotel prices rise and the Australian Open tennis rolls into town, along with a slew of summer festivals and markets. Winter is the quietest season but offers a wealth of undercover cultural events and happenings.

MELBOURNE'S MAJOR FESTIVALS

There's a festival in Melbourne to cater to just about every interest, from fashion to football. Here's a rundown of the major festivals and events through the year.

Check www.visitmelbourne.com/events for more inspiration.

January
Australian Open Tennis
Midsumma LGBTIQ+ Festival
Sugar Mountain Festival

February
Sustainable Living Festival
Lonsdale Street (Greek) Festival

March
Moomba Festival
Formula 1 Australian Grand Prix
Melbourne International Coffee Expo
Virgin Australia Melbourne Fashion Festival
Melbourne Design Week
Melbourne International Flower and Garden Show
Melbourne Food and Wine Festival
Melbourne International Comedy Festival

April
Melbourne International Comedy Festival

May
Next Wave Festival
Melbourne Knowledge Week
Good Beer Week
Human Rights Arts & Film Festival

June
Melbourne International Jazz Festival
Mind Body Spirit Festival

July
Open House Melbourne

August
Melbourne International Film Festival
White Night Melbourne
Melbourne Writers Festival

September
Melbourne Fashion Week
Royal Melbourne Show
Melbourne Fringe Festival
AFL Grand Final

October
Melbourne Festival
Melbourne Marathon

November
Melbourne Cup Carnival
Melbourne Music Week

December
The Big Design Market

PUBLIC HOLIDAYS

1 January – New Years Day
26 January – Australia Day
March – Labour Day
March/April – Good Friday, Easter Monday
25 April – Anzac Day
June – Queen's Birthday
September – Grand Final Parade
November – Melbourne Cup Day
25 December – Christmas Day
26 December – Boxing Day

LGBTIQ+

LGBTIQ+ travellers are drawn to the rich culture of this artsy, cosmopolitan city. Melbourne has a vibrant and diverse local queer community, with the majority of gay venues to be found in Fitzroy/Collingwood and South Yarra/Prahran. The annual **Midsumma Festival** (Jan–Feb, (midsumma.org.au) is a citywide celebration of queer culture and creativity. About 1.5 hours from Melbourne, **Daylesford** (see p.165) is Victoria's gayest country town and hosts the annual **Chill Out** pride festival in March (www.chilloutfestival.com.au).

TRAVEL TIPS

EATING & DRINKING

Reservations
The Melbourne dining scene has shifted from bookings-only to a no-bookings trend in recent years, with an increasing number of large, casual eateries. Most restaurants will gladly accept walk-ins, but it's worth checking the door policy if hoping to eat at a particularly well-known, popular and/or high-end eatery.

International food mecca
Melbourne is a multicultural city, which means there's a dazzling choice of international food on offer. It's a veritable melting pot here, but each culinary culture has its heartland – from the food mecca of Chinatown, the mini Greek precinct on Lonsdale Street and Italian section of Lygon Street in Carlton, to Brunswick for Middle Eastern and Halal and Vietnamese in Richmond and Footscray.

Vegetarian and vegan food
Plant-based protein is totally on-trend and easy to get your hands on in Melbourne. The inner northern suburbs of Fitzroy and Collingwood are the traditional vegetarian haunts, with several meat-free cafes and restaurants, but numerous plant-based eateries can be found throughout the inner suburbs, often casual cafes. Most restaurants offer some vegetarian or vegan options; if unsure, check their menu online before you go.

Tipping
Workers in Australia are paid a minimum wage and do not rely on tips, though some venues encourage tips or demand a surcharge on weekends and public holidays. Basically, you don't ever have to tip in Melbourne, but if you want to show your appreciation for a particularly memorable meal and/or exceptional service, you're most welcome to do so.

OPENING HOURS

Melbourne's retail stores and shopping centres generally open at 10am and close at 6pm or 7pm, though many businesses offer late-night shopping. Most cafes operate from 7am to 4pm, when the city's restaurants, bars and entertainment venues come to life. Melbourne is slated to become a 24-hour city, with plenty of late-night dining options and a healthy bar and club scene that can take you into the wee hours. There are no lock-out laws, here. Public transport runs all night on weekends.

MAPS

Bookstores and newsagents sell good travel guides and folded maps, but you can also use smartphone apps like Google Maps for navigating your way around the city. The Public Transport Victoria (PTV) app has handy public transport maps and detailed travel information.

VOLTAGE & CONVERTERS

Mains voltage in Australia is 230V 50Hz, which is compatible with most electrical appliances sold in Asia, Europe and Africa. However, the three-pin system here requires most international travellers to invest in an adapter plug, available at convenience stores and vending machines. Appliances from Japan, USA and Canada also require a voltage convertor or a convertor/adapter in one.

WEIGHTS & MEASURES

Australia follows the modern metric weight and measurement system, so it's all about the kilograms and metres. But you can still buy an 'Imperial pint' of beer at certain pubs!

173

MELBOURNE CITY MAPS

MELBOURNE

- SUNSHINE
- MARIBYRNONG
- MOONEE PONDS
- MAIDSTONE
- ASCOT VALE
- BRAYBROOK
- FLEMINGTON
- WEST FOOTSCRAY
- FOOTSCRAY
- SUNSHINE WEST
- TOTTENHAM
- 200-1
- SEDDON
- BROOKLYN
- YARRAVILLE
- 199
- WEST MELBOURNE
- SOUTH KINGSVILLE
- SPOTSWOOD
  - SCIENCEWORKS
- ALTONA NORTH
- PORT MELBOURNE
- ALTONA
- NEWPORT
- WILLIAMSTOWN

174

Map Index

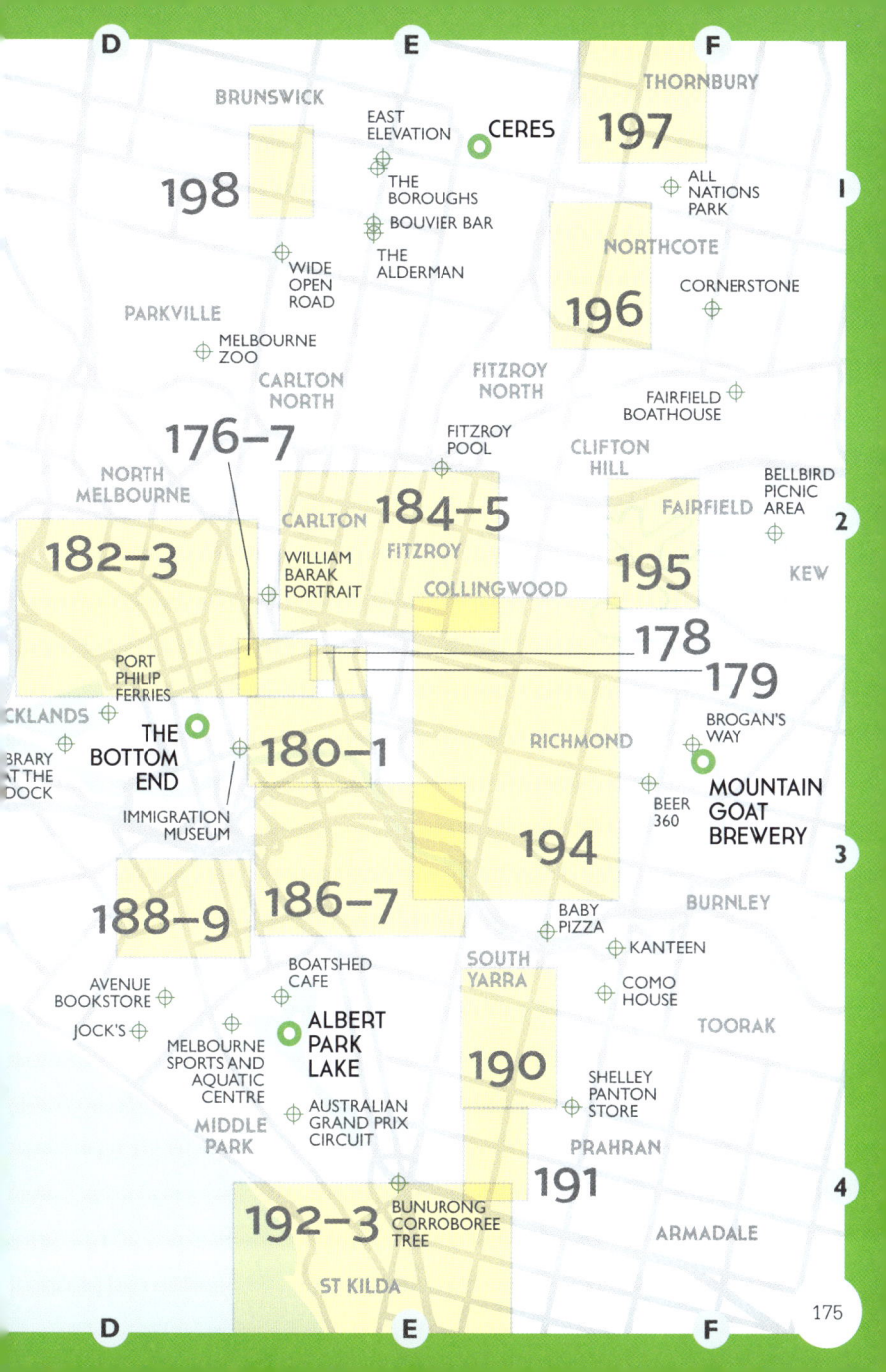

D **E** **F**

BRUNSWICK

EAST ELEVATION — CERES

197 THORNBURY

198

THE BOROUGHS
BOUVIER BAR
THE ALDERMAN

ALL NATIONS PARK

1

WIDE OPEN ROAD

NORTHCOTE

PARKVILLE

MELBOURNE ZOO

196

CORNERSTONE

CARLTON NORTH

FITZROY NORTH

FAIRFIELD BOATHOUSE

FITZROY POOL

176–7

CLIFTON HILL

NORTH MELBOURNE

CARLTON

184–5

FAIRFIELD

BELLBIRD PICNIC AREA

2

182–3

FITZROY

195

KEW

WILLIAM BARAK PORTRAIT

COLLINGWOOD

178

179

PORT PHILIP FERRIES

DOCKLANDS

180–1

RICHMOND

BROGAN'S WAY

LIBRARY AT THE DOCK

THE BOTTOM END

BEER 360

MOUNTAIN GOAT BREWERY

IMMIGRATION MUSEUM

3

188–9

186–7

194

BURNLEY

BABY PIZZA

KANTEEN

BOATSHED CAFE

SOUTH YARRA

COMO HOUSE

AVENUE BOOKSTORE

JOCK'S

MELBOURNE SPORTS AND AQUATIC CENTRE

ALBERT PARK LAKE

TOORAK

190

SHELLEY PANTON STORE

AUSTRALIAN GRAND PRIX CIRCUIT

MIDDLE PARK

PRAHRAN

191

4

192–3

BUNURONG CORROBOREE TREE

ARMADALE

ST KILDA

175

D **E** **F**

Map

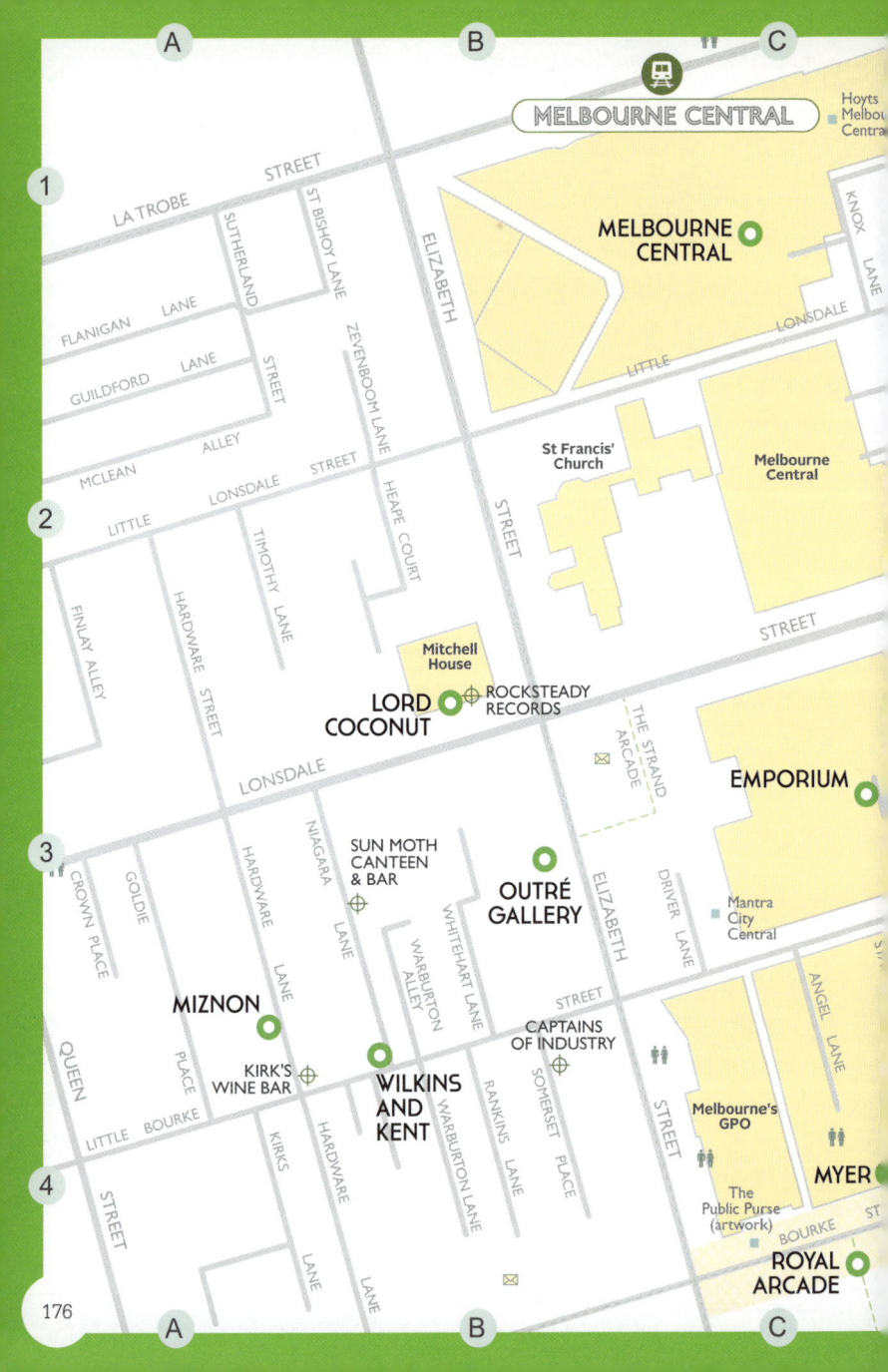

Grid references: A, B, C (columns); 1, 2, 3, 4 (rows)

Streets and Lanes

- LA TROBE STREET
- SUTHERLAND STREET
- ST BISHOY LANE
- FLANIGAN LANE
- GUILDFORD LANE
- MCLEAN ALLEY
- ZEVENBOOM LANE
- ELIZABETH STREET
- LITTLE LONSDALE STREET
- LONSDALE STREET
- FINLAY ALLEY
- HARDWARE STREET
- TIMOTHY LANE
- HEAPE COURT
- KNOX LANE
- THE STRAND ARCADE
- DRIVER LANE
- CROWN PLACE
- GOLDIE PLACE
- NIAGARA LANE
- WHITEHART LANE
- WARBURTON ALLEY
- WARBURTON LANE
- RANKINS LANE
- SOMERSET PLACE
- ANGEL LANE
- QUEEN STREET
- LITTLE BOURKE STREET
- KIRKS LANE
- HARDWARE LANE
- BOURKE STREET

Landmarks

- **MELBOURNE CENTRAL** (train station, B1/C1)
- Hoyts Melbourne Central (C1)
- Melbourne Central (shopping, C2)
- St Francis' Church (B2)
- Mitchell House (B2)
- **LORD COCONUT** (B2/B3)
- ROCKSTEADY RECORDS (B2/B3)
- **EMPORIUM** (C3)
- SUN MOTH CANTEEN & BAR (B3)
- **OUTRÉ GALLERY** (B3)
- Mantra City Central (C3)
- **MIZNON** (A3/B3)
- KIRK'S WINE BAR (B3)
- **WILKINS AND KENT** (B3/B4)
- CAPTAINS OF INDUSTRY (B3/B4)
- Melbourne's GPO (C4)
- **MYER** (C4)
- The Public Purse (artwork) (C4)
- **ROYAL ARCADE** (C4)

176

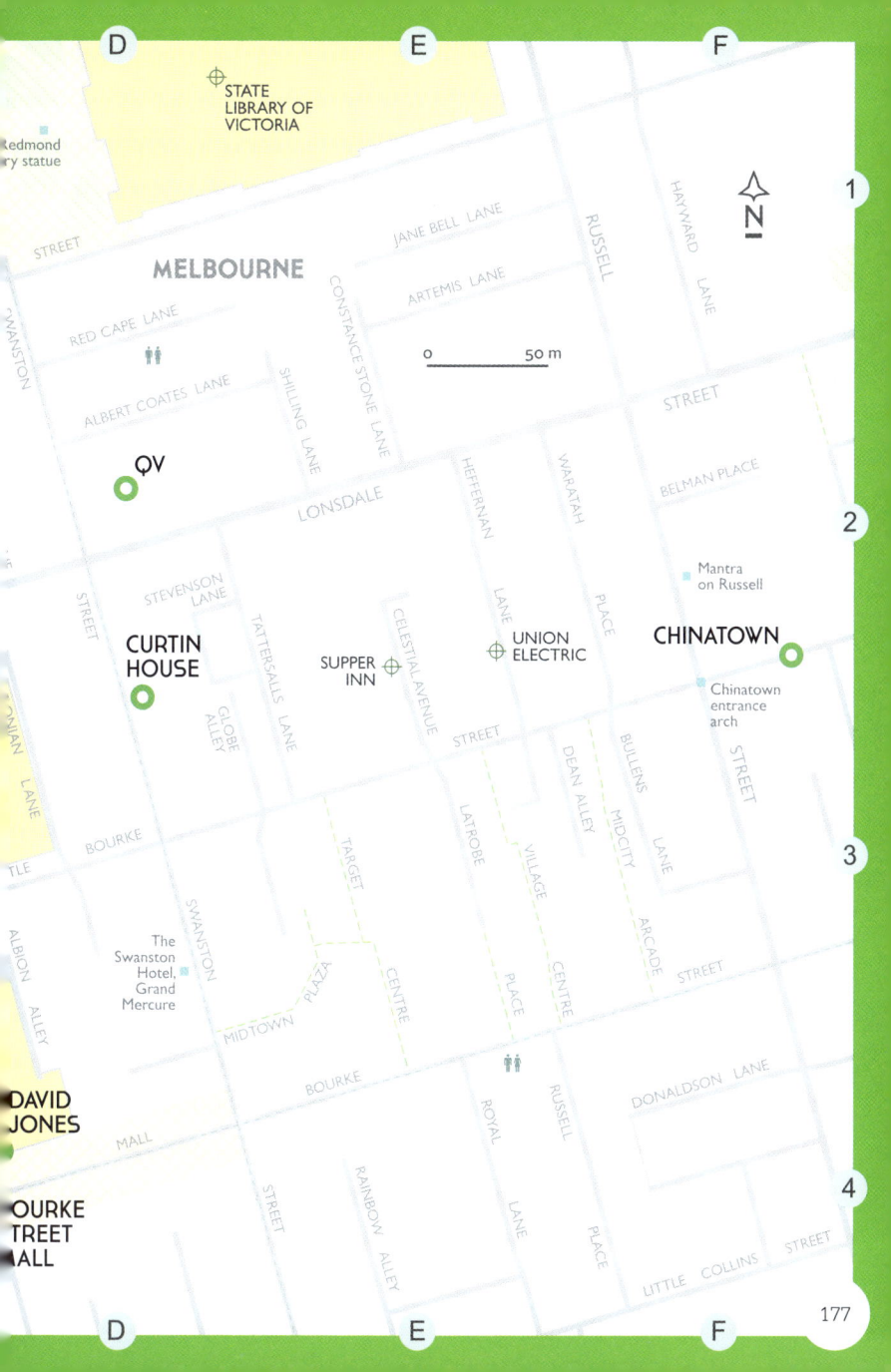

MELBOURNE

STATE LIBRARY OF VICTORIA

Redmond ry statue

RED CAPE LANE
ALBERT COATES LANE
SWANSTON STREET
CONSTANCE STONE LANE
SHILLING LANE
JANE BELL LANE
ARTEMIS LANE
RUSSELL STREET
HAYWARD LANE

N

0 — 50 m

QV

LONSDALE

HEFFERNAN LANE
WARATAH PLACE
BELMAN PLACE

Mantra on Russell

STEVENSON LANE

CURTIN HOUSE

TATTERSALLS LANE
GLOBE ALLEY

SUPPER INN

CELESTIAL AVENUE

UNION ELECTRIC

DEAN ALLEY
BULLENS LANE
MIDCITY

CHINATOWN

Chinatown entrance arch

BOURKE STREET

TARGET
LATROBE
VILLAGE
ARCADE

The Swanston Hotel, Grand Mercure

SWANSTON STREET
MIDTOWN PLAZA
CENTRE PLACE
CENTRE

ALBION ALLEY

BOURKE

DAVID JONES

MALL

ROYAL LANE
RAINBOW ALLEY
RUSSELL PLACE
DONALDSON LANE

BOURKE STREET MALL

LITTLE COLLINS STREET

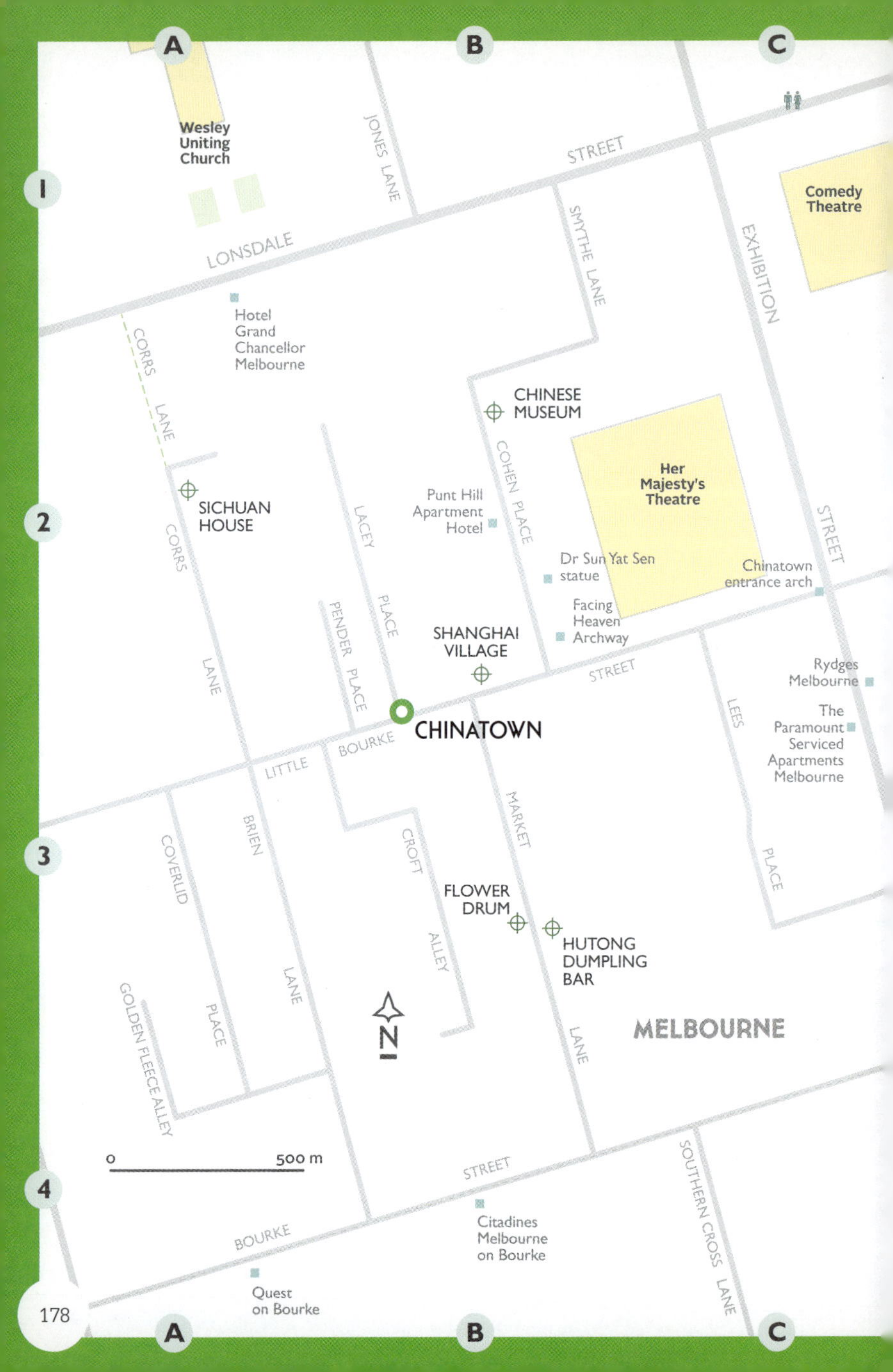
A
B
C
1
2
3
4
Wesley Uniting Church
JONES LANE
STREET
Comedy Theatre
LONSDALE
SMYTHE LANE
EXHIBITION
STREET
Hotel Grand Chancellor Melbourne
CORRS LANE
CHINESE MUSEUM
Her Majesty's Theatre
SICHUAN HOUSE
CORRS LANE
LACEY PLACE
Punt Hill Apartment Hotel
COHEN PLACE
Dr Sun Yat Sen statue
Chinatown entrance arch
Facing Heaven Archway
PENDER PLACE
SHANGHAI VILLAGE
STREET
Rydges Melbourne
CHINATOWN
LITTLE BOURKE
LEES PLACE
The Paramount Serviced Apartments Melbourne
MARKET LANE
BRIEN LANE
COVERLID PLACE
CROFT ALLEY
FLOWER DRUM
HUTONG DUMPLING BAR
GOLDEN FLEECE ALLEY
N
MELBOURNE
0
500 m
BOURKE STREET
Citadines Melbourne on Bourke
SOUTHERN CROSS LANE
Quest on Bourke

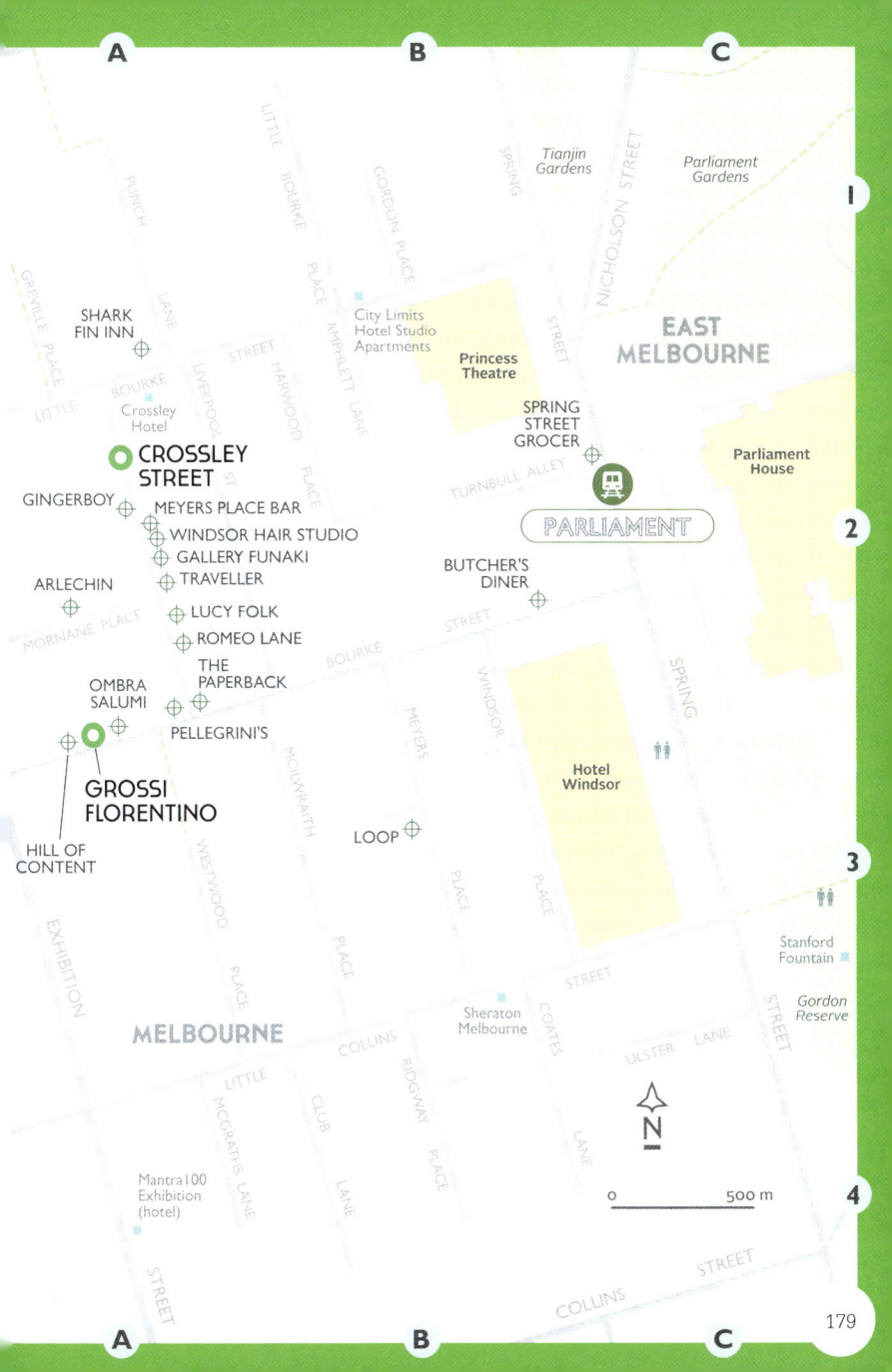

Map: Crossley Street & Parliament area, Melbourne

Grid references: A, B, C (columns) / 1, 2, 3, 4 (rows)

Areas & Landmarks
- EAST MELBOURNE
- MELBOURNE
- Tianjin Gardens
- Parliament Gardens
- Parliament House
- Princess Theatre
- Parliament (station)
- Gordon Reserve
- Stanford Fountain

Streets & Lanes
- PUNCH LANE
- LITTLE BOURKE STREET
- GREVILLE PLACE
- LIVERPOOL STREET
- AMPHLETT LANE
- HARWOOD PLACE
- GORDON PLACE
- SPRING STREET
- NICHOLSON STREET
- TURNBULL ALLEY
- MORNANE PLACE
- BOURKE STREET
- MEYERS PLACE
- WINDSOR PLACE
- McILWRAITH PLACE
- WESTWOOD PLACE
- RIDGWAY PLACE
- COATES LANE
- ULSTER LANE
- EXHIBITION STREET
- LITTLE COLLINS STREET
- McGRATH'S LANE
- CLUB LANE
- COLLINS STREET

Featured Locations

O CROSSLEY STREET (A2)

O GROSSI FLORENTINO (A3)

Dining & Bars
- SHARK FIN INN
- GINGERBOY
- MEYERS PLACE BAR
- ARLECHIN
- TRAVELLER
- ROMEO LANE
- OMBRA SALUMI
- PELLEGRINI'S
- SPRING STREET GROCER
- BUTCHER'S DINER

Shopping
- GALLERY FUNAKI
- LUCY FOLK
- THE PAPERBACK
- HILL OF CONTENT
- LOOP
- WINDSOR HAIR STUDIO

Hotels
- Crossley Hotel
- City Limits Hotel Studio Apartments
- Hotel Windsor
- Sheraton Melbourne
- Mantra 100 Exhibition (hotel)

N

0 — 500 m

179

Map

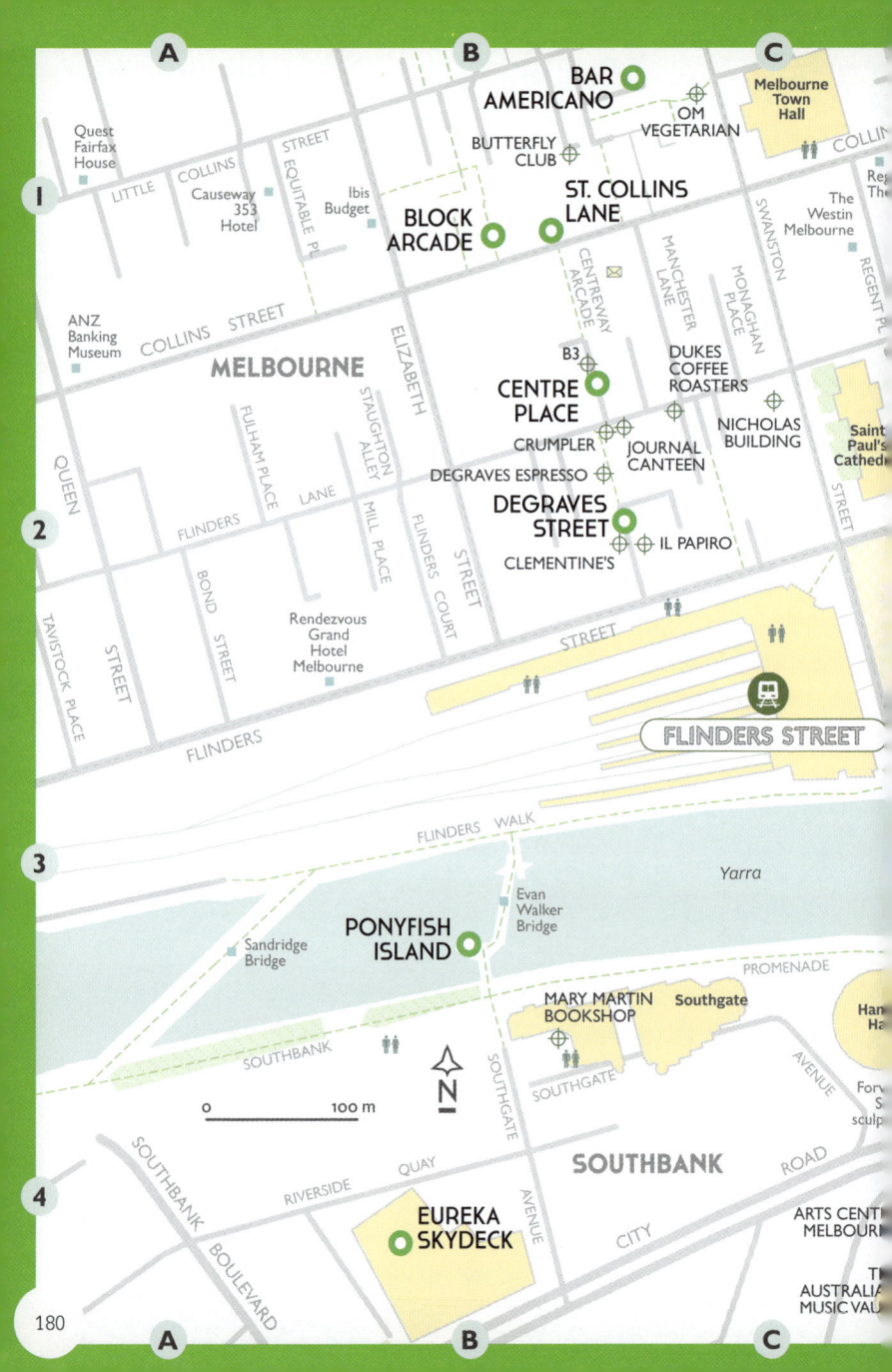

Grid A
- Quest Fairfax House (A1)
- Causeway 353 Hotel (A1)
- ANZ Banking Museum (A1)

Grid B
- BAR AMERICANO (B1)
- BUTTERFLY CLUB (B1)
- OM VEGETARIAN (B1)
- Ibis Budget (B1)
- BLOCK ARCADE (B1)
- ST. COLLINS LANE (B1)
- B3 (B1)
- CENTRE PLACE (B1/B2)
- DUKES COFFEE ROASTERS (B1)
- CRUMPLER (B2)
- JOURNAL CANTEEN (B2)
- NICHOLAS BUILDING (B2)
- DEGRAVES ESPRESSO (B2)
- DEGRAVES STREET (B2)
- IL PAPIRO (B2)
- CLEMENTINE'S (B2)
- Rendezvous Grand Hotel Melbourne (B2)
- FLINDERS STREET (station) (B2)
- Evan Walker Bridge (B3)
- PONYFISH ISLAND (B3)
- Sandridge Bridge (A3)
- MARY MARTIN BOOKSHOP (B3)
- Southgate (B3)
- EUREKA SKYDECK (B4)

Grid C
- Melbourne Town Hall (C1)
- The Westin Melbourne (C1)
- Saint Paul's Cathedral (C2)
- ARTS CENTRE MELBOURNE (C4)
- AUSTRALIAN MUSIC VAULT (C4)

Streets
- LITTLE COLLINS STREET
- COLLINS STREET
- EQUITABLE PLACE
- ELIZABETH STREET
- CENTREWAY ARCADE
- MANCHESTER LANE
- MONAGHAN PLACE
- SWANSTON STREET
- REGENT PLACE
- FULHAM PLACE
- STAUGHTON ALLEY
- FLINDERS LANE
- MILL PLACE
- FLINDERS COURT
- QUEEN STREET
- BOND STREET
- TAVISTOCK PLACE
- FLINDERS STREET
- FLINDERS WALK
- SOUTHBANK PROMENADE
- SOUTHGATE AVENUE
- SOUTHBANK BOULEVARD
- RIVERSIDE QUAY
- CITY ROAD

Yarra

0 — 100 m

MELBOURNE

SOUTHBANK

180

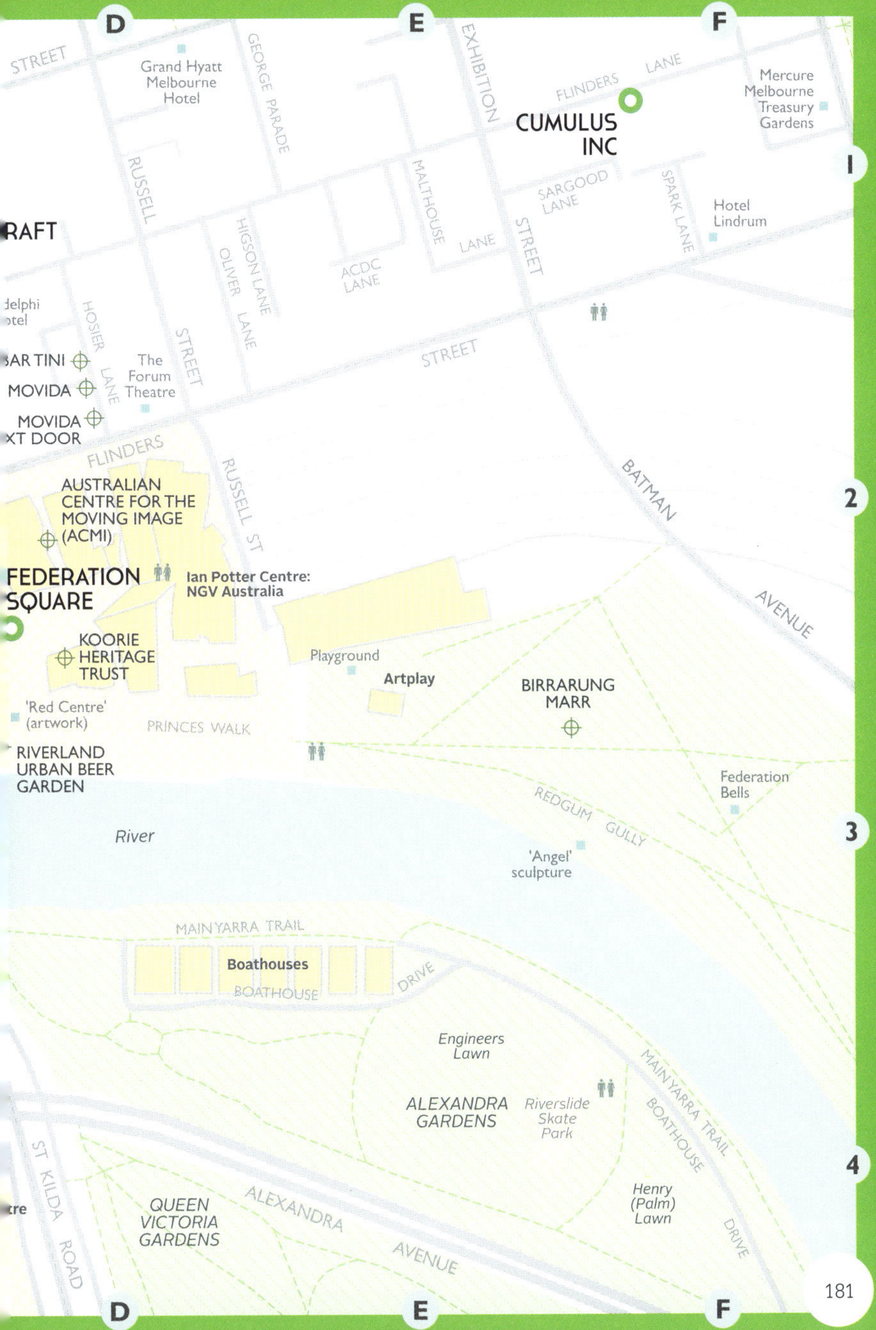

D
E
F
STREET
Grand Hyatt Melbourne Hotel
GEORGE PARADE
EXHIBITION
FLINDERS LANE
CUMULUS INC
Mercure Melbourne Treasury Gardens
RUSSELL
MALTHOUSE
SARGOOD LANE
SPARK LANE
Hotel Lindrum
RAFT
HIGSON LANE
OLIVER LANE
ACDC LANE
LANE
STREET
delphi otel
HOSIER LANE
BAR TINI
MOVIDA
MOVIDA NEXT DOOR
The Forum Theatre
STREET
STREET
FLINDERS
RUSSELL ST
AUSTRALIAN CENTRE FOR THE MOVING IMAGE (ACMI)
BATMAN AVENUE
FEDERATION SQUARE
Ian Potter Centre: NGV Australia
KOORIE HERITAGE TRUST
Playground
Artplay
BIRRARUNG MARR
'Red Centre' (artwork)
PRINCES WALK
RIVERLAND URBAN BEER GARDEN
Federation Bells
REDGUM GULLY
River
'Angel' sculpture
MAIN YARRA TRAIL
Boathouses
BOATHOUSE DRIVE
Engineers Lawn
ALEXANDRA GARDENS
Riverslide Skate Park
MAIN YARRA TRAIL
BOATHOUSE DRIVE
ST KILDA ROAD
QUEEN VICTORIA GARDENS
ALEXANDRA AVENUE
Henry (Palm) Lawn
tre
1
2
3
4
D
E
F

North Melbourne & Docklands

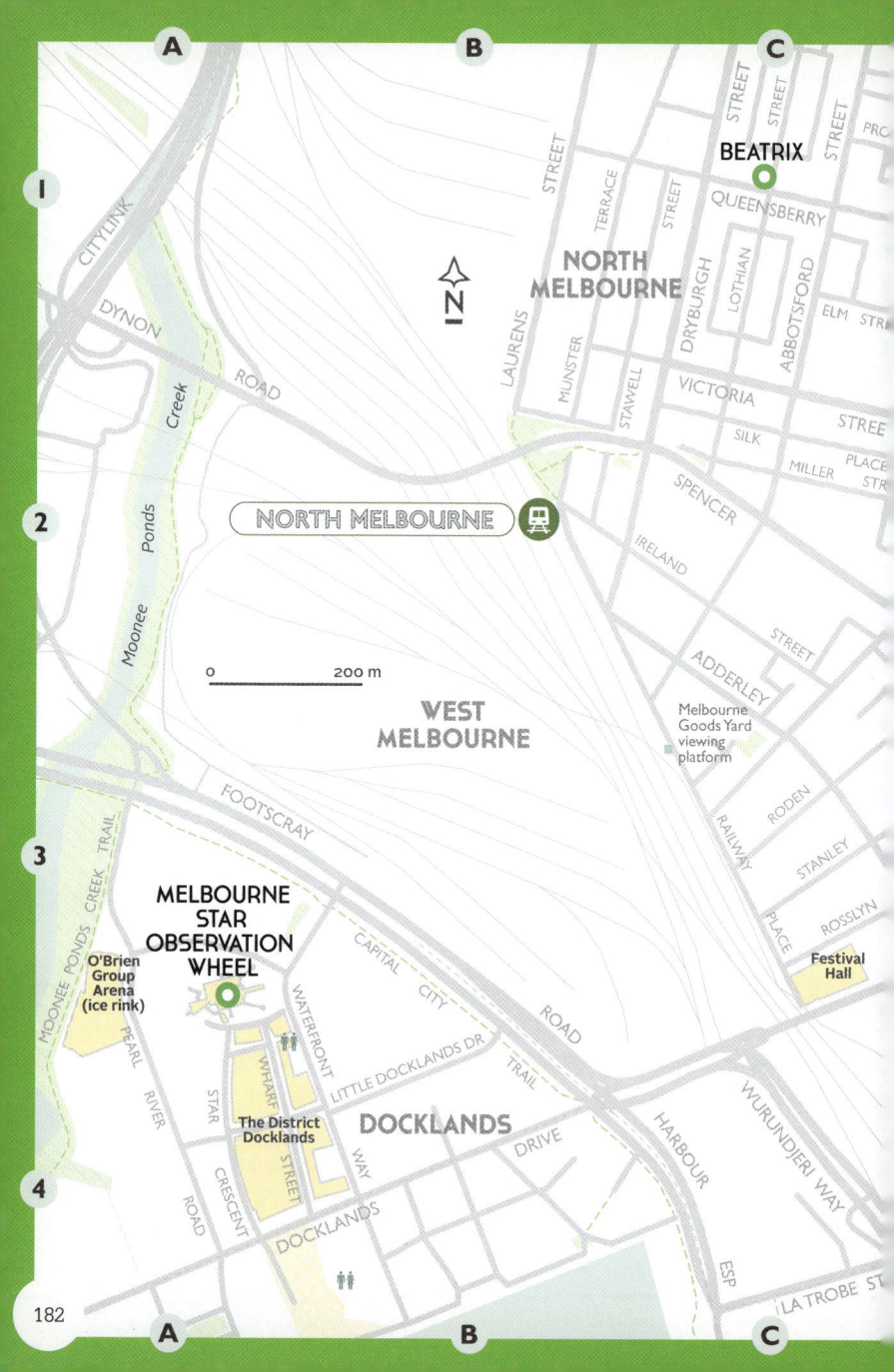

BEATRIX (C1)

NORTH MELBOURNE station (B2)

WEST MELBOURNE

MELBOURNE STAR OBSERVATION WHEEL (A3)

O'Brien Group Arena (ice rink)

The District Docklands

DOCKLANDS

Melbourne Goods Yard viewing platform

Festival Hall

Streets and features

- Citylink
- Dynon Road
- Moonee Ponds Creek
- Laurens Street
- Munster Terrace
- Stawell Street
- Dryburgh Street
- Lothian Street
- Abbotsford Street
- Elm Street
- Queensberry Street
- Victoria Street
- Silk Street
- Miller Street
- Place
- Spencer Street
- Ireland Street
- Adderley Street
- Roden Street
- Railway Place
- Stanley Street
- Rosslyn Street
- Footscray
- Moonee Ponds Creek Trail
- Capital City Trail
- Waterfront
- Little Docklands Dr
- Pearl River
- Star Crescent
- Wharf Street
- Harbour Esp
- Wurundjeri Way
- Docklands Drive
- La Trobe St

0 — 200 m

182

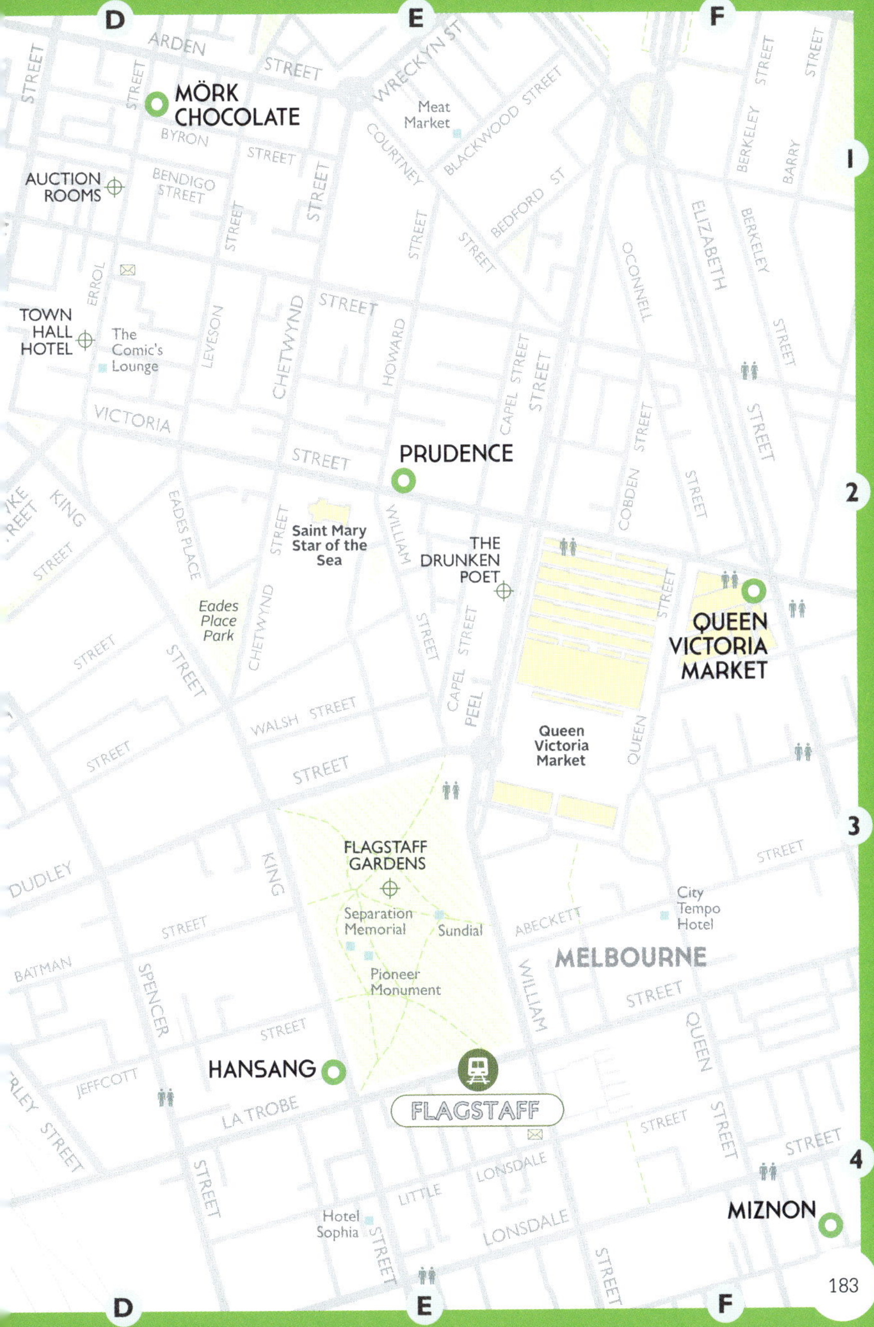
D
E
F
I
2
3
4
ARDEN STREET
MÖRK CHOCOLATE
BYRON STREET
AUCTION ROOMS
BENDIGO STREET
WRECKYN ST
Meat Market
COURTNEY STREET
BLACKWOOD STREET
BEDFORD ST
BERKELEY STREET
BARRY STREET
ELIZABETH STREET
ERROL STREET
TOWN HALL HOTEL
The Comic's Lounge
LEVESON STREET
CHETWYND STREET
HOWARD STREET
CAPEL STREET
O'CONNELL STREET
VICTORIA STREET
PRUDENCE
COBDEN STREET
KING STREET
EADES PLACE
Saint Mary Star of the Sea
WILLIAM STREET
THE DRUNKEN POET
PEEL STREET
QUEEN VICTORIA MARKET
Eades Place Park
WALSH STREET
Queen Victoria Market
QUEEN STREET
FLAGSTAFF GARDENS
Separation Memorial
Sundial
Pioneer Monument
DUDLEY STREET
ABECKETT STREET
City Tempo Hotel
MELBOURNE
BATMAN STREET
SPENCER STREET
HANSANG
JEFFCOTT STREET
LA TROBE STREET
FLAGSTAFF
LITTLE LONSDALE STREET
LONSDALE STREET
Hotel Sophia
MIZNON

Map: Carlton, Melbourne

Streets and locations:

- Palmerston Street
- Elgin Street
- Faraday Street
- Grattan Street
- Pelham Street
- Queensberry Street
- Victoria Street
- Princes Street
- Kay Street
- Macarthur Place
- Canning Street
- Nicholson Street
- Rathdowne Street
- Drummond Street
- Lygon Street
- Cardigan Street
- Swanston Street
- Ormond Place
- Barkly Street / Little Barkly St
- Carlton Street
- Owen Street
- David Street
- Moor Street
- King William Street
- Hanover Street
- Palmer Street
- Royal Lane
- Marion Street

Points of interest:

- Green Man's Arms (B1)
- Readings (A1/B1)
- Pidapipó
- Cinema Nova
- La Mama Courthouse Theatre
- D.O.C. Delicatessen
- D.O.C. Espresso
- D.O.C Pizzeria & Mozzarella Bar
- Carlton Yacht Club (A2/B2)
- Best Western Plus Travel Inn Hotel
- Carlton
- Murchison Square
- Argyle Square
- Carlton Gardens
- Playground
- Melbourne Museum
- IMAX Melbourne
- Royal Exhibition Building
- French Fountain
- The Obelisk
- Hochgurtel Fountain
- Quest Carlton on Finlay
- Quality Hotel Downtowner on Lygon
- Quest Royal Gardens
- Old Melbourne Gaol (A4)
- Space Hotel

0 — 100 m

184

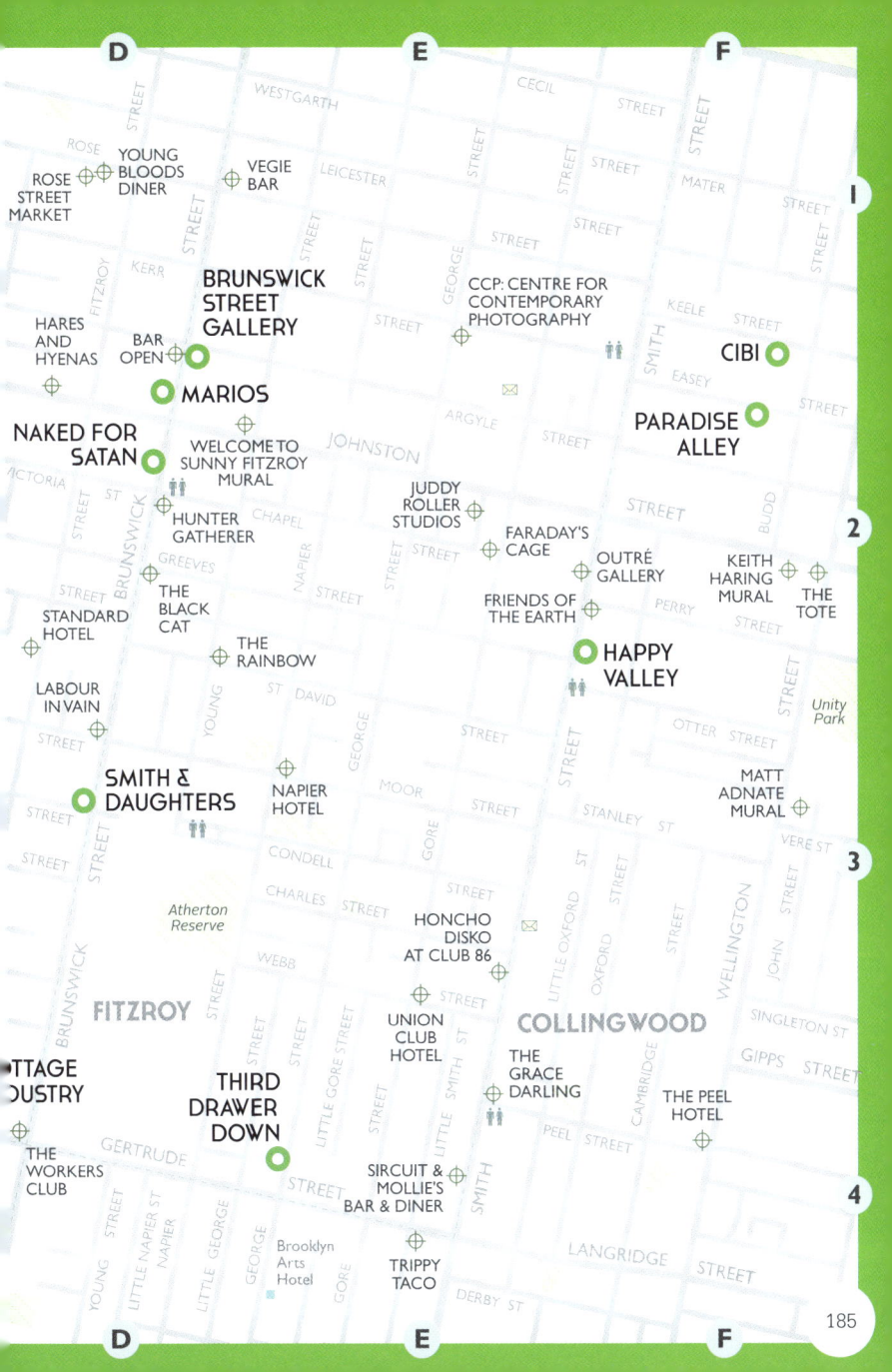

Fitzroy & Collingwood

Streets & Locations:
- Westgarth Street
- Rose Street
- Leicester Street
- Cecil Street
- Mater Street
- Kerr Street
- George Street
- Keele Street
- Smith Street
- Easey Street
- Argyle Street
- Johnston Street
- Chapel Street
- Greeves Street
- Napier Street
- Budd Street
- Perry Street
- Young Street
- St David Street
- Otter Street
- Moor Street
- Stanley Street
- Vere Street
- Condell Street
- Charles Street
- Webb Street
- Little Oxford Street
- Oxford Street
- Wellington Street
- John Street
- Singleton St
- Gipps Street
- Cambridge Street
- Peel Street
- Gertrude Street
- Little Napier Street
- Little George Street
- Little Gore Street
- Little Smith Street
- Langridge Street
- Derby St
- Brunswick Street
- Fitzroy Street
- Victoria Street

Places of Interest:
- Rose Street Market
- Young Bloods Diner
- Vegie Bar
- Hares and Hyenas
- Bar Open
- Brunswick Street Gallery
- CCP: Centre for Contemporary Photography
- CIBI
- Marios
- Naked for Satan
- Welcome to Sunny Fitzroy Mural
- Paradise Alley
- Hunter Gatherer
- Juddy Roller Studios
- Faraday's Cage
- Outré Gallery
- Keith Haring Mural
- The Tote
- Standard Hotel
- The Black Cat
- Friends of the Earth
- Happy Valley
- The Rainbow
- Labour In Vain
- Unity Park
- Smith & Daughters
- Napier Hotel
- Matt Adnate Mural
- Atherton Reserve
- Honcho Disko at Club 86
- Fitzroy
- Collingwood
- Union Club Hotel
- The Grace Darling
- The Peel Hotel
- Cottage Industry
- Third Drawer Down
- The Workers Club
- Brooklyn Arts Hotel
- Sircuit & Mollie's Bar & Diner
- Trippy Taco

185

SOUTHBANK

- NGV
- Iwaki Auditorium
- Melbourne Recital Centre
- Melbourne Theatre Company
- BUXTON CONTEMPORARY
- Margaret Lawrence Gallery
- Vault sculpture
- ACCA: AUSTRALIAN CENTRE FOR CONTEMPORARY ART
- Victoria Barracks

SOUTH MELBOURNE

- Sturt Street Reserve
- Quest on Dorcas Apartment Hotel
- Eastern North Reserve
- Eastern South Reserve
- THE KETTLE BLACK

Kings Domain

- Floral Clock
- Walker Fountain
- Eternal Flame
- SHRINE OF REMEMBRANCE
- MacRobertson Fountain

0 — 100 m

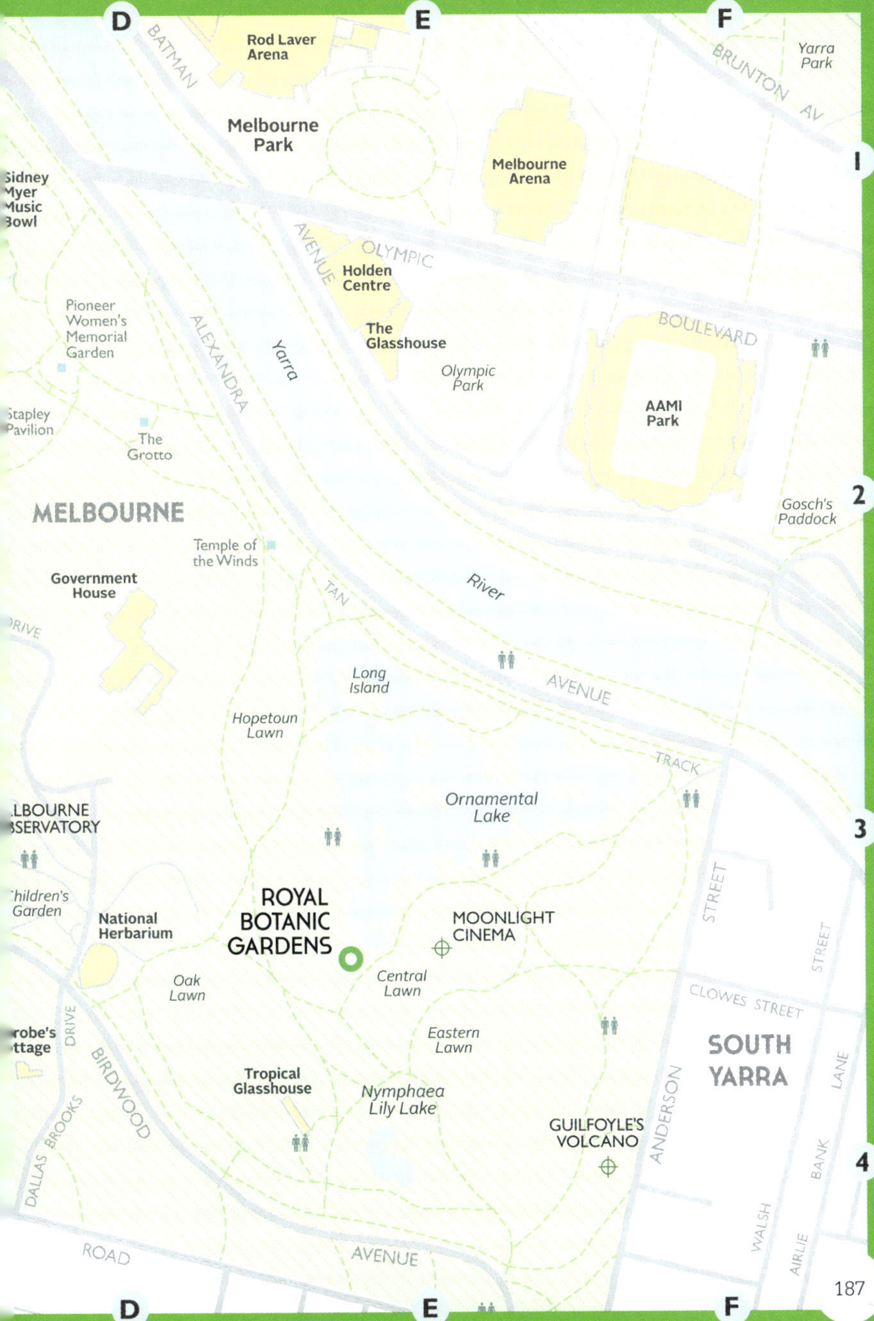
D
E
F
Rod Laver Arena
BATMAN
BRUNTON AV
Yarra Park
Melbourne Park
Melbourne Arena
Sidney Myer Music Bowl
AVENUE
OLYMPIC
Holden Centre
The Glasshouse
BOULEVARD
Olympic Park
AAMI Park
Pioneer Women's Memorial Garden
ALEXANDRA
Yarra
Stapley Pavilion
The Grotto
Gosch's Paddock
MELBOURNE
Temple of the Winds
River
Government House
TAN
DRIVE
Long Island
AVENUE
Hopetoun Lawn
TRACK
Ornamental Lake
MELBOURNE OBSERVATORY
ROYAL BOTANIC GARDENS
MOONLIGHT CINEMA
STREET
STREET
Children's Garden
National Herbarium
Oak Lawn
Central Lawn
CLOWES STREET
DRIVE
Eastern Lawn
SOUTH YARRA
BIRDWOOD
Tropical Glasshouse
Nymphaea Lily Lake
ANDERSON
LANE
BROOKS
GUILFOYLE'S VOLCANO
DALLAS
BANK
WALSH
AIRLIE
ROAD
AVENUE
1
2
3
4

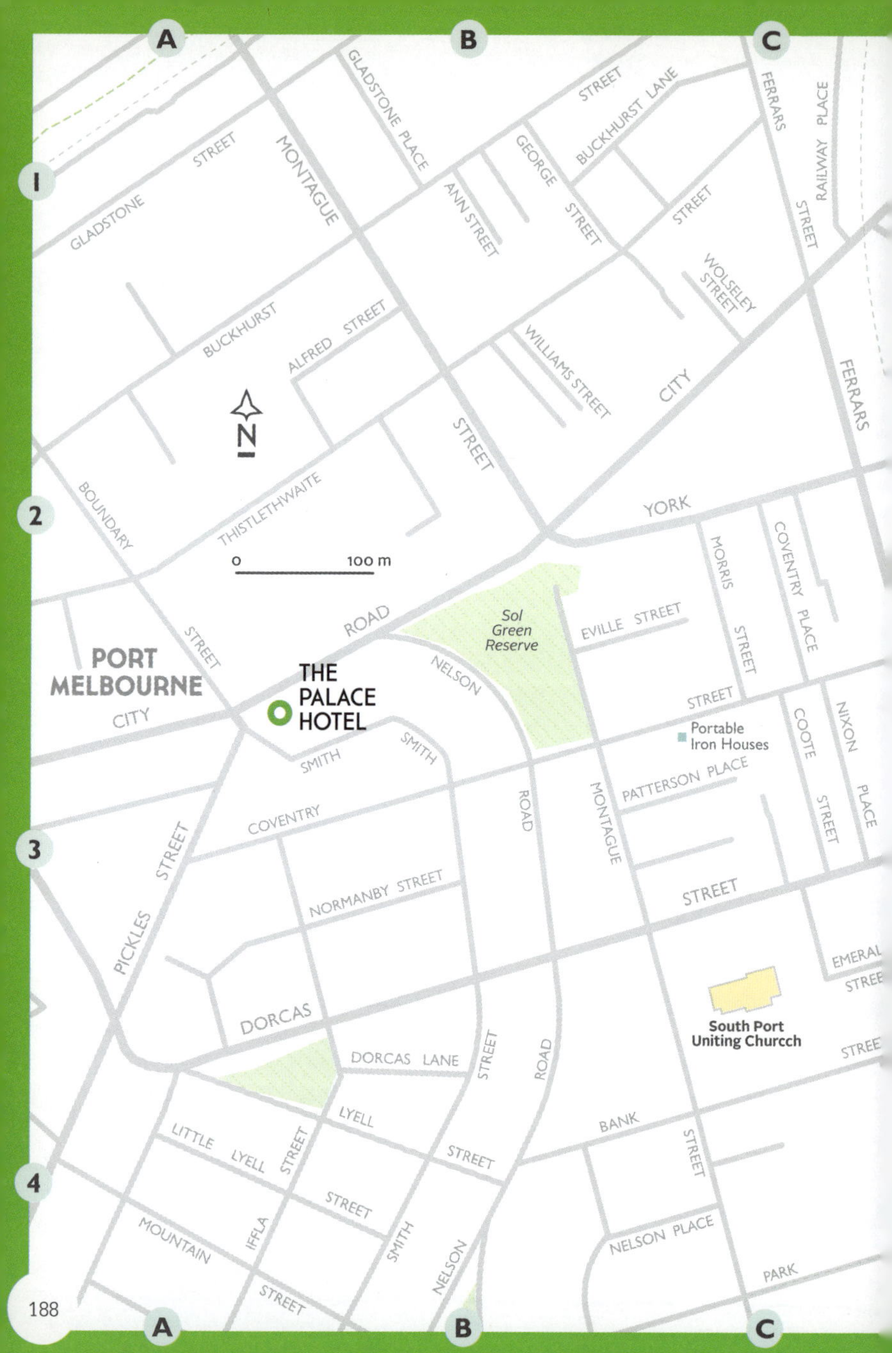
A
B
C
1
2
3
4
N
0
100 m
PORT MELBOURNE
THE PALACE HOTEL
Sol Green Reserve
Portable Iron Houses
South Port Uniting Churcch
GLADSTONE STREET
MONTAGUE STREET
GLADSTONE PLACE
ANN STREET
GEORGE STREET
BUCKHURST LANE
BUCKHURST STREET
FERRARS STREET
RAILWAY PLACE
WOLSELEY STREET
ALFRED STREET
WILLIAMS STREET
CITY ROAD
THISTLETHWAITE
BOUNDARY STREET
YORK STREET
MORRIS STREET
COVENTRY PLACE
EVILLE STREET
NELSON ROAD
SMITH
COVENTRY STREET
COOTE STREET
NIXON PLACE
PATTERSON PLACE
PICKLES STREET
NORMANBY STREET
DORCAS STREET
EMERAL STREE
DORCAS LANE
SMITH STREET
LYELL STREET
LITTLE LYELL STREET
BANK STREET
IFFLA
MOUNTAIN STREET
NELSON PLACE
PARK STREE

SOUTHBANK

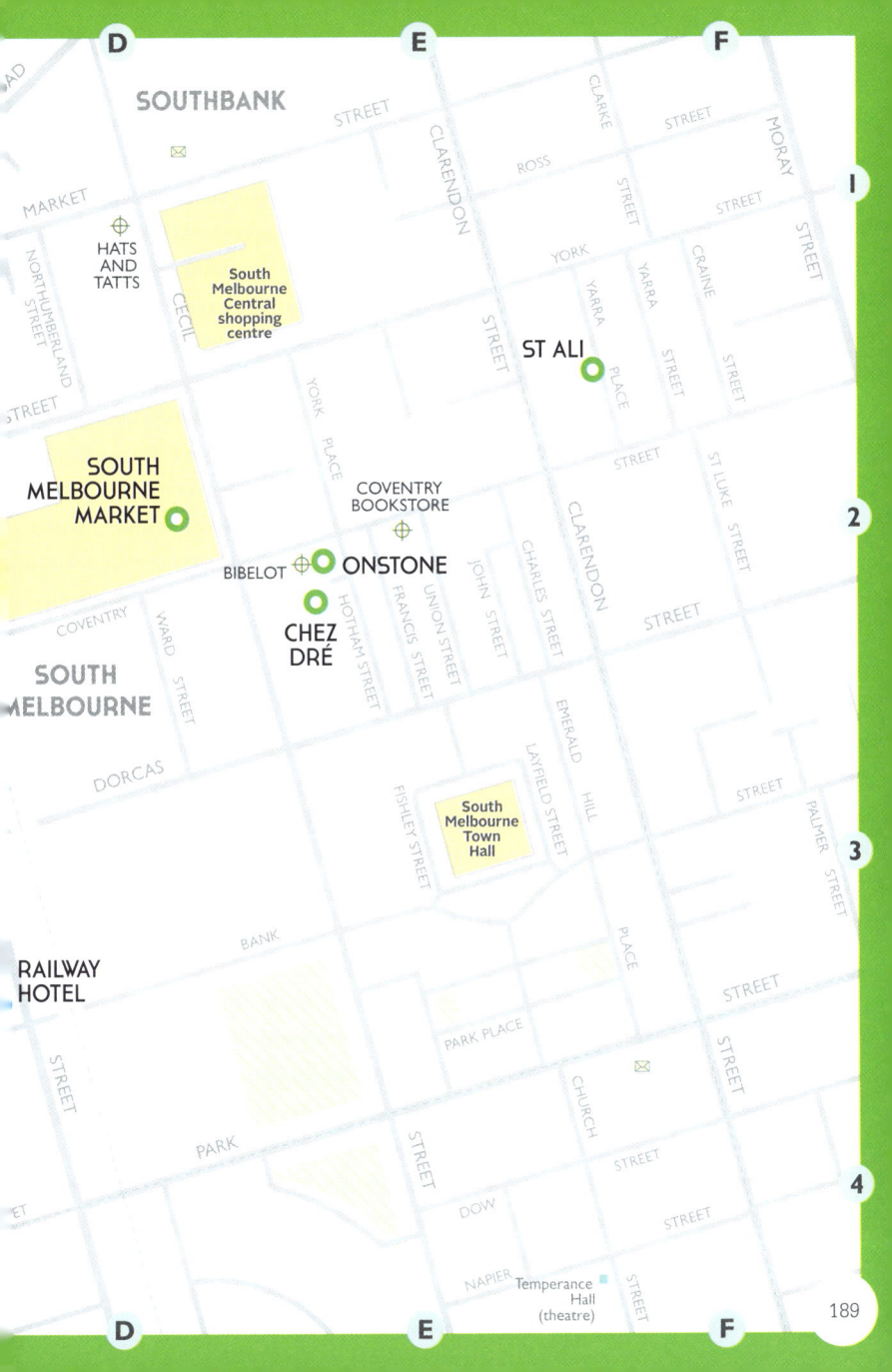

- HATS AND TATTS
- South Melbourne Central shopping centre
- ST ALI
- SOUTH MELBOURNE MARKET
- COVENTRY BOOKSTORE
- BIBELOT
- ONSTONE
- CHEZ DRÉ
- SOUTH MELBOURNE
- South Melbourne Town Hall
- RAILWAY HOTEL
- Temperance Hall (theatre)

A
B
C
1
2
3
4
BURCH & PURCHESE SWEET STUDIO
CHAPEL STREET
SOUTH YARRA
SOUTH YARRA
PRAHRAN
Quest on Chapel
LE LOUVRE
The Lyall Hotel
The Olsen Hotel
The Como Melbourne
Hotel Claremont Guesthouse
Como Centre
PALACE CINEMA COMO
TIVOLI ROAD BAKERY
COUNTRY ROAD
SABA
MARIMEKKO
ARTHUR GALAN
SCANLAN & THEODORE
GORMAN
ALICE MCCALL
SASS & BIDE
KOOKAI
Jam Factory
Village Cinemas
South Yarra Siding Reserve
Argo Reserve
Grosvenor Reserve
Dyeworks Park
Quest Prahran
PRAHRAN MARKET
POOF DOOF
SACRED HEART MISSION SHOP
The Cullen
Grattan Gardens
Chapel off Chapel (theatre)
N
0 100 m
CAROLINE ST
AVOCA ST
MURPHY STREET
DARLING STREET
YARRA STREET
CLAREMONT ST
RIVER STREET
STATION STREET
TOORAK ROAD
MACFARLAN STREET
MYRTLE STREET
POWELL STREET
AVENUE STREET
WILLIAM STREET
CHAMBERS STREET
OXFORD ST
CUNNINGHAM ST
LANE
OXFORD
DAVIS
OSBORNE
ARTHUR STREET
PLACE
FAWKNER STREET
PALERMO STREET
FITZGERALD STREET
NICHOLSON STREET
ALBION STREET
PORTLAND STREET
CLIFF STREET
GARDEN STREET
GARDEN LANE
PHOENIX
HOWARD ST
ARGO STREET
WILSON STREET
ELLIS STREET
GROSVENOR STREET
MOORE STREET
HARDY STREET
OSBORNE
BALMORAL STREET
LARA ST
BARRY STREET
SIMMONS STREET
ELIZABETH STREET
COMMERCIAL ROAD
CHAPEL
BRAY STREET
MALVERN ROAD
CHARLES STREET
PORTER STREET
GRATTAN STREET
IZETT STREET
WATTLE STREET

A
B
C
DAS T-SHIRT AUTOMART
AESOP
PARDON
FOOL CLOTHING
SIGNED AND NUMBERED
ONEPOINTSEVENFOUR
LADRO
GREVILLE RECORDS
PRAHRAN
GREVILLE STREET
CHATHAM STREET
PRINCES CLOSE
LITTLE CHAPEL ST
KING STREET
1
PRAHRAN
REVOLVER UPSTAIRS
REVOLVER LANE
DAVID'S
CECIL PLACE
CHAPEL STREET BAZAAR
PRAHRAN MISSION
ANCHOR PLACE
CLIFTON
PORTER STREET
PERCY PLACE
PERCY STREET
HIGH STREET
ST EDMONDS ROAD
MACQUARIE STREET
2
CRUMPLER
LUCKY COQ
BORSCH, VODKA AND TEARS
ST JOHN STREET
THOMAS STREET
MECHANICS LANE
VICTORIA STREET
EASTBOURNE STREET
0
100 m
GREEN STREET
TUSK
FARRELL WAY
LANE
EARL STREET
3
SHAG
SALVOS STORES
WINDSOR
ARTISTS
CHAPEL STREET
DUKE STREET
UNION STREET
JAMES STREET
James Street Reserve
PRIMROSE
Windsor Siding Reserve
STOREHOUSE THRIFT
SACRED HEART MISSION SHOP
SAVE THE CHILDREN
PEEL STREET
WHITE STREET
FREDERICK STREET
HORNBY STREET
4
N
WINDSOR
MCILWRICK STREET
MECWACARE OPPORTUNITY SHOP
ALBERT STREET
A
B
C

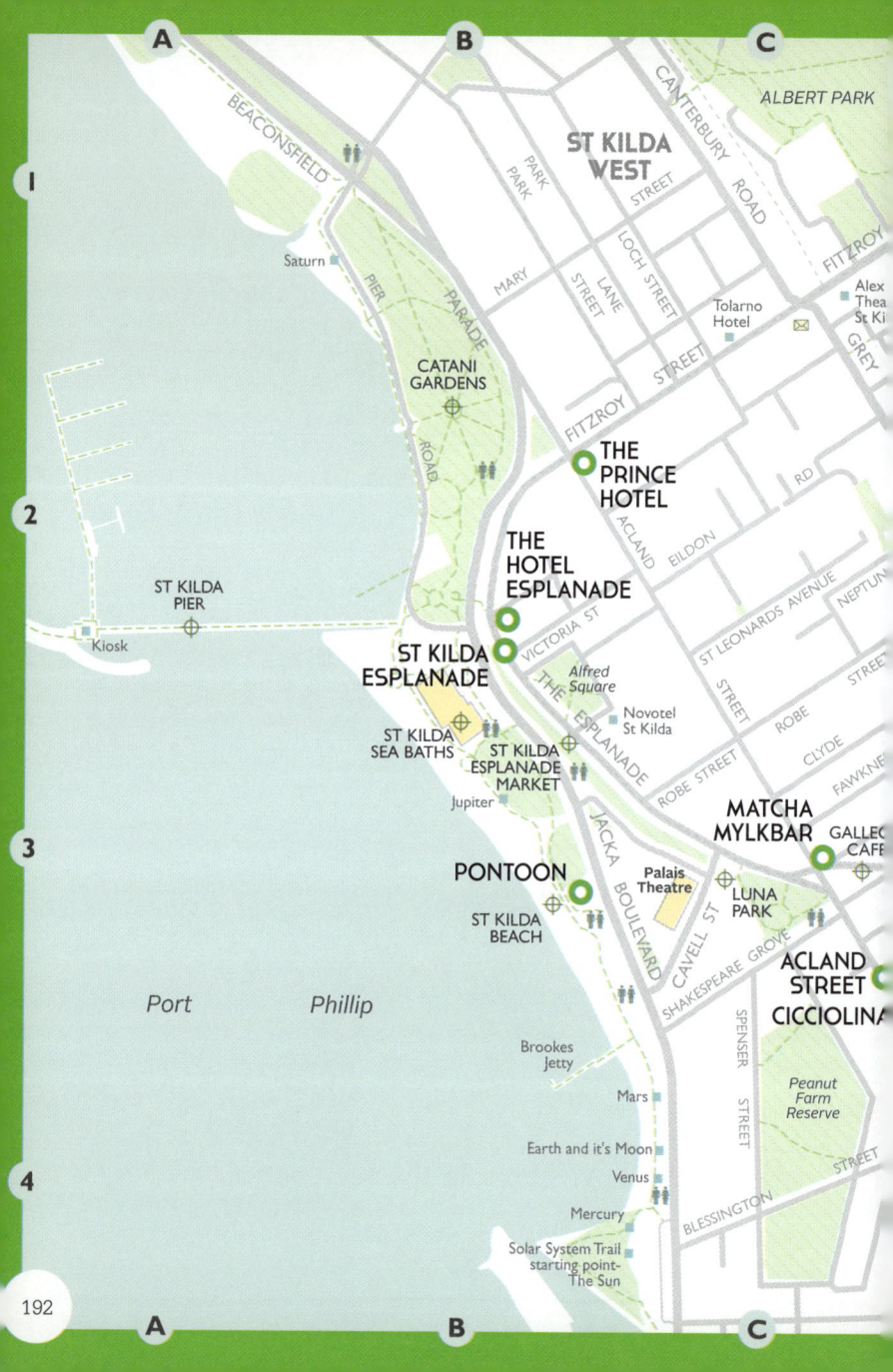

St Kilda

Grid A1–C4

- Beaconsfield Parade
- Saturn
- Pier Road
- Catani Gardens
- St Kilda Pier
- Kiosk
- The Prince Hotel
- The Hotel Esplanade
- St Kilda Esplanade
- Victoria St
- Alfred Square
- St Kilda Sea Baths
- St Kilda Esplanade Market
- Jupiter
- Novotel St Kilda
- The Esplanade
- Tolarno Hotel
- Alex Theatre St Kilda
- Fitzroy Street
- Acland Street
- Eildon Road
- St Leonards Avenue
- Neptune Street
- Robe Street
- Clyde Street
- Fawkner Street
- Matcha Mylkbar
- Gallec Cafe
- Pontoon
- St Kilda Beach
- Palais Theatre
- Jacka Boulevard
- Cavell St
- Luna Park
- Shakespeare Grove
- Acland Street Cicciolina
- Spenser Street
- Peanut Farm Reserve
- Brookes Jetty
- Mars
- Earth and it's Moon
- Venus
- Mercury
- Solar System Trail starting point - The Sun
- Blessington Street

Port Phillip

Albert Park

ST KILDA WEST

192

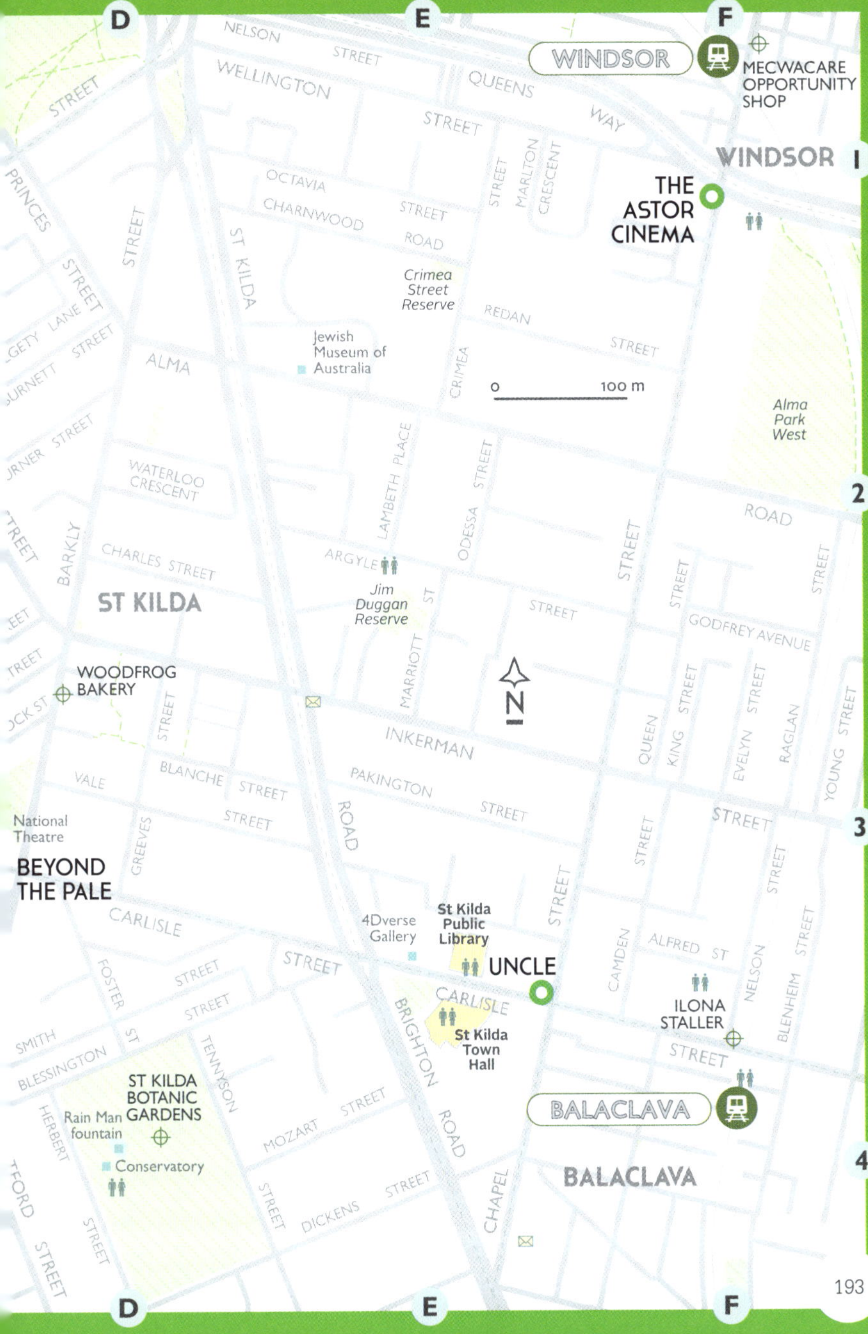
D
E
F
I
2
3
4
WINDSOR
MECWACARE
OPPORTUNITY
SHOP
WINDSOR
THE
ASTOR
CINEMA
NELSON STREET
WELLINGTON STREET
QUEENS WAY
STREET
PRINCES STREET
OCTAVIA STREET
CHARNWOOD ROAD
ST KILDA ROAD
MARLTON CRESCENT
Crimea
Street
Reserve
REDAN STREET
Jewish
Museum of
Australia
ALMA
CRIMEA STREET
0 100 m
Alma
Park
West
ALMA ROAD
WATERLOO
CRESCENT
LAMBETH PLACE
ODESSA STREET
BARKLY STREET
CHARLES STREET
ARGYLE STREET
Jim
Duggan
Reserve
MARRIOTT ST
ST KILDA
GODFREY AVENUE
WOODFROG
BAKERY
N
INKERMAN STREET
QUEEN STREET
KING STREET
EVELYN STREET
RAGLAN STREET
YOUNG STREET
BLANCHE STREET
VALE STREET
PAKINGTON STREET
National
Theatre
BEYOND
THE PALE
GREEVES STREET
CARLISLE STREET
4Dverse
Gallery
St Kilda
Public
Library
UNCLE
CAMDEN
ALFRED ST
NELSON STREET
BLENHEIM STREET
FOSTER ST
SMITH STREET
BLESSINGTON STREET
TENNYSON STREET
BRIGHTON ROAD
St Kilda
Town
Hall
ILONA
STALLER
ST KILDA
BOTANIC
GARDENS
Rain Man
fountain
Conservatory
HERBERT STREET
MOZART STREET
BALACLAVA
BALACLAVA
DICKENS STREET
CHAPEL STREET
D
E
F

A
B
C
1
2
3
4
TRIPPY TACO
COLLINGWOOD
ABBOTSFORD
AU79
MINH MINH SAIGON SOUL
I LOVE PHO
NORTH RICHMOND
EAST MELBOURNE
FITZROY GARDENS
River God Fountain
Model Tudor Village
The Fairies Tree
Darling Square
WEST RICHMOND
RICHMOND
JOLIMONT
TROPHY WIFE NAIL ART
NATIONAL SPORTS MUSEUM
Melbourne Cricket Ground
Yarra Park
TOFU SHOP INTERNATIONAL
A THOUSAND BLESSINGS
Citizens Park
GLOBAL VINTAGE COLLECTIVE
PURVIS BEER
Melbourne Arena
AAMI Park
Gosch's Paddock
THE CORNER HOTEL
FEAST OF MERIT
CREMORNE
EAST RICHMOND
Yarra River
Yarra Bend Park
LANGRIDGE
VICTORIA PARADE
WELLINGTON ST
ALBERT STREET
SMITH ST
NICHOLSON STREET
ELIZABETH STREET
YORK STREET
EGAN ST
CLARENDON STREET
POWLETT STREET
HOTHAM STREET
SIMPSON STREET
HODDLE STREET
WELLINGTON PARADE
ERIN ST
BRIDGE ROAD
LENNOX STREET
ROWENA PARADE
ABINGER STREET
FIREBELL LANE
BRUNTON AVENUE
RICHMOND TERRACE
GIPPS STREET
CHURCH STREET
OLYMPIC BOULEVARD
SWAN STREET
PUNT ROAD
MARY STREET
COPP STREET
N
0 200 m

Map: Yarra Bend Park and surrounds

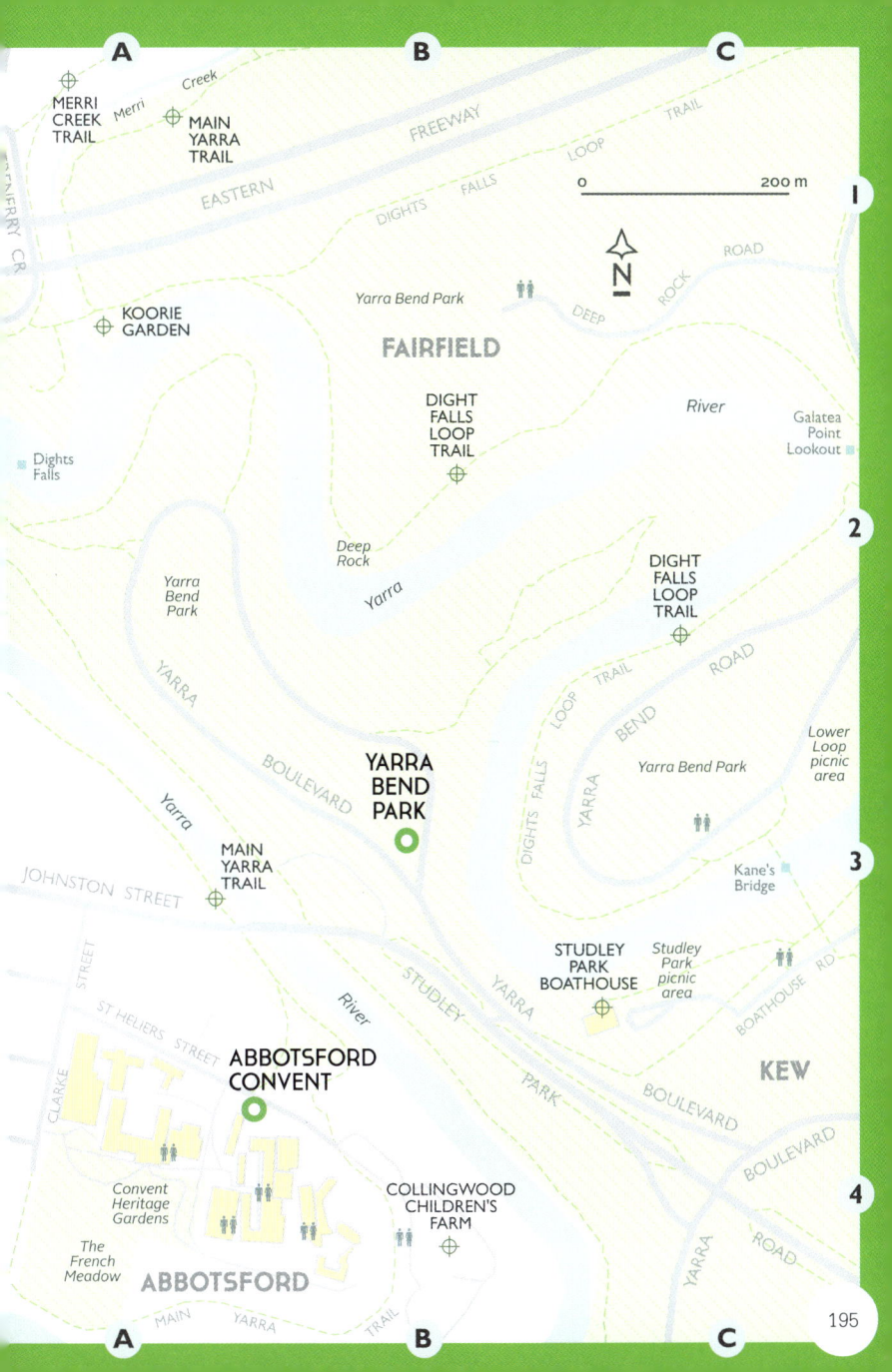

Grid references: A, B, C (columns) / 1, 2, 3, 4 (rows)

0 — 200 m

N

Labels

- MERRI CREEK TRAIL
- Merri Creek
- MAIN YARRA TRAIL
- EASTERN FREEWAY
- DIGHTS FALLS LOOP TRAIL
- DEEP ROCK ROAD
- Yarra Bend Park
- FAIRFIELD
- KOORIE GARDEN
- DIGHT FALLS LOOP TRAIL
- Galatea Point Lookout
- Dights Falls
- Yarra Bend Park
- Deep Rock
- Yarra River
- DIGHT FALLS LOOP TRAIL
- YARRA BOULEVARD
- DIGHTS FALLS LOOP TRAIL
- YARRA BEND ROAD
- Yarra Bend Park
- Lower Loop picnic area
- YARRA BEND PARK
- MAIN YARRA TRAIL
- Kane's Bridge
- JOHNSTON STREET
- STUDLEY PARK BOATHOUSE
- Studley Park picnic area
- BOATHOUSE RD
- ST HELIERS STREET
- CLARKE STREET
- Yarra River
- STUDLEY PARK
- BOULEVARD
- KEW
- YARRA BOULEVARD
- ABBOTSFORD CONVENT
- Convent Heritage Gardens
- COLLINGWOOD CHILDREN'S FARM
- The French Meadow
- ABBOTSFORD
- MAIN YARRA TRAIL
- YARRA ROAD

195

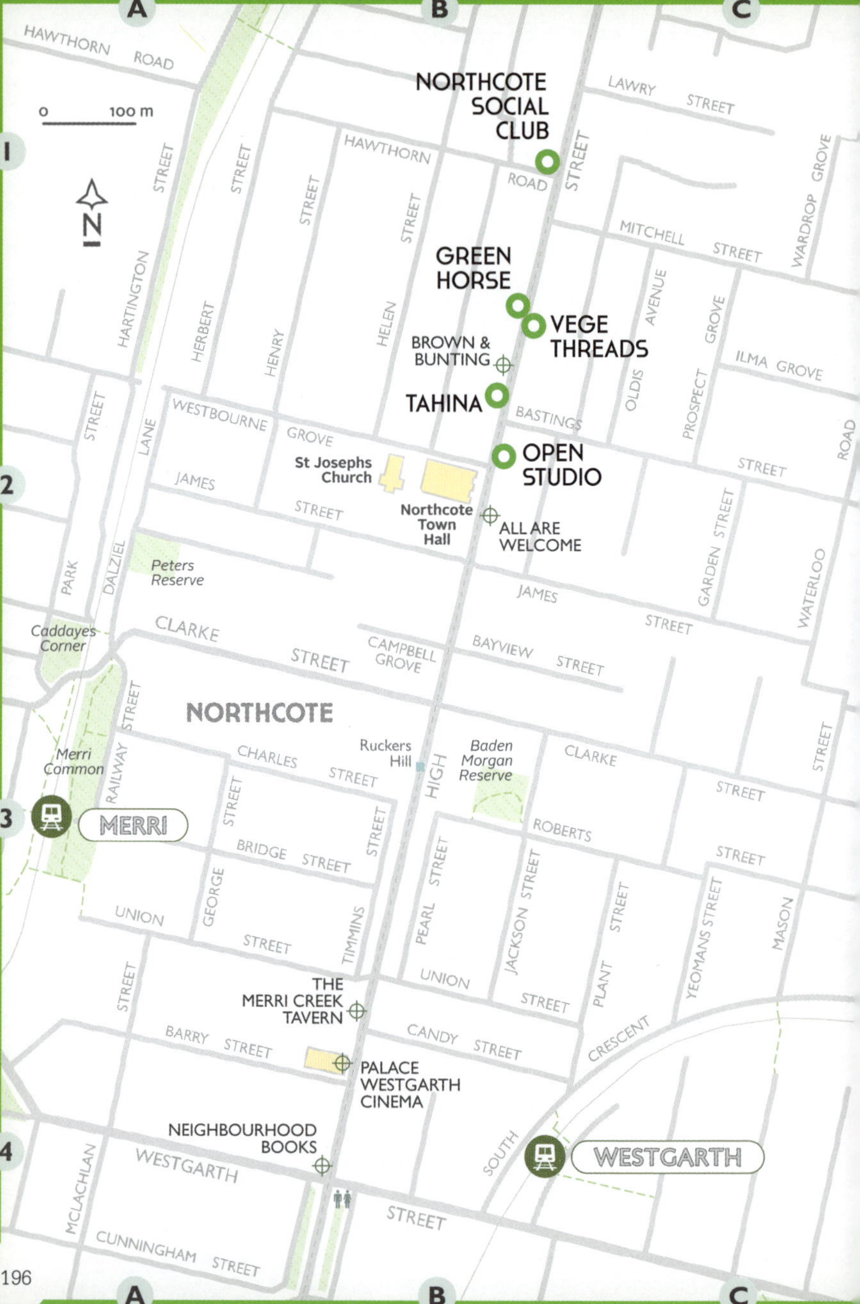

A
B
C
1
2
3
4
0 100 m
N
NORTHCOTE SOCIAL CLUB
GREEN HORSE
VEGE THREADS
BROWN & BUNTING
TAHINA
OPEN STUDIO
St Josephs Church
Northcote Town Hall
ALL ARE WELCOME
Peters Reserve
Caddayes Corner
Merri Common
MERRI
NORTHCOTE
Ruckers Hill
Baden Morgan Reserve
THE MERRI CREEK TAVERN
PALACE WESTGARTH CINEMA
NEIGHBOURHOOD BOOKS
WESTGARTH
HAWTHORN ROAD
LAWRY STREET
MITCHELL STREET
WARDROP GROVE
ILMA GROVE
PROSPECT GROVE
OLDIS AVENUE
BASTINGS STREET
HARTINGTON STREET
HERBERT STREET
HENRY STREET
HELEN STREET
HIGH STREET
WESTBOURNE GROVE
JAMES STREET
LANE
PARK STREET
DALZIEL
CLARKE STREET
CAMPBELL GROVE
BAYVIEW STREET
GARDEN STREET
WATERLOO ROAD
RAILWAY STREET
CHARLES STREET
GEORGE STREET
BRIDGE STREET
TIMMINS STREET
UNION STREET
PEARL STREET
JACKSON STREET
PLANT STREET
ROBERTS STREET
YEOMANS STREET
MASON STREET
CANDY STREET
BARRY STREET
SOUTH CRESCENT
WESTGARTH STREET
MCLACHLAN STREET
CUNNINGHAM STREET

Thornbury Map

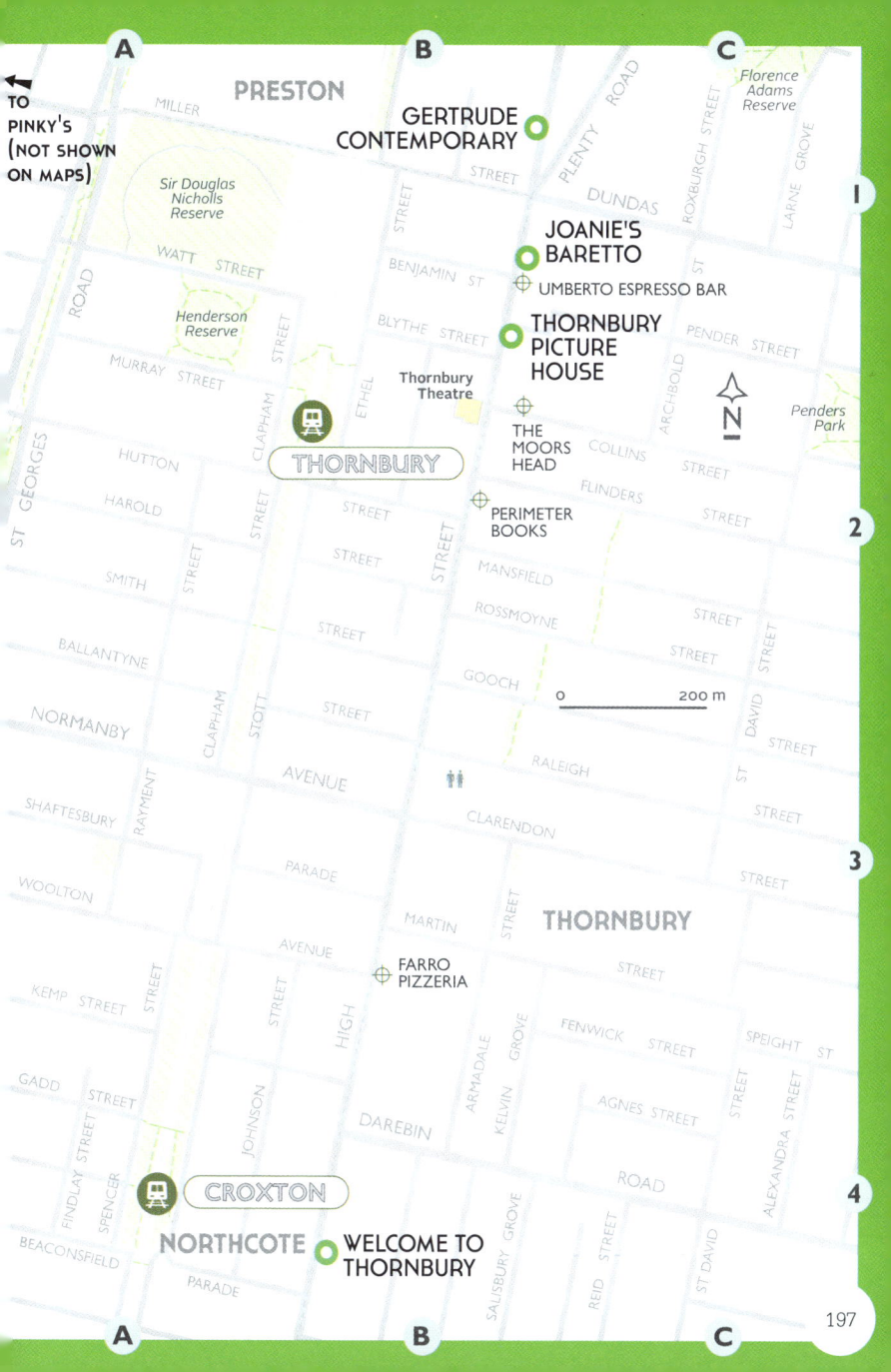

PRESTON

TO PINKY'S (NOT SHOWN ON MAPS) ←

- GERTRUDE CONTEMPORARY
- JOANIE'S BARETTO
- UMBERTO ESPRESSO BAR
- THORNBURY PICTURE HOUSE
- THE MOORS HEAD
- PERIMETER BOOKS
- FARRO PIZZERIA
- WELCOME TO THORNBURY

THORNBURY

NORTHCOTE

Florence Adams Reserve
Sir Douglas Nicholls Reserve
Henderson Reserve
Thornbury Theatre
Penders Park

Stations: THORNBURY, CROXTON

Streets: MILLER, WATT STREET, BENJAMIN ST, BLYTHE STREET, MURRAY STREET, HUTTON, HAROLD, SMITH, BALLANTYNE, NORMANBY, SHAFTESBURY, WOOLTON, KEMP STREET, GADD STREET, BEACONSFIELD, ST GEORGES ROAD, CLAPHAM, STOTT, ETHEL STREET, FINDLAY STREET, SPENCER, JOHNSON, RAYMENT, HIGH, PLENTY ROAD, ROXBURGH STREET, LARNE GROVE, DUNDAS STREET, PENDER STREET, ARCHBOLD, COLLINS STREET, FLINDERS, MANSFIELD, ROSSMOYNE STREET, GOOCH, RALEIGH, CLARENDON, PARADE, MARTIN AVENUE, FENWICK STREET, AGNES STREET, SPEIGHT ST, ALEXANDRA STREET, ARMADALE, KELVIN, GROVE, DAREBIN, SALISBURY GROVE, REID STREET, ST DAVID STREET, ROAD, PARADE

0 — 200 m

N ↑

Brunswick

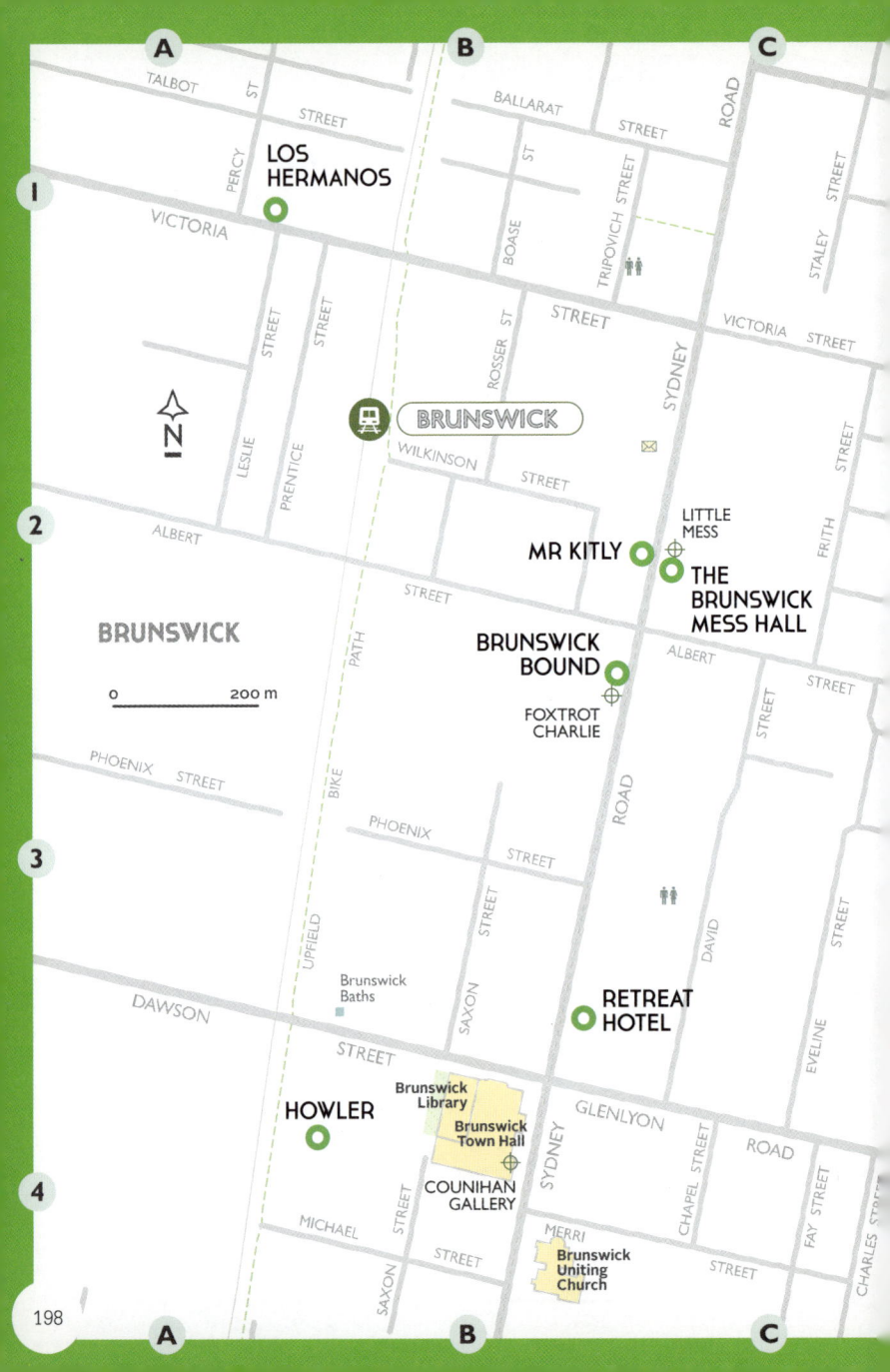

Map Grid

A1: Talbot Street, Percy Street, Victoria Street, Los Hermanos, Leslie Street, Prentice Street

B1: Ballarat Street, Boase St, Rosser St, Tripovich Street

C1: Road, Staley Street, Victoria Street

A2: Albert Street, Brunswick (0 – 200 m)

B2: Brunswick (station), Wilkinson Street, Bike Path

C2: Sydney Road, Little Mess, Mr Kitly, The Brunswick Mess Hall, Brunswick Bound, Foxtrot Charlie, Albert Street, Frith Street

A3: Phoenix Street, Dawson Street

B3: Phoenix Street, Brunswick Baths, Saxon Street

C3: Retreat Hotel, David Street, Eveline Street

A4: Howler, Michael Street, Saxon Street

B4: Brunswick Library, Brunswick Town Hall, Counihan Gallery, Brunswick Uniting Church, Merri Street, Glenlyon Road

C4: Sydney Road, Chapel Street, Fay Street, Charles Street

N (north arrow shown)

198

199

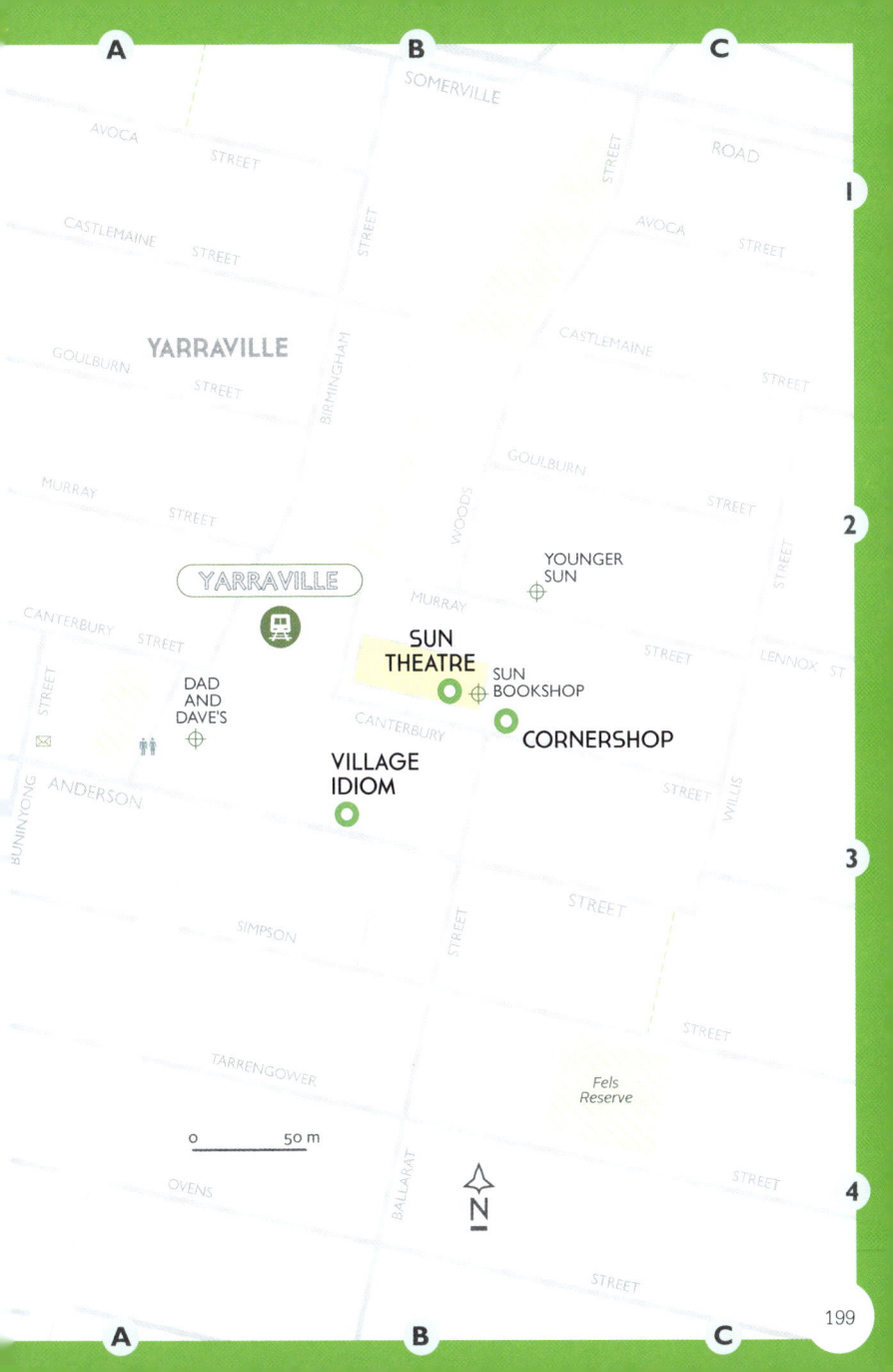

Map: Footscray / Seddon

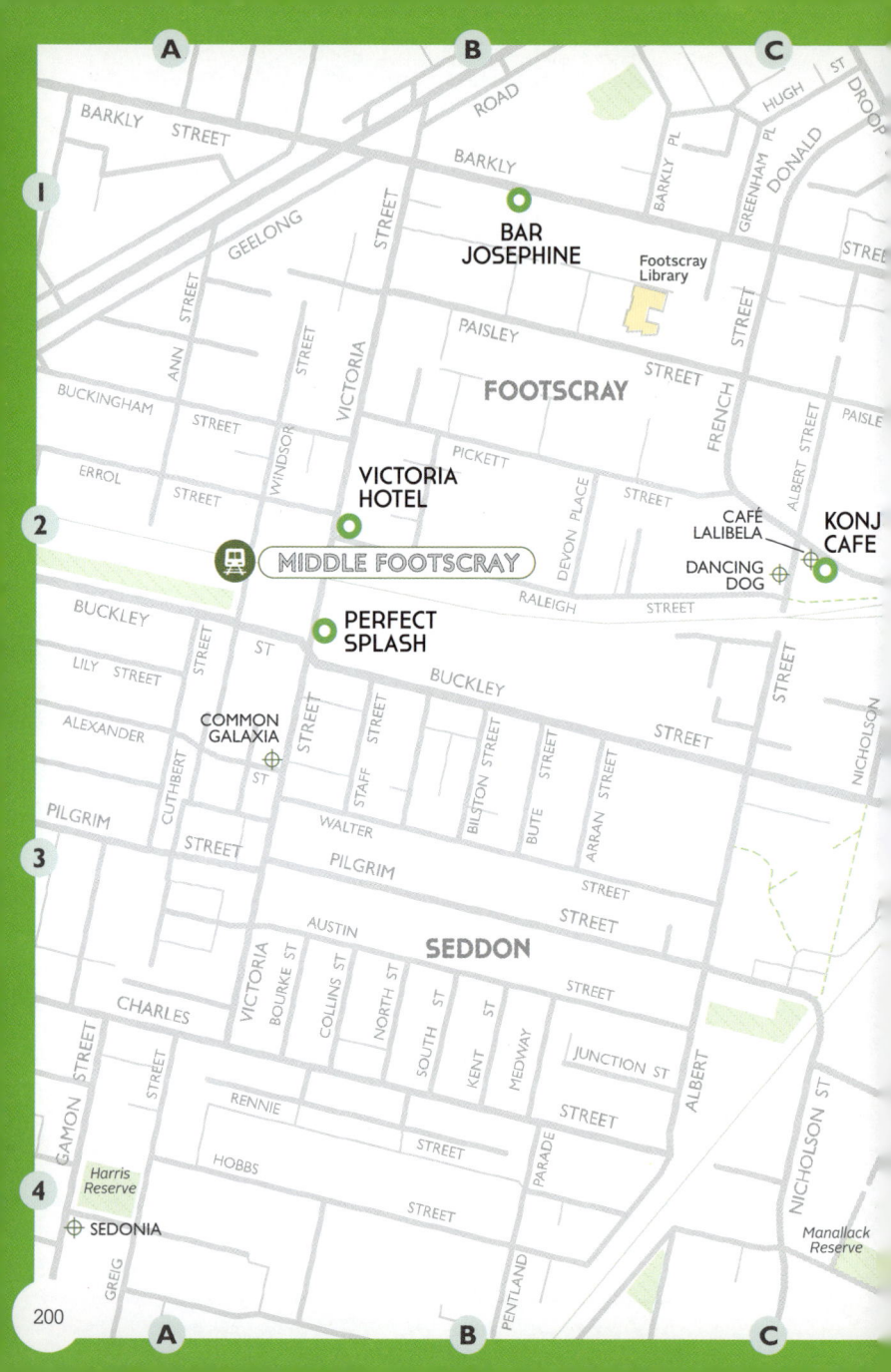

Grid references: A, B, C (columns) × 1, 2, 3, 4 (rows)

Points of interest

- BAR JOSEPHINE
- Footscray Library
- VICTORIA HOTEL
- MIDDLE FOOTSCRAY (train station)
- CAFÉ LALIBELA
- KONJ CAFE
- DANCING DOG
- PERFECT SPLASH
- COMMON GALAXIA
- SEDONIA
- Harris Reserve
- Manallack Reserve

Streets and areas

FOOTSCRAY

- BARKLY STREET
- ROAD
- BARKLY
- HUGH ST
- DROOP
- GEELONG
- VICTORIA STREET
- BARKLY PL
- GREENHAM PL
- DONALD
- ANN STREET
- WINDSOR STREET
- PAISLEY STREET
- FRENCH STREET
- ALBERT STREET
- PAISLE
- BUCKINGHAM STREET
- ERROL STREET
- PICKETT STREET
- DEVON PLACE
- RALEIGH STREET
- BUCKLEY
- ST
- CUTHBERT ST
- STAFF STREET
- BILSTON STREET
- BUTE STREET
- ARRAN STREET
- NICHOLSON STREET
- LILY STREET
- ALEXANDER
- BUCKLEY STREET
- PILGRIM STREET
- WALTER
- PILGRIM STREET

SEDDON

- AUSTIN STREET
- VICTORIA ST
- BOURKE ST
- COLLINS ST
- NORTH ST
- SOUTH ST
- KENT ST
- MEDWAY
- JUNCTION ST
- ALBERT STREET
- CHARLES STREET
- GAMON STREET
- RENNIE STREET
- HOBBS STREET
- PARADE
- NICHOLSON ST
- PENTLAND
- GREIG

200

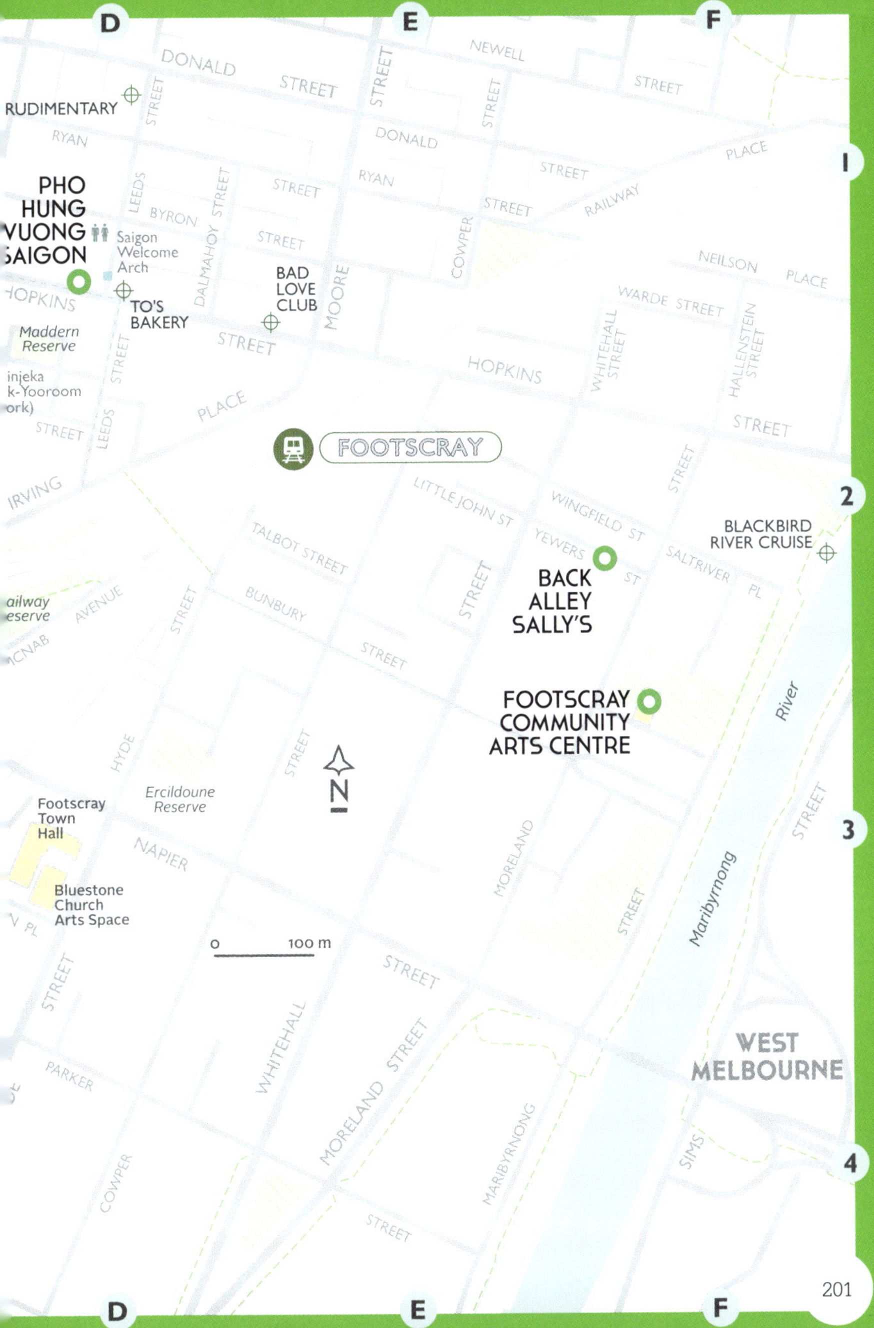

D
E
F
DONALD STREET
NEWELL STREET
DONALD
RUDIMENTARY
RYAN
RYAN
PHO HUNG VUONG SAIGON
Saigon Welcome Arch
LEEDS
BYRON STREET
DALMAHOY STREET
STREET
STREET
BAD LOVE CLUB
MOORE
COWPER
STREET
RAILWAY PLACE
I
NEILSON PLACE
WARDE STREET
HOPKINS STREET
TO'S BAKERY
Maddern Reserve
WHITEHALL STREET
HALLENSTEIN STREET
HOPKINS STREET
PLACE
STREET
LEEDS
FOOTSCRAY
IRVING
LITTLE JOHN ST
WINGFIELD ST
2
BLACKBIRD RIVER CRUISE
TALBOT STREET
YEWERS ST
SALTRIVER PL
BACK ALLEY SALLY'S
BUNBURY STREET
AVENUE
STREET
FOOTSCRAY COMMUNITY ARTS CENTRE
River
HYDE
STREET
N
Ercildoune Reserve
Footscray Town Hall
NAPIER
MORELAND
Maribyrnong
3
STREET
Bluestone Church Arts Space
0 100 m
STREET
WHITEHALL
MORELAND STREET
WEST MELBOURNE
PARKER
MARIBYRNONG
SIMS
4
COWPER
STREET
D
E
F

INDEX

12 Apostles Visitor Information Centre 160
400 Gradi at Rochford Wines 147

A Thousand Blessings 137
Abbotsford 128–41
Abbotsford Convent 130–1, 195 A4
Aboriginal heritage walk 3
ACCA vii
Acland Street 92, 192 C3
Aesop 104
Agathé Patisserie 35
Aireys Inlet 157
Albert Park Lake 34, 175 E4
Alderman, The 70
Alice McCall 103
All Are Welcome 79
All Nations Park 82
Amelia Shaw 69
Andy's Remedy cafe 116
Anglesea 157
Anglesea General Store 157
Apollo Bay 158–9
Apostles, Arches and Gorges 160
Arlechin 11
Arthur Galan 103
Arts Centre Melbourne vii
Astor Cinema, The 102, 193 F1
Atypic Chocolate 35
AU79 135, 194 C1
Australian Centre for the Moving Image (ACMI) 2
Australian Grand Prix 34
Australian Music Vault vii, 32
Australian National Surfing Museum, The 156
Australian Wildlife Centre 146

B3 5
Baby Pizza 141
Back Alley Sally's vii, 125, 201 F2
Back Bar 93
Bad Love Club 124
Ballarat 164

Ballarat Art Gallery and Museum 164
Bar Americano 13, 180 C1
Bar Josephine 124, 200 B1
Bar Open 54–5
Bar Tini 2
Basement Discs 5
Bayside 86–99
Bayside Coastal Trail 88
Bayside Trail 88–9
Beatrix 25, 182 C1
Beer 360 138
Bellbird Picnic Reserve 132
Bells Beach 156–7
Bendigo 166
Bendigo Art Gallery 166
Bendigo Pottery 166
Beyond the Pale 91, 193 D3
Bibelot 37
Black Cat, The 50
Blackbird River Cruise 116
Blackman's Brewery 156
Block Arcade vii, 5
Blood on the Southern Cross 164
Boatshed cafe 34
Boroughs, The 63
Borsch, Vodka and Tears 108, 191 B2
Bottle of Milk, The 158
Bottom End, The 28, 175 D3
Bourke Street Mall 6
Bouvier Bar 69
Bridge Road 134
Brighton Beach bathing boxes 88
Brogan's Way 139
Brown & Bunting 77
Brunswick 56–71
Brunswick Bound 62, 198 B2
Brunswick Mess Hall, The 66, 198 C2
Brunswick Street Gallery 44, 185 D1
Budj Bim National Park 160–1
Bunjilaka Aboriginal Cultural Centre 60
Bunurong Corroboree Tree 34
Burch & Purchese Sweet Studio 106, 190 C1
Burnam Beeches 145
Butterfly Club 15
Buxton Contemporary vii, 33

c3 Contemporary Art Space 130

Cafe Lalibela 121
Cam's Kiosk 130
Cape Otway Lighthouse 159
Cape Woolamai 153
Captains of Industry 22
Carlton 56–71
Carlton Yacht Club 68, 184 A2
Castlemaine 167
Castlemaine Art Museum 167
Castlemaine Vintage Bazaar 167
Catani Gardens 90
Central Deborah Gold Mine 166
Centre for Contemporary Photography 44
Centre Place vii, 5
Centreway vii
Cerberus Beach House 88
CERES 58–9, 175 E1
Chapel Street 103, 190 C1
Chapel Street Bazaar 105
Chez Dré 37, 189 E2
Chill Out 165, 171
Chinatown vii, 9, 177 F2, 178 B3
Chinese Museum 9
Churchill Island 153
CIBI 49, 185 F1
Cicciolina 93, 192 C4
Cinema Nova 61
City East x–15
City West 16–29
Claypots 35
Clementine's 5
Cliffy's 165
Clunes 167
Coldstream 147
Coldstream Brewery 147
Collingwood 42–55
Collingwood Children's Farm 131
Collins Settlement Historic Site 150
Colonel Tan's Thai 112
Common Galaxia 119
Como House 103
Continental Hotel 150
Convent Bakery 130
Convent Gallery, The 165
Cook Street Collective 152
Cookie 12
Corner Hotel, The 140–1, 194 B4
Cornershop 123, 199 B3
Cornerstone 81
Cottage Industry 48, 185 D4

Counihan Gallery 60
Country Road 103
Craft 7, 181 D1
Crafty Squirrel, The 164
Crossley Street 7, 179 A2
Crumpler 5, 103
Cubby Haus Brewing 164
Cumulus Inc 10, 181 F1
Cumulus Up 10
Curtin House vii, 12, 177 D3

D. O. C. Pizza & Mozzarella Bar 64, 184 B2
Dad and Dave's 123
Dancing Dog 126
Dandenong Ranges 144
Dandenong Ranges Botanic Garden 144
Dandenong Ranges National Park 144
Dandenongs 142–7
Das Kaffeehaus 167
Das T-Shirt Automart 104
David Jones 6
David's 110, 191 C2
Daylesford 165, 171
Degraves Street vii, 5
Degraves Street Espresso 5
Deli Hall 18
Dights Falls Loop Trail 132
Drunken Poet, The 18
Dukes Coffee Roasters vii, 5

Emporium 6
Espy Kitchen 96
Eureka Skydeck 33, 180 B4
Europa 92

Fairfield Boathouse 132
Faraday's Cage 45
Farmers Arms 165
Farri Pizzeria 85
Feast of Merit 137, 194 B4
Federation Square 2, 181 D2
Fitzroy 42–55
Fitzroy Pool 52
Fitzroy Pub Crawl 53, 185 D4
Flagstaff Gardens 26
Flinders 151
Flinders Blowhole 152
Flinders Hotel 152
Flinders Sourdough 152
Florentino Cellar Bar 11
Florentino Grill 11
Florentino's 11
Flower Drum 9
Fool Clothing 104

202

INDEX

Footscray 114–27
Footscray Community Arts Centre 116, 201 F3
Foundry 164
400 Gradi at Rochford Wines 147
Foxtrot Charlie 62
Frank & Connie's Kitchen 165
Frankie's Story 35
Friends of the Earth 49

Galleon Cafe 94
Gallery Funaki 7
Georgie Bass Cafe and Cookery 152
Gershwin Room 96
Gertrude Contemporary 74, 197 B1
Gin Castro Hair and Makeup 133
Gingerboy 7
Glicks 95
Global Vintage Collective 134, 194 C3
Gold Museum 164
Goldfields 162–7
Gorman 103
Grace Darling, The 53
Grand Hotel, The 19
Great Ocean Road 154–61
Green Horse 78, 196 B1
Green Man's Arms 67, 184 B1
Greville Records 104
Greville Street 104, 191 B1
Grossi Florentino 11, 179 A3
Growlers 156
Guilfoyle's Volcano 3

Haigh's vii, 5
Half Moon Bay 88
Hamer Lawn vii
Hansang 26–7, 183 E4
Happy Valley 47, 185 F2
Harbour Fish and Chip Shop, The 159
Hares and Hyenas 47
Hats and Tatts 40
Healesville 146
Healesville Sanctuary 146
Heide Museum of Modern Art 132
Hepburn Bathhouse 165
Hepburn Pool 165
Hepburn Springs 165
Hill of Content 7
Honcho Disko 53
Hopetoun Tea Rooms 3

Hosier Lane 2
Hotel Esplanade, The 96–7, 192 B2
Hotel Sorrento 150
Howler 70–1, 198 A4
Hunter Gatherer 5, 48
Hutong Dumpling Bar 9

I Love Pho 136, 194 C1
Il Papiro 5
Ilona Staller 93

Jerry's Milkbar 88
Joanie's Baretto 84, 197 B1
Jock's 38
Johnston Street Art Walk 45, 185 D2
Journal Canteen vii
Juddy Roller Street 45

Kanteen 103
Kappaya 130
Keith Haring mural 45
Kilderkin Distillery 164
Kinki Gerlinki 5
Kirk;s Wine Bar 23
Kittos 156
Koala Conservation Centre 153
Koko Black 5
Kokoda Walk 144
Konjo Cafe 121, 200 C2
Koorie Cultural Walk 156
Koorie Garden 132
Koorie Heritage Trust 2

Labour in Vain 53
Ladro 104
Lake House Restaurant 165
Lake Wendouree 164
Lanes and Arcades 5, 180 B2
Lavendula 165
Le Bon 92
Le Louvre 103
Leaf Store, The 89
Leica 6
Lentil as Anything 130
L'Espresso 164
Library at the Dock 28
LIFEwithBIRD 103
Little Mess 66
Logans Beach Whale Watching Platform 160
Loop 12
Lord Coconut 21, 176 B3
Lorne 157–8
Lorne Beach Books 158
Lorne Corner Store 158

Lorne Visitor Information Centre 158
Los Hermanos 65, 198 A1
Lucky Coq 111, 191 B2
Lucky Panda Kitchen 66
Lucy Folk 7
Luna Park 90
Lyrebird Track 144

Mabu Mabu 35
Maddens Rise 146
Main Yarra Trail 132
Mallow, The 164
Mamasita 82
Marimekko 103
Marios 50, 185 D2
Market Imports 35
Mary Martin Bookshop 36
Matcha Mylkbar 94, 192 C3
Matt Adnate's 20-storey mural 45
Mecwaware Opportunity Shop 105
Melbourne Central 6
Melbourne Gallery 60
Melbourne Museum 60, 184 B3
Melbourne Sports and Aquatic Centre 34
Melbourne Star Observation Wheel 19, 182 A3
Melinda Grace Beauty 133
Merchants of Change 35
Merri Creek Tavern, The 83
Merri Creek Trail 78
Merri Table 58
Mesa Verde 12
Metropolis vii, 12
Meyers Place Bar vii, 7
Midi Boutique 158
Midsumma Festival 171
Mill, The 176
Minh Minh Saigon Soul 136
Miznon vii, 23, 176 A4, 183 F4
Monarch 92
Monster Threads 5
Montalto Winery 152
Moonlight Cinema 3
Moors Head, The 85
Mörk Chocolate 24, 183 D1
Mornington Peninsula 148–53
Mornington Peninsula Chocolaterie and Ice Creamery 152
Mountain Goat Brewery 139, 175 F3
Movida 2

Movida Next Door 2
Mr Kitly 63, 198 C2
Mr Wares vii
Mushroom Reef Marine Sanctuary 152
Mya Tiger 96
Myer 6

Nails by Kirsten 133
Naked for Satan 54, 185 D2
Naked in the Sky 54
Napier Hotel 53
National Sports Museum 4, 194 A3
National Surfing Reserve 153
Neighbourhood Books 77
NGV International vii, 32, 186 B1
NGV's Australian gallery 2
Nicholas Building 8
night markets 18
No Vacancy Gallery 6
Nobbies Centre 153
Northcote 72–85
Northcote Social Club 83, 196 B1

Ocean Beach Road 150
Old Melbourne Observatory 3
Olinda 144
Olinda Tea House 144
Olsen, The 103
OM Vegetarian 13
Ombra Salumi 11
One Tree Hill 144
onepointsevenfour 104
Onstone 36, 189 E2
Open Studio 85, 196 B2
Otway Fly Tree Top Walk 159
Otway Ranges 159
Outré Gallery 20, 176 B3
Overlook bar 102

Padre Coffee 18
Paint n Powder vii, 5
Palace Cinema Como 103
Palace Hotel, The 40–1, 188 A3
P.A.M. vii, 12
Paperback, The 7
Paradise Alley 52, 185 F2
Pardon 104
Peel Hotel, The 53
Pellegrini's Espresso Bar 7
Penguin Parade Visitor Centre, The 153

203

INDEX

Perfect Splash 118–19, 200 B2
Perimeter Books 77
Phillip Island 148, 153
Pho Hung Vuong Saigon vii, 122, 201 D1
Pho Nom 6
Pidapipo 67
Piggery, The 145
Pinky's 76–7
Pinnacles, The 153
Point Nepean National Park 151
Pontoon 99, 192 B3
Ponyfish Island 14, 180 B3
Poof Doof 112
Port Fairy 160–1
Prahran 100–13
Prahran Market 105
Prahran Mission 105
Preston 72–85
Preston Market 74
Prince Bandroom 98
Prince Dining Room 98
Prince Hotel, The 98, 192 B2
Prudence 29, 183 E2
Public Bar 98
Puffing Billy 144
Purvis Beer 138, 194 C3

Quarantine Station 151
Queen Victoria Market 18, 183 F2
Queenscliff 150
QV 6

Railway Hotel 39, 189 D3
Rainbow, The 53
Rare Hare Wine & Food Store 151
Readings 61, 92, 184 A1
Readings Kids 61
Red Duck 164
Restorers Barn 167
Retreat Hotel 69, 198 B3
Revolver Lane 108
Revolver Upstairs vii, 112–13, 191 B2
Rhyll Inlet 153
Richmond 128–41
Riverland Urban Beer Garden 14
Rockysteady Records 21
Romeo Lane 7
Rooftop Bar 12
Rosalind Park 166
Rose Street Market 46
Royal Arcade vii, 5

Royal Botanic Gardens 3, 187 E3
Royal Exhibition Building 60
Royal Park 66
Rudimentary 125

Saba 103
Sacred Heart Mission Shop 105
St Ali 38, 189 F2
St Cloud Cakes 167
St Collins Lane 6
St Helier's Street Gallery 130
St Kilda 86–99
St Kilda Baths 90
St Kilda Beach 90
St Kilda Esplanade 88, 90, 192 B2
St Kilda Esplanade Market 90
St Kilda Gardens 90
St Kilda Pier 90
Salvos Stores 105
Sandringham Yacht Club 88
Sass & Bide 103
Sassafras 144
Save the Children 105
Scanlan & Theodore 103
Seal Rock 153
Sedonia 119
Shag 105
Shanghai Village 9
Shark Finn Inn 9
Shelley Panton Store 111
Shrine of Remembrance 3
ShyHigh Mount Dandenong 144
Sichuan House 9
Signed and Numbered 104
Sircuit and Mollie's Bar & Diner 53
Slice Girls West 125
Slow Food Farmers Market 130
Smith & Daughters 51, 185 D3
Sorrento 150
Sorrento–Portsea Artists Trail 150
South Melbourne 30–41
South Melbourne Market 35, 189 D2
South Yarra 100–13
Southbank 30–41
Sovereign Hill 164
Spa Country 162–7
Spirits of the Sky 146

Split Point Lighthouse 157
Spring St Grocer vii, 11
Sprout Bakery 167
Standard, The 53
state Library of Victoria vii
Storehouse Thrift 105
String Bean Alley 18
Studley Park Boathouse 132
Sun Bookshop 117
Sun Moth Canteen & Bar 20
Sun Theatre 117, 199 B2
Sunday Market 165
Super Cool, The 35
Supper Inn 9

Tahina 80–1, 196 B2
Tarrawarra Museum of Art 146
The Alderman 70
The Astor Cinema 102
The Australian National Surfing Museum 156
The Black Cat 50
The Boroughs 63
The Bottle of Milk 158
The Bottom End 28
The Brunswick Mess Hall 66
The Convent Gallery 165
The Corner Hotel 140–1
The Corner Shop 123
The Crafty Squirrel 164
The Drunken Poet 18
The Grace Darling 53
The Grand Hotel 19
The Harbour Fish and Chip Shop 159
The Hotel Esplanade 96–7
The Leaf Store 91
The Mallow 164
The Merri Creek Tavern 83
The Mill 176
The Moors Head 85
The Olsen 103
The Palace Hotel 40–1
The Paperback 7
The Peel Hotel 53
The Penguin Parade Visitor Centre 153
The Piggery 145
The Pinnacles 153
The Prince Hotel 98
The Rainbow 53
The Retreat Hotel 69
The Standard 53
The Super Cool 35
The Toff in Town 12
The Tote 53
The Vineyard 92

The Workers Club 53
Theatre Royal 167
Third Drawer Down 46, 185 E4
Thornbury 72–85
Thornbury Picture House 75, 197 B1
Thousand Blessings, A 137
Tivoli Road Bakery 106
Toff in Town, The 12
Tofu Shop International 135
Torquay 156
To's Bakery 122
Tote, The 53
Town Hall Hotel 29
Traveller 7
Trophy Wife Nail Art 133, 194 B2
Tusk 107, 191 B3
12 Apostles Visitor Information Centre 160

Ultimate Foodie Tour 18
Umberto Espresso Bar 84
Uncle 95, 193 E3
Union Club Hotel 53
Union Electric 9
Unlocked Tours 6
Urban Attitude 92

Vege Threads 79, 196 B2
Vegie Bar 51
Victoria Hotel 126–7, 200 B2
Village Idiom 120, 199 B3
Vineyard, The 92
Vintage Shop Crawl 105, 191 B2

Welcome to Sunny Fitzroy 45
Welcome to Thornbury vii, 82, 197 B4
Westgarth Cinema 75
Wide Open Road 86
Wilkins and Kent 22, 176 B4
Windsor 110–13
Workers Club, The 53
Wye River General Store 158

Yarra Bend Park 132, 195 B3
Yarra Valley 142–7
Yarra Valley Gateway Estate 147
Yarraville 114–27
Yering Station 147
Young Bloods Diner 46
Younger Sun 117

ABOUT THE AUTHORS

Dale Campisi and Brady Michaels know Melbourne inside and out. They've lived in more than a dozen different suburbs and in the city, and spent more than a decade exploring Melbourne's history, architecture, cafe, bar and foodie scenes. They co-founded cult publisher Arcade Publications and souvenir store Melbournalia, and now they share stories about Australia as The Gents, including the popular Unlocked Tours of Melbourne Central. They are the authors of *Signs of Australia*, a visual history of sign-making in Australia, and the owners of Tasmanian country getaway Hunting Ground. Find out more at: thegentsaustralia.com

ACKNOWLEDGEMENTS

This is for you, Melbourne. Thanks for constantly evolving and for always providing something new to see or do, find and explore. And Alice Barker, gentlewoman.

Big thanks to the team at Hardie Grant who helped make this book possible: Megan Cuthbert for her stellar project management, Melissa Kayser for her long-term support and guidance, Michelle Mackintosh for the sparkling book design, Emily Maffei for making the beautiful maps and Megan Ellis for typesetting our words.

PHOTO CREDITS

All images copyright Brady Michaels and Dale Campisi, except the following (letters indicate where multiple images appear on a page, from left to right, top to bottom):

i, 96-97 The Hotel Esplanade; Visit Victoria ii, iv-v, x-1, 2, 4, 6, 7, 9a, 9c, 11a, 12, 15b, 16-17, 32a, 32b, 33a, 46b, 50a, 55a, 60, 61b, 90c, 92a, 92c, 103b, 103c, 142-143, 144, 145b, 146a, 146b, 147, 150, 151, 152, 153, 154-155, 156, 157a, 157b, 160, 161, 162-163, 164, 165, 166, 167, 205c, 205d; 8 Lauren Bamford; 10a J McGann; 10b, 10c Kristoffer Paulson; 11b Grossi Florentino; 18, 30-31, 32c Tourism Australia; 20 Outre Gallery; 21 Lord Coconut; 22 Wilkins and Kent; 24 Mork Chocolate; 25 Beatrix; 27 Hansang; 28 The Bottom End; 29 Prudence; 33a Eureka Skydeck; 36 Onstone; 37 Chez Dre; 44a Indrid K Brooker, 44b Sharon Peoples; 46b Third Drawer Down; 47 Happy Valley; 49 Cibi; 50b Marios; 51a Nicole Goodwin; 51b Benn Wood; 51c, 123 Rosanna Dutson; 52 Paradise Alley; 54, 55b Naked for Satan; 65 Los Hermanos; 66 Brunswick Mess Hall; 67 Green Man's Arms; 70-71 Sean Fennessy; 74a Jake Roden; 74b Daniel Gardezabel,

(continued on next page)

74c Fraser Stanley; 75a, 75b, Tinny Tang; 76-77 Annette O'Brien; 78 Green Horse; 79 Veg Threads; 80-81 Tahina; 72-73, 82 Welcome to Thornbury; 83b, 83c Northcote Social Club; 84a Daniel Mazzarella; 84b Hi Sylvia Photography; 85 Open Studio; 91 Beyond the Pale; 93 Cicciolina; 95a Martina Gemmola; 98 The Prince Hotel; 99 Pontoon; 108-109 Borsch, Vodka and Tears; 110 David's; 110-111 Lucky Coq; 112-113 Revolver Upstairs; 116a, 116c Jody Haines; 118-119 Perfect Splash; 120b Village Idiom; 121 Konjo Café; 126-127 Victoria Hotel; 128-129, 130-131 Abbotsford Convent; 133 Heather Lighton; 134 Global Vintage Collective; 137 Feast of Merit; 139 Mountain Goat Brewery; 140-141 The Corner Hotel; 146 Andrew Curtis; 157c Alamy Stock Photo; 159b, 159c iStock Photo

---

Some of the material in this book originally appeared in *Melbourne Precincts*, published by Explore Australia Publishing Pty Ltd, 2013, where full acknowledgements for individual contributions appear.

Published in 2019 by Hardie Grant Travel, a division of Hardie Grant Publishing

Hardie Grant Travel (Melbourne)
Building 1, 658 Church Street
Richmond, Victoria 3121

Hardie Grant Travel (Sydney)
Level 7, 45 Jones Street
Ultimo, NSW 2007

www.hardiegrant.com/au/travel

All rights reserved. No part of this publication may be reproduced, stored in a retrieval system or transmitted in any form by any means, electronic, mechanical, photocopying, recording or otherwise, without the prior written permission of the publishers and copyright holders.

The moral rights of the author have been asserted.

Copyright text © Dale Campisi and Brady Michaels 2019

Copyright concept, maps and design © Hardie Grant Publishing 2019

The maps in this publication incorporate data from:

© Imprint and currency – VAR Product and PSMA Data "Copyright based on data provided under licence from PSMA Australia Limited (www.psma.com.au)".
Hydrography Data (May 2006)
Transport Data (November 2018)

© OpenStreetMap contributors
OpenStreetMap is made available under the Open Data Commons Open Database License (ODbL) by the OpenStreetMap Foundation (OSMF):
http://opendatacommons.org/licenses/odbl/1.0/.
Any rights in individual contents of the database are licensed under the Database Contents License: http://opendatacommons.org/licenses/dbcl/1.0/
OSM data extracts via Geofabrik GmbH https://www.geofabrik.de

A catalogue record for this book is available from the National Library of Australia

Melbourne Pocket Precincts
ISBN 9781741176292

10 9 8 7 6 5 4 3 2 1

Publisher
Melissa Kayser

Project editor
Megan Cuthbert

Editor
Alice Barker

Editorial assistance
Rosanna Dutson

Proofreader
Helena Holmgren

Cartographer
Emily Maffei

Design
Michelle Mackintosh

Typesetting
Megan Ellis

Index
Max McMaster

Prepress
Megan Ellis and Splitting Image Colour Studio

Printed and bound in China by LEO Paper Group

Disclaimer: While every care is taken to ensure the accuracy of the data within this product, the owners of the data (including the state, territory and Commonwealth governments of Australia) do not make any representations or warranties about its accuracy, reliability, completeness or suitability for any particular purpose and, to the extent permitted by law, the owners of the data disclaim all responsibility and all liability (including without limitation, liability in negligence) for all expenses, losses, damages (including indirect or consequential damages) and costs which might be incurred as a result of the data being inaccurate or incomplete in any way and for any reason.

Publisher's Disclaimers: The publisher cannot accept responsibility for any errors or omissions. The representation on the maps of any road or track is not necessarily evidence of public right of way. The publisher cannot be held responsible for any injury, loss or damage incurred during travel. It is vital to research any proposed trip thoroughly and seek the advice of relevant state and travel organisations before you leave.

Publisher's Note: Every effort has been made to ensure that the information in this book is accurate at the time of going to press. The publisher welcomes information and suggestions for correction or improvement.